A-Z NOTT[...]

CONTENT[...]

REFERENCE

Motorway	M1	Map Continuation	32 / Large Scale City Centre 4
A Road	A609	Car Park (selected)	P
Proposed		Church or Chapel	†
B Road	B684	Fire Station	■
Dual Carriageway		House Numbers (A & B Roads only)	20 / 8
One-way Street	→	Hospital	H
Traffic flow on A Roads is indicated by a heavy line on the driver's left.		Information Centre	i
All one way streets are shown on Large Scale Pages 4-5	⇒	National Grid Reference	450
Restricted Access		Police Station	▲
Pedestrianized Road		Post Office	★
Residential Walkway	....	Toilet	▽
Track & Footpath	--------	with facilities for the Disabled	♿
Local Authority Boundary	— · — · —	Educational Establishment	
Postcode Boundary	— — —	Hospital or Hospice	
Railway	Tunnel / Station / Level Crossing	Industrial Building	
Nottingham Express Transit	Stops / One-Way / Two-Way	Leisure or Recreational Facility	
		Place of Interest	
		Public Building	
Built-up Area	DEAN AV.	Shopping Centre or Market	
		Other Selected Buildings	

SCALE

Map Pages 6-81	Map Pages 4-5
1:15840 (4 inches to 1 mile) 6.31cm to 1km	1:7920 (8 inches to 1 mile) 12.63cm to 1km
0 ¼ ½ Mile	0 ⅛ ¼ Mile
0 250 500 750 Metres	0 100 200 300 400 Metres

Geographers' A-Z Map Company Ltd.

Head Office:
Fairfield Road, Borough Green, Sevenoaks, Kent, TN15 8PP
Telephone 01732 781000 (General Enquiries & Trade Sales)
Showrooms:
44 Gray's Inn Road, London, WC1X 8HX
Telephone 020 7440 9500 (Retail Sales)
www.a-zmaps.co.uk

RIPLEY

Codnor

Linby

Papplewic

Friezeland

Moorgreen

Aldercar

6 **7** **8**
HUCKNALL
Westville

Smalley

HEANOR
14 **15**
Langley

Marlpool

EASTWOOD Newthorpe
16 **17** **18** **19** **20**
Kimberley BULWELL

Bestwoo Village

Giltbrook

Shipley

Cotmanhay

Nuthall

Old Basford

26 **27** **28** **29** **30** **31** **32**
Mapperley Bilborough

West Hallam

ILKESTON
TROWELL (S)

NOTTINGHAM

38 **39** **40** **41** **42** **43** **44**
Kirk Hallam Trowell Woollaton Lenton

Bramcote

STAPLEFORD
52 **53** **54** **55** **56**
Sandiacre BEESTON

Rylands

Spondon

Ockbrook

Chilwell

Attenborough

Clifto

Borrowash

Breaston

Toton
62 **63** **64** **65** **66**

LONG EATON

Barton in Fabis

Sawley
72 **73** **74** **75** **76**
Trentlock

Gotham

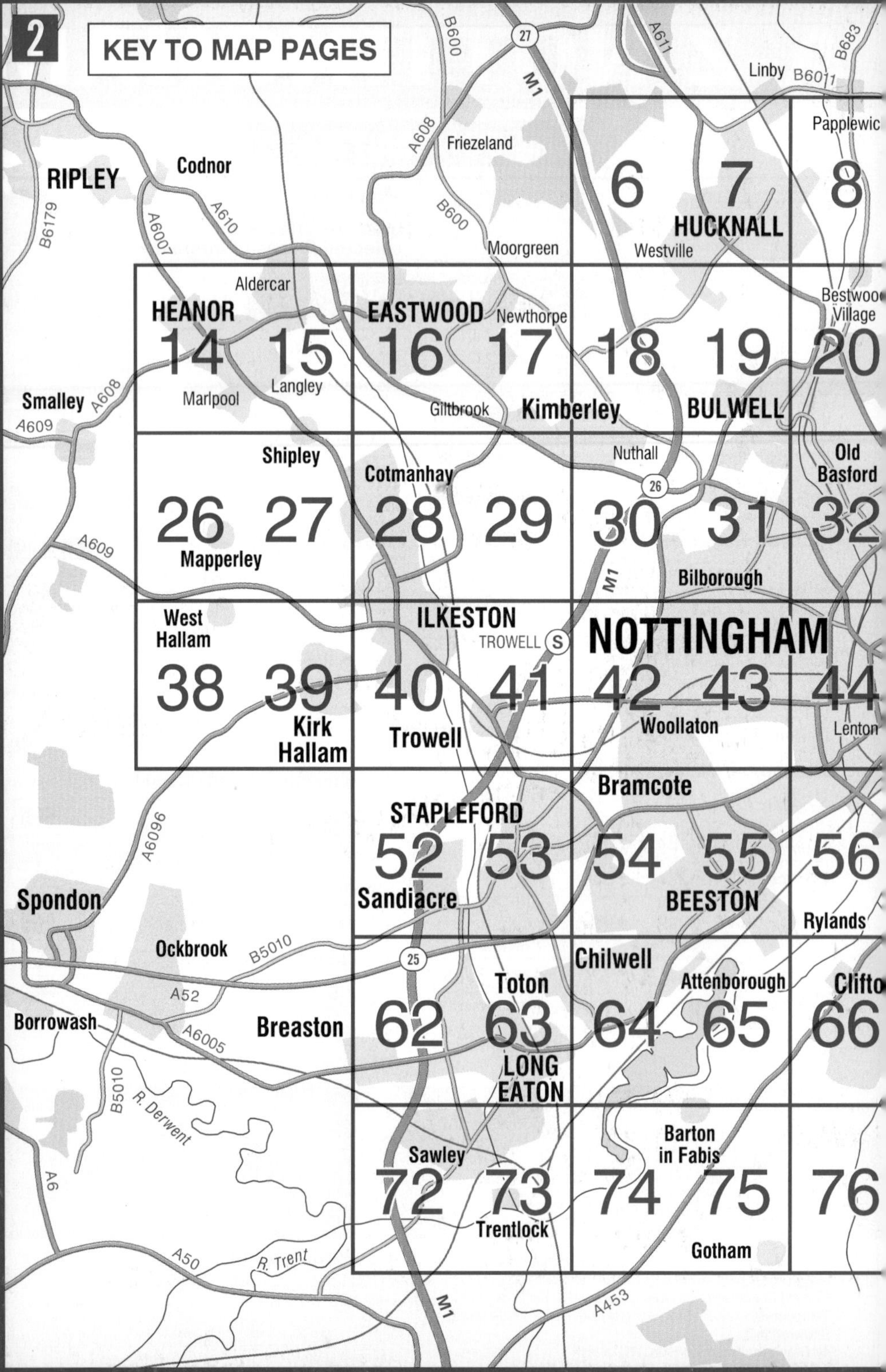

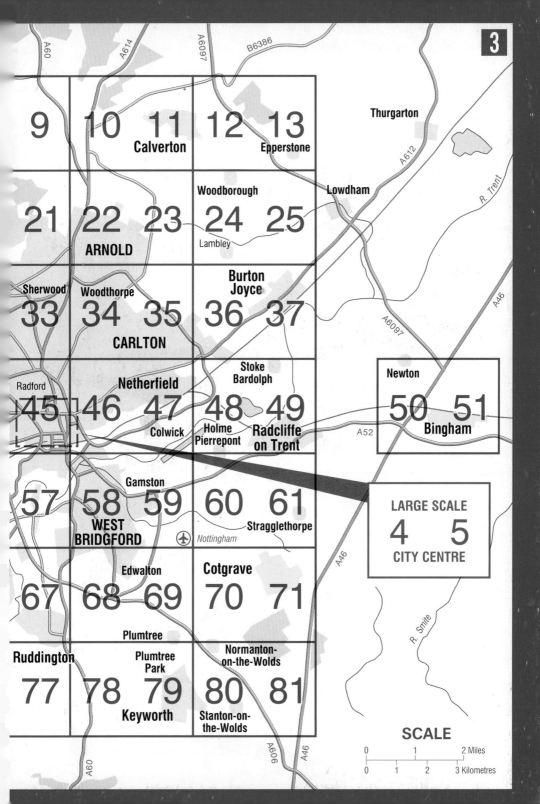

3

9 | 10 | 11 Calverton | 12 | 13 Epperstone

Thurgarton

21 | 22 ARNOLD | 23 | 24 Woodborough | 25

Lambley

Lowdham

33 Sherwood | 34 Woodthorpe | 35 | 36 Burton Joyce | 37

CARLTON

45 Radford | 46 Netherfield | 47 Colwick | 48 Holme Pierrepont | 49 Stoke Bardolph Radcliffe on Trent

Newton
50 | 51 Bingham

A52

57 | 58 WEST BRIDGFORD | 59 Gamston | 60 | 61 Stragglethorpe

Nottingham

LARGE SCALE
4 5
CITY CENTRE

67 | 68 Edwalton | 69 | 70 Cotgrave | 71

Plumtree

77 Ruddington | 78 Plumtree Park | 79 Keyworth | 80 Normanton-on-the-Wolds Stanton-on-the-Wolds | 81

SCALE

0 ... 1 ... 2 Miles
0 ... 1 ... 2 ... 3 Kilometres

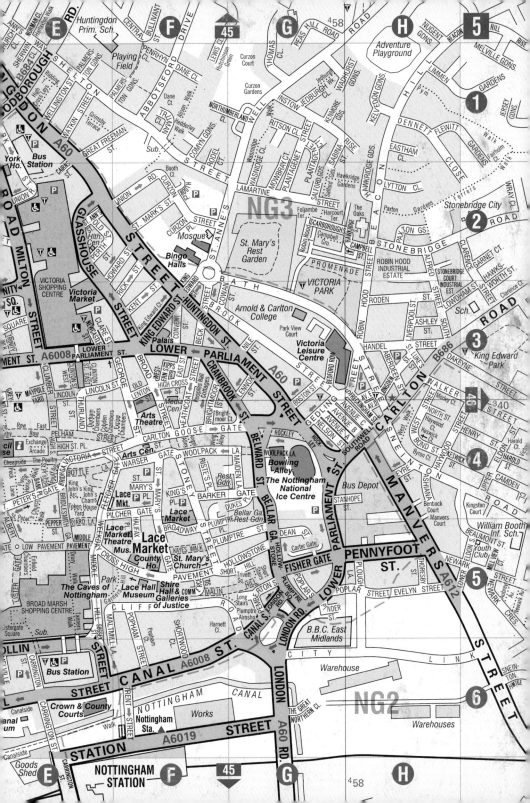

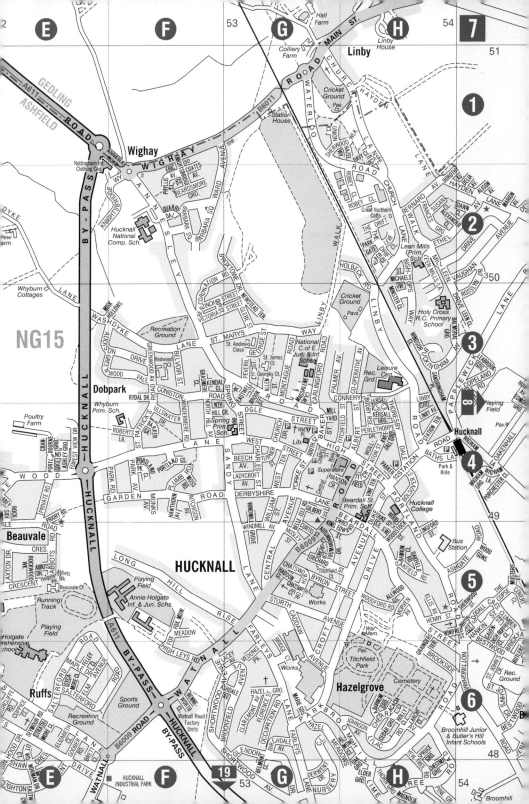

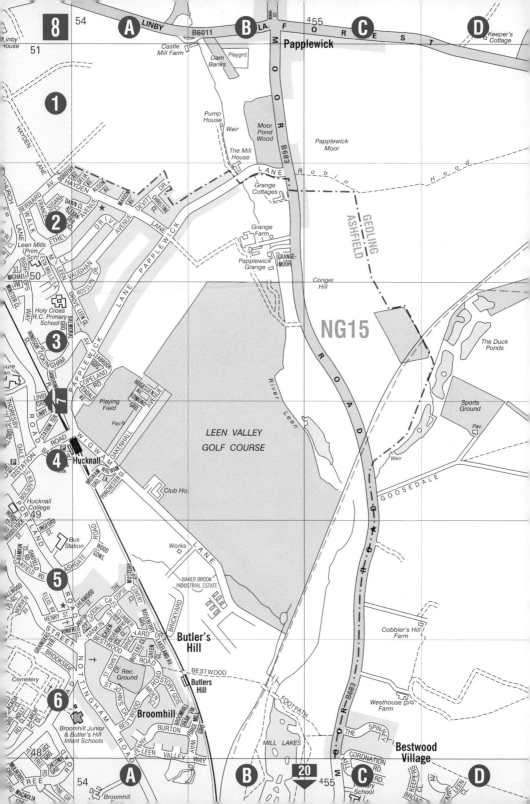

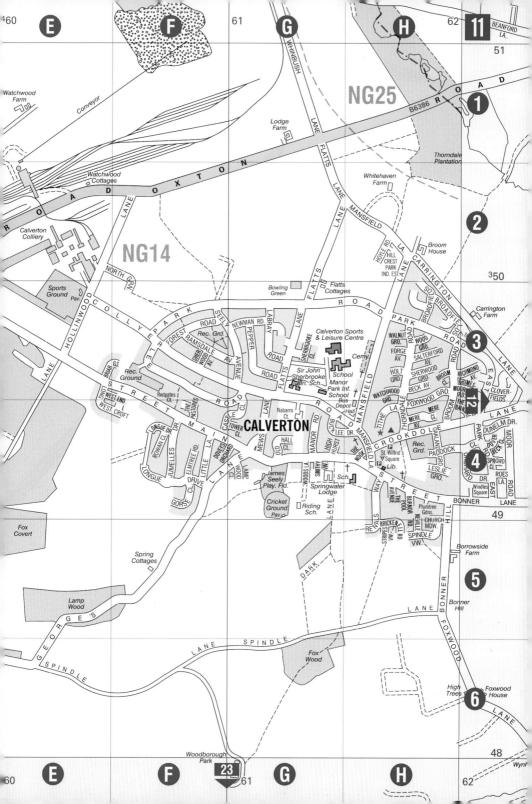

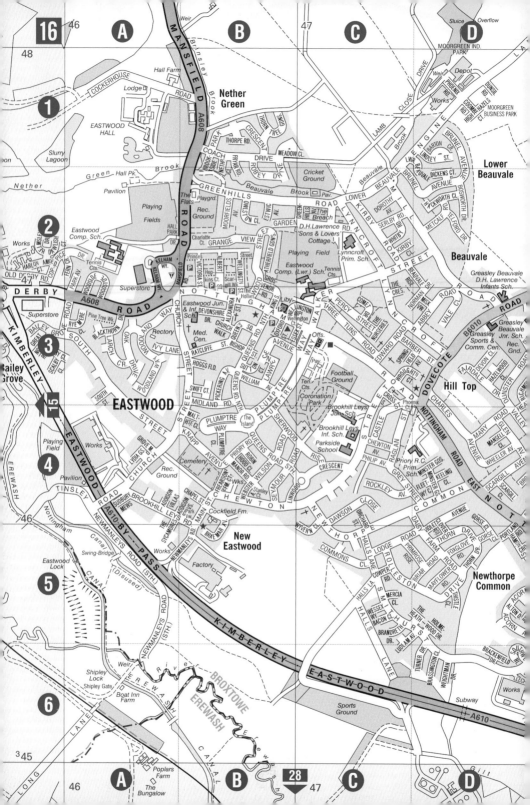

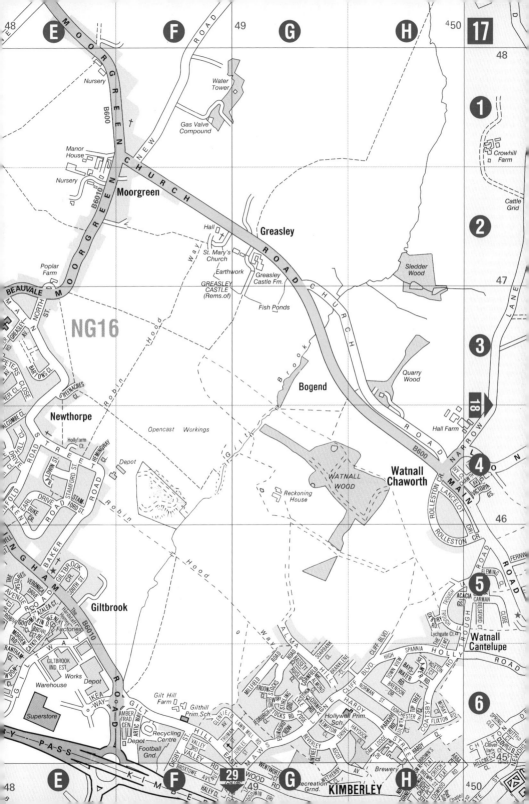

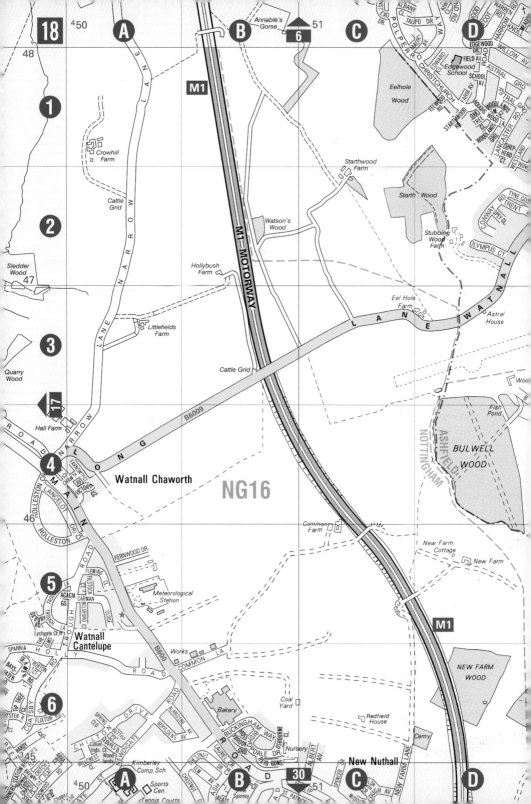

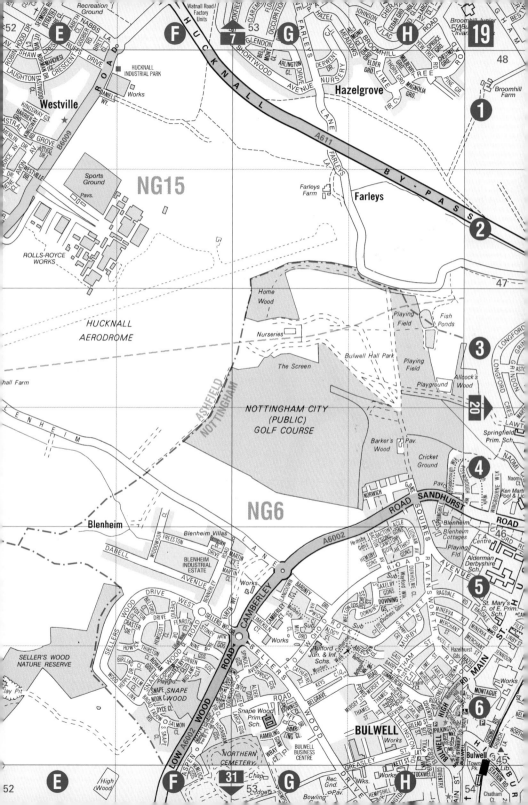

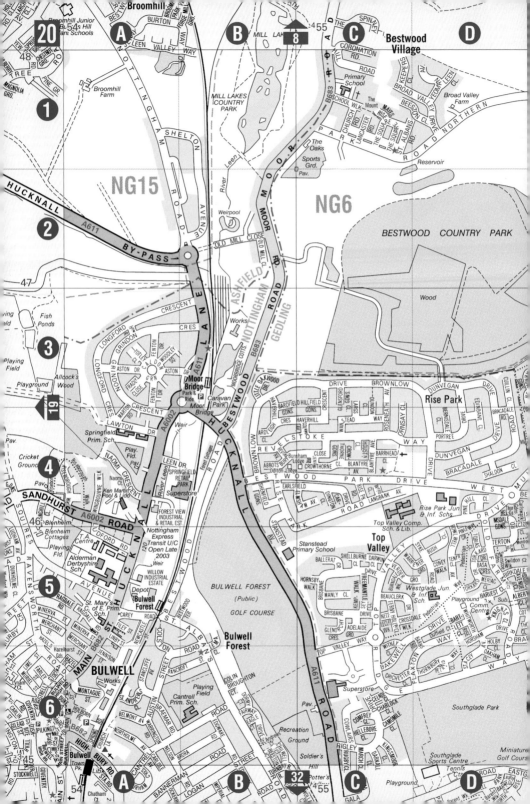

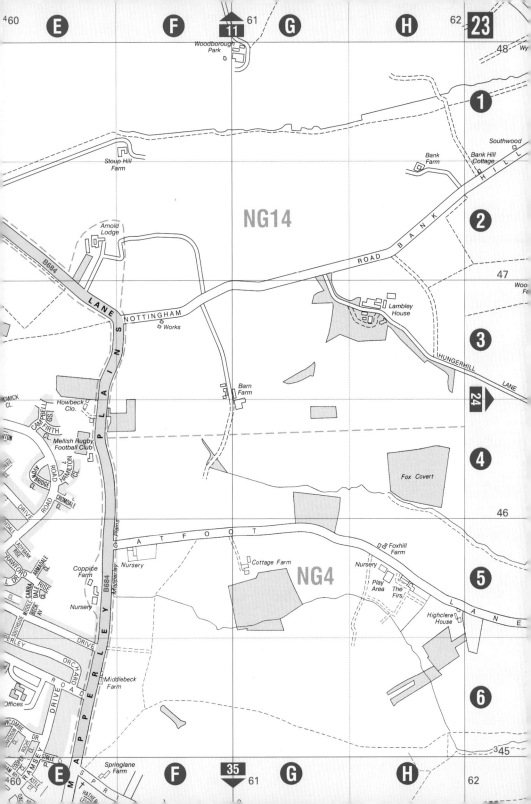

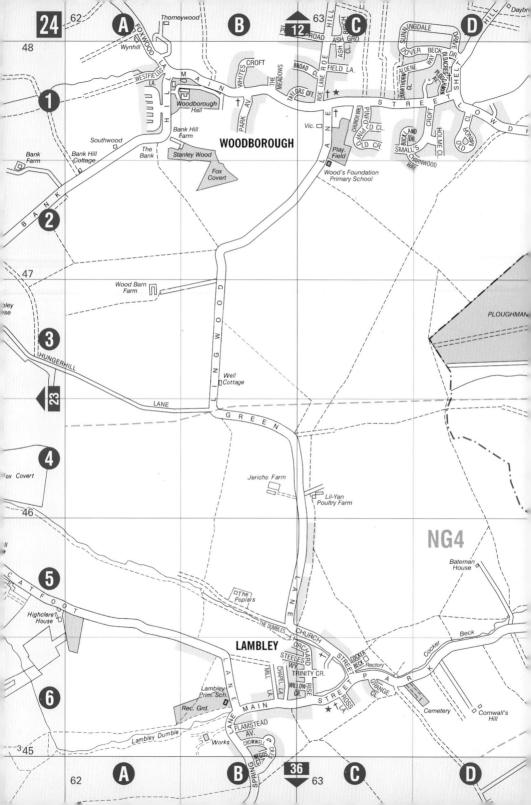

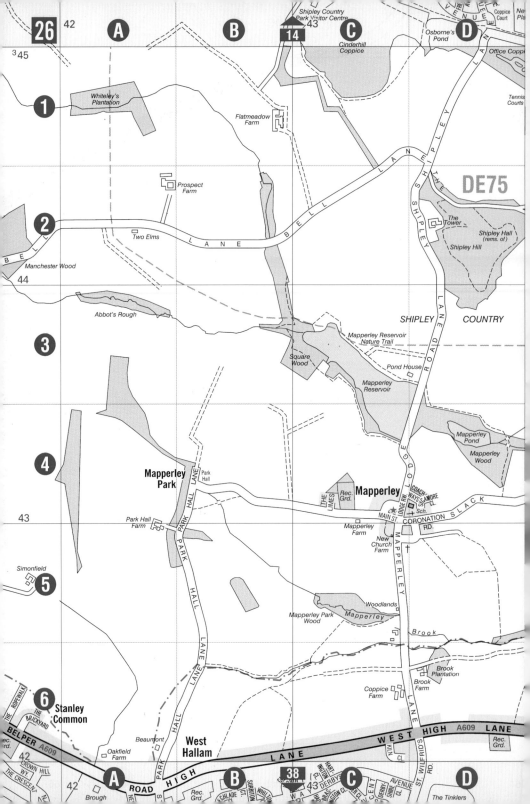

³45

A   B   C   D

Shipley Country
Park Visitor Centre
14
43

Cinderhill
Coppice

Osborne's
Pond

Coppice
Court

Office Copp

Tennis
Courts

1   Whiteley's
Plantation

Flatmeadow
Farm

Prospect
Farm

DE75

The
Tower

Shipley Hall
(rems. of)

2   Two Elms

BELL   LANE

Shipley Hill

SHIPLEY   LANE

THE   SHIPLEY

Manchester Wood

44

BELL

Abbot's Rough

SHIPLEY   COUNTRY

3

Square
Wood

Mapperley Reservoir
Nature Trail

Pond House

Mapperley
Reservoir

GODGE   ROW   ROAD

Mapperley
Pond

Mapperley
Wood

4

**Mapperley
Park**

Park
Hall

PARK   HALL   LANE

THE LIMES

Rec.
Grd.

Mapperley

COACH-
WAYS
Sch.

SYCAMORE
CL.

SLACK

43

Park Hall
Farm

Mapperley
Farm

Main St.

CORONATION   RD.

New Church
Farm

Simonfield

5

Mapperley Park
Wood

Mapperley

Woodlands

MAPPERLEY

Brook

Brook
Plantation

Coppice
Farm

Brook
Farm

6   **Stanley
Common**

THE BRICKYARD

THE RIDGEWALKS

BELPER   A609

Beaumont

Oakfield
Farm

**West
Hallam**

PARK   HALL   LANE

HIGH

WEST   HIGH   A609   LANE

Rec.
Grd.

42

CROWN HILL

THE CRESCENT

THE CROWN WY

A   ROAD   HIGH   B   **38**   43   C   ST. WILFRID'S RD.   D

42

Brough

Rec.
Grd.

ESCHLADE CT.

WHITTON

SURBITON

WAY

WEST

ING.

HART-
INGTON CL.
 DERBY

VINCENT

BRAS-
INGTON CL.

SHIRE CL.

AVENUE

The Tinklers

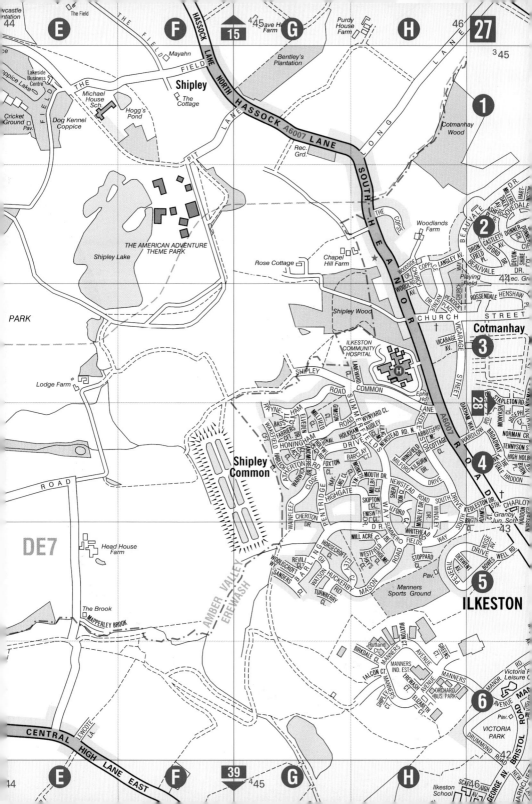

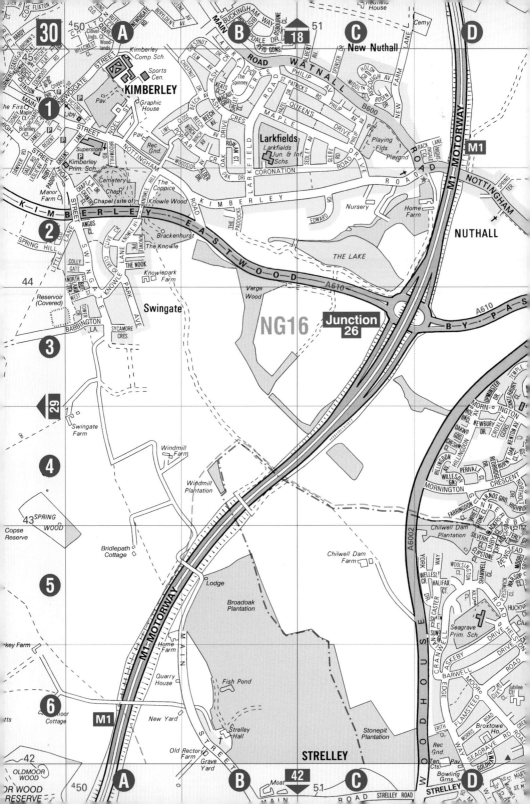

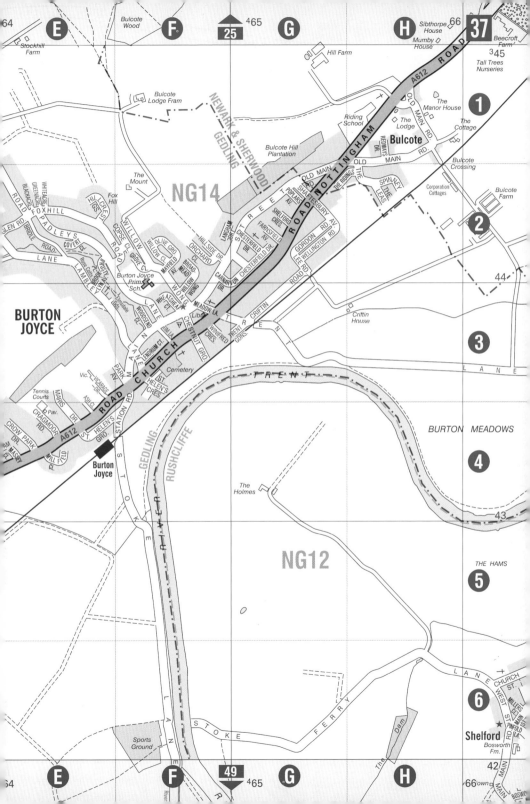

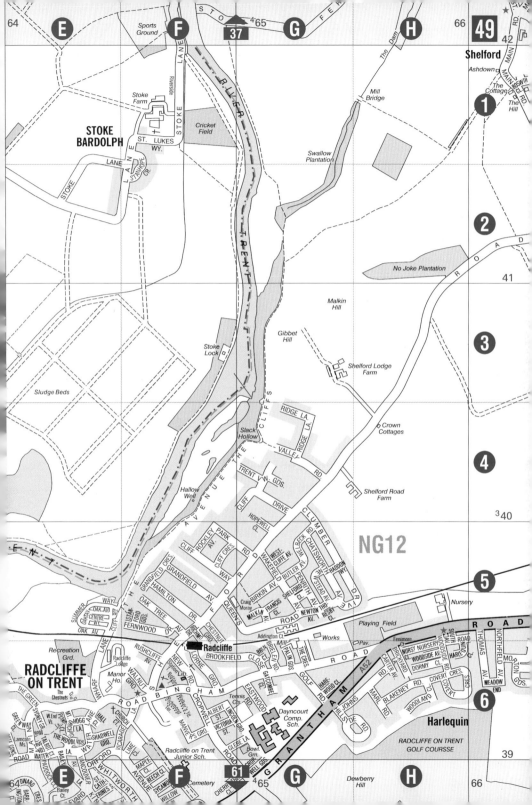

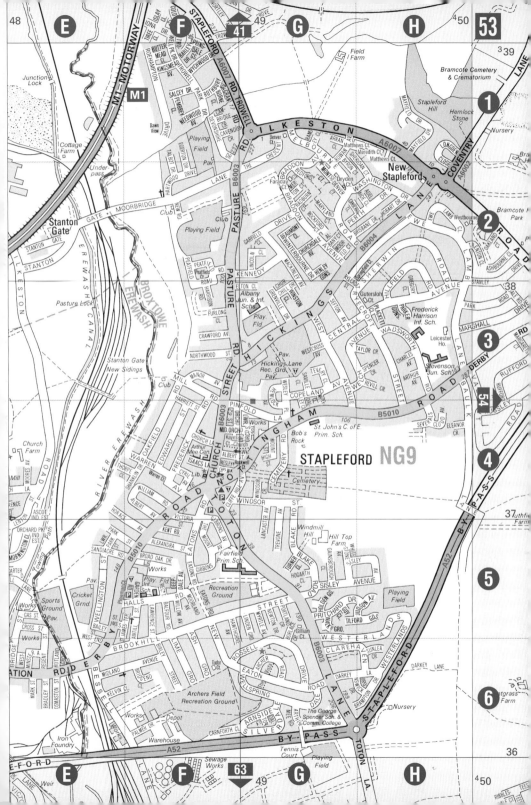

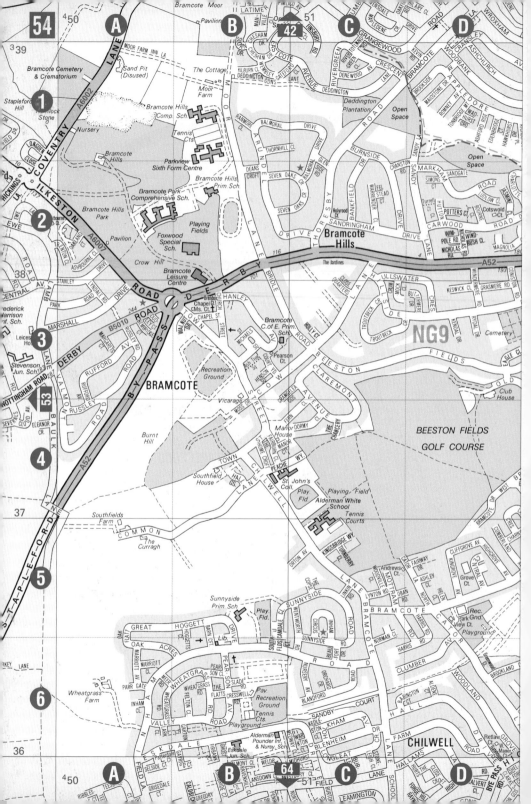

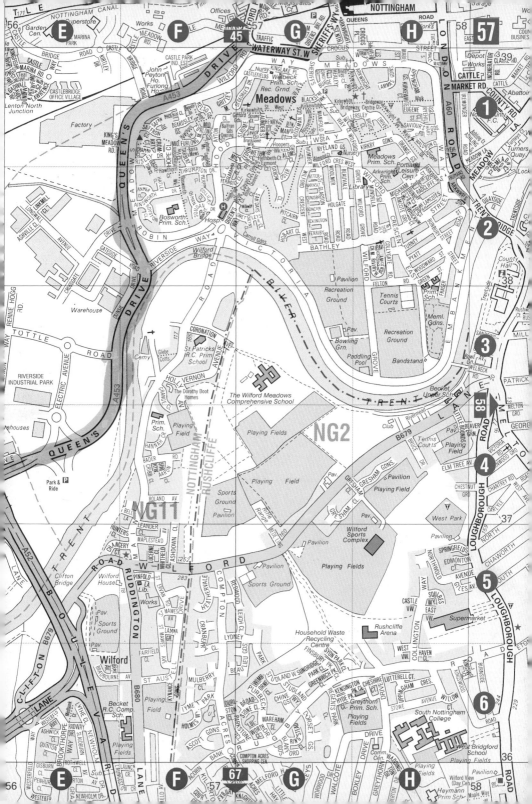

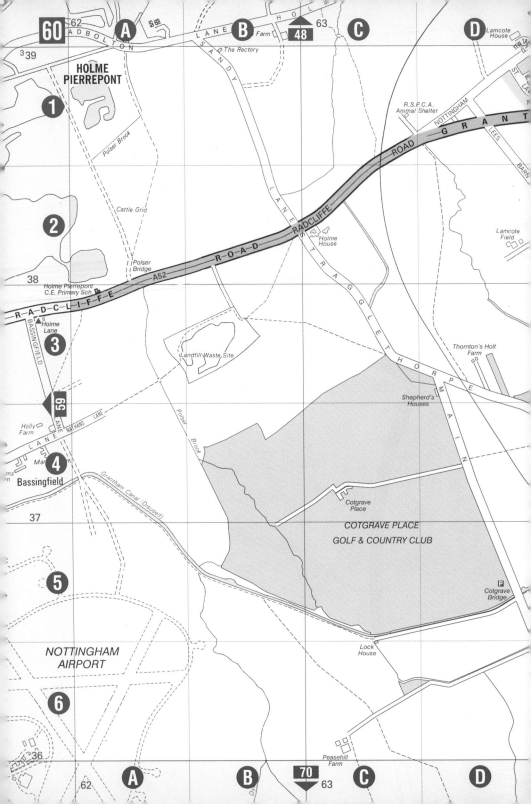

60

62

A ADBOLTON LANE **B** Farm **C** 63 **D** Lamcote House

3 39

HOLME PIERREPONT

1

Polser Brook

SANDY LANE

The Rectory

48

HOLM

R.S.P.C.A. Animal Shelter

NOTTINGHAM

FEN LANE

ST. PE LA.

2

Cattle Grid

ROAD GRANT

LEES BARN

RADCLIFFE

Lamcote Field

38

Polser Bridge

A52

ROAD

RADCLIFFE

Holme House

Holme Pierrepont C.E. Primary Sch.

BASSINGFIELD

R—A—D—C—L—I—F—F—E

6 Holme Lane

STRAGGLETHORPE

3

59

Holly Farm

LANE

NATHANS LANE

Landfill Waste Site

Thornton's Holt Farm

MAIN

Shepherd's Houses

Mar

ms

m

4

Bassingfield

Polser Brook

Grantham Canal (Disused)

Cotgrave Place

COTGRAVE PLACE GOLF & COUNTRY CLUB

37

5

P

Cotgrave Bridge

NOTTINGHAM AIRPORT

6

Lock House

36

62 **A** **B** 70 63 **C** Peasehill Farm **D**

E **F** **G** **H** 66

³39

Dewberry
Hill

Comp. Sch.

Victoria
St

Radcliffe on Trent
Junior School

Cemetery

Club
House

49

1

RADCLIFFE ON TRENT
GOLF COURSE

RADCLIFFE
ON TRENT

Lees Barn

Sunpit
Plantation

2

Radcliffe Barn
Farm

38

Works

Hall
Farm

3

NG12

Cockedhat
Plantation

North
Farm

Stragglethorpe

4

Paddock
Cottages

37

COTGRAVE COUNTRY

PARK

Brown's
Cotts.

5

Hollygate
Farm

Lock

6

Brown's
Bridge

Lock

Weirs

Gozen
Lodge

Homefields

Canal

(Disused)

36

E **F** **71** **G** **H** 66

Windmill
Hill

⁴65

Grantham

64

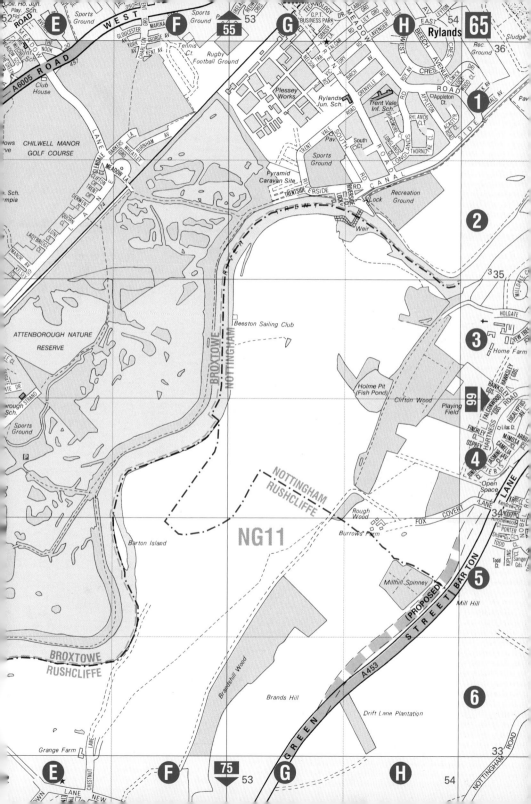

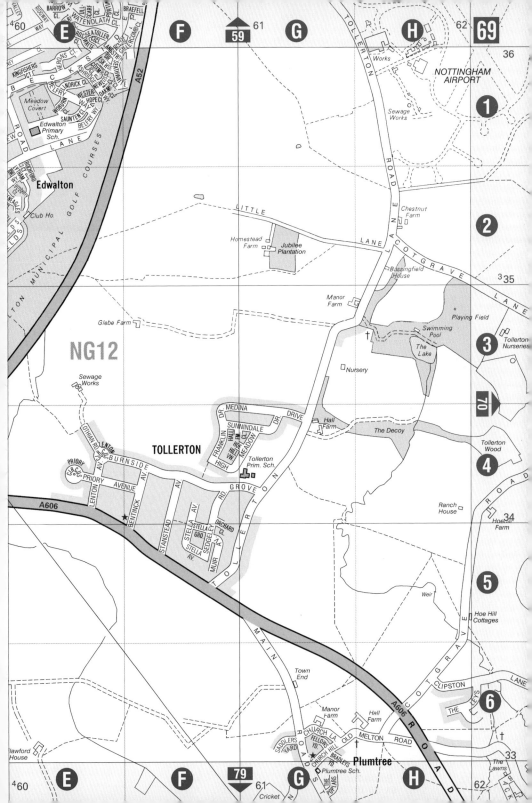

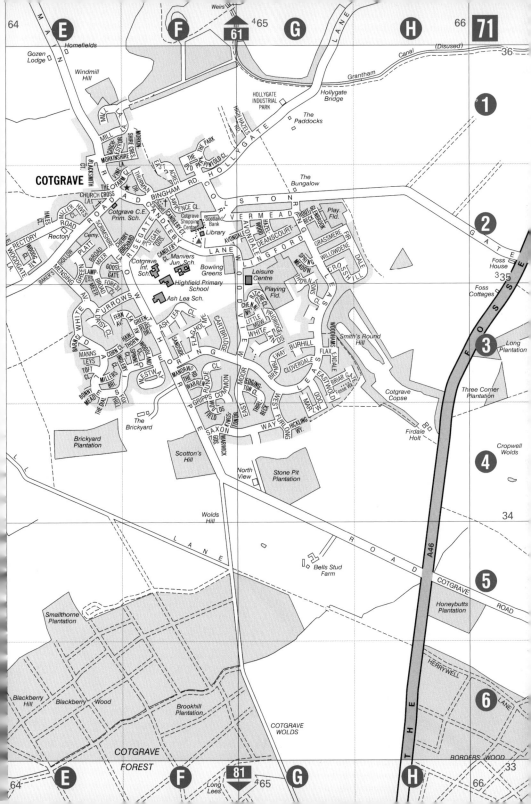

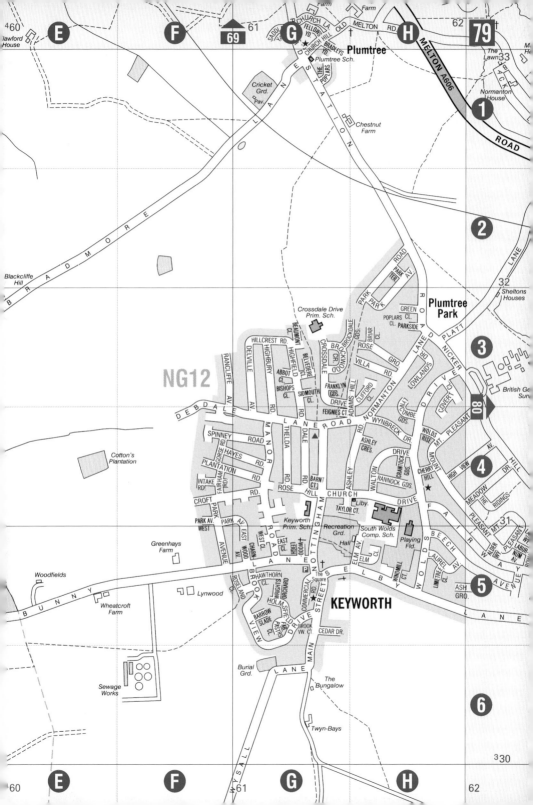

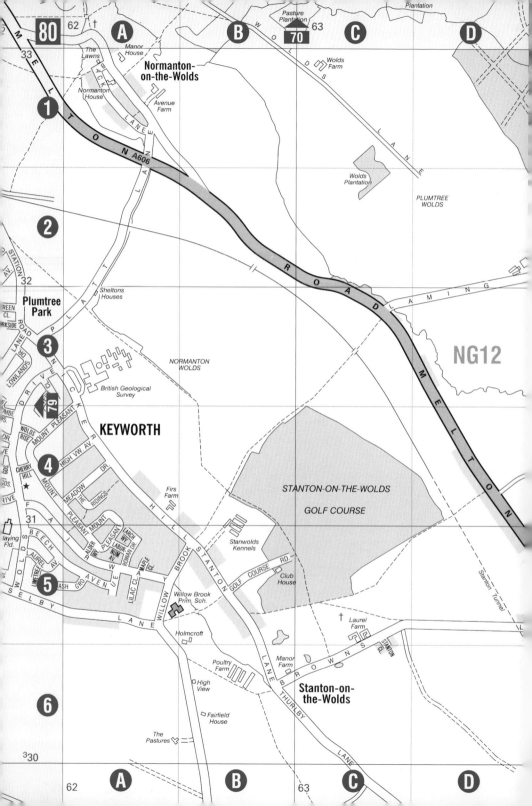

80

62 †

A

B

63

C

D

Plantation

Pasture Plantation

70

1

33

The Lawns

Manor House

Normanton House

Normanton-
on-the-Wolds

Avenue Farm

Wolds Farm

2

MELTON A606

ROAD

Wolds Plantation

PLUMTREE WOLDS

32

STATION AV.

Sheltons Houses

GREEN CL.
PARKSIDE

Plumtree Park

NORMANTON WOLDS

LAMING

NG12

3

LOWLANDS

PLATT LANE

DRIVE

British Geological Survey

ROAD

79

WOLDS RISE

MOUNT PLEASANT

KEYWORTH

MELTON

DR.

COMBE
DRIVE
WDS.

CHERRY HILL

HIGH VW. AV.

MEADOW DR.

THE RIDINGS

Firs Farm

STANTON-ON-THE-WOLDS

4

★

5

31

MOUNT PLEASANT
ALDER DR.
PLEASANT

LARCH WY.
LABUR.
NUM AV.
ROWAN DR.

MAPLE CL.
LILAC CL.

HILL

WILLOW BROOK

STANTON

GOLF COURSE

Stanwolds Kennels

GOLF COURSE

GOLF COURSE

RD.

Club House

Stanton Tunnel

laying Fld.

BEECH
LAUREL
LIMETREE AV.
ASH GRO.

WOLDS
SELBY

LANE

Willow Brook Prim. Sch.

Holmcroft

Poultry Farm

High View

Manor Farm

BROWNS

† Laurel Farm

STANTON CL.

Stanton-on-
the-Wolds

6

330

62

A

B

63

C

THURLBY LANE

Fairfield House

The Pastures

D

INDEX

Including Streets, Selected Subsidiary Addresses
and Selected Places of Interest.

HOW TO USE THIS INDEX

1. Each street name is followed by its Posttown or Postal Locality and then by its map reference; e.g. Aaron Clo. *Nott* —4F **57** is in the Nottingham Posttown and is to be found in square 4F on page **57**. The page number being shown in bold type. A strict alphabetical order is followed in which Av., Rd., St., etc. (though abbreviated) are read in full and as part of the street name; e.g. Abbotsbury Clo. appears after Abbot Rd. but before Abbots Clo.

2. Streets and a selection of Subsidiary names not shown on the Maps, appear in the index in *Italics* with the thoroughfare to which it is connected shown in brackets; e.g. *Albert Sq. Nott* —6C **44** *(off Church St.)*

3. An example of a selected place of interest is **Albion Leisure Cen.** —1B **40**

4. Map references shown in brackets; e.g. Abbotsford Dri. *Nott* —3H **45** (1F **5**) refer to entries that also appear on the large scale pages 4 & 5.

GENERAL ABBREVIATIONS

All : Alley	Ct : Court	Lit : Little	Rd : Road
App : Approach	Cres : Crescent	Lwr : Lower	Shop : Shopping
Arc : Arcade	Cft : Croft	Mc : Mac	S : South
Av : Avenue	Dri : Drive	Mnr : Manor	Sq : Square
Bk : Back	E : East	Mans : Mansions	Sta : Station
Boulevd : Boulevard	Embkmt : Embankment	Mkt : Market	St : Street
Bri : Bridge	Est : Estate	Mdw : Meadow	Ter : Terrace
B'way : Broadway	Fld : Field	M : Mews	Trad : Trading
Bldgs : Buildings	Gdns : Gardens	Mt : Mount	Up : Upper
Bus : Business	Gth : Garth	Mus : Museum	Va : Vale
Cvn : Caravan	Ga : Gate	N : North	Vw : View
Cen : Centre	Gt : Great	Pal : Palace	Vs : Villas
Chu : Church	Grn : Green	Pde : Parade	Vis : Visitors
Chyd : Churchyard	Gro : Grove	Pk : Park	Wlk : Walk
Circ : Circle	Ho : House	Pas : Passage	W : West
Cir : Circus	Ind : Industrial	Pl : Place	Yd : Yard
Clo : Close	Info : Information	Quad : Quadrant	
Comn : Common	Junct : Junction	Res : Residential	
Cotts : Cottages	La : Lane	Ri : Rise	

POSTTOWN AND POSTAL LOCALITY ABBREVIATIONS

Ann : Annesley	*Colw P* : Colwick Park	*L'by* : Linby	*Sand* : Sandiacre
Arn : Arnold	*Coss* : Cossall	*Locki* : Lockington	*Shard* : Shardlow
Att : Atterton	*Cotg* : Cotgrave	*Long E* : Long Eaton	*Shelf* : Shelford
Aws : Awsworth	*C But* : Cropwell Butler	*Los* : Loscoe	*Sher* : Sherwood
Bar F : Barton-in-Fabis	*Dal A* : Dale Abbey	*Low* : Lowdham	*Sher R* : Sherwood Rise
Bees : Beeston	*Day* : Daybrook	*Man I* : Manners Ind. Est.	*Ship* : Shipley
B Vil : Bestwood Village	*Den V* : Denby Village	*M'ley* : Mapperley (Ilkeston)	*Smal* : Smalley
Bilb : Bilborough	*Dray* : Draycott	*Map* : Mapperley (Nottingham)	*Snei* : Sneinton
Bing : Bingham	*Eastw* : Eastwood	*N'fld* : Netherfield	*Stan* : Stanley
Blen I : Bleneim Ind. Est.	*Edw* : Edwalton	*New B* : New Basford	*Stan C* : Stanley Common
Borr : Borrowash	*Epp* : Epperstone	*Newt* : Newthorpe	*Stan D* : Stanton-by-Dale
Bradm : Bradmore	*For F* : Forest Fields	*New* : Newton (Alfreton)	*S'fd* : Stapleford
Bramc : Bramcote	*Gam* : Gamston	*Nwtn* : Newton (Nottingham)	*Stock* : Stockhill
Breas : Breaston	*Ged* : Gedling	*Nott* : Nottingham	*Strel* : Strelley
Brins : Brinsley	*Gilt* : Giltbrook	*Nut* : Nuthall	*T'wd* : Thorneywood
Bul : Bulcote	*Got* : Gotham	*Old B* : Old Basford	*Thrum* : Thrumpton
Bulw : Bulwell	*Greas* : Greasley	*Oxt* : Oxton	*Toll* : Tollerton
Bun : Bunny	*Hean* : Heanor	*Pap* : Papplewick	*Trow* : Trowell
Bur J : Burton Joyce	*Hol P* : Holme Pierrepont	*Park T* : Park, The	*Wat* : Waterthorpe
C'tn : Calverton	*Huck* : Hucknall	*Plum* : Plumtree	*Watn* : Watnall
Cltn : Carlton	*Ilk* : Ilkeston	*Quar H* : Quarry Hill Ind. Est.	*W Bri* : West Bridgford
Carr : Carrington	*Keyw* : Keyworth	*Q Dri* : Queens Drive Ind. Est.	*W Hal* : West Hallam
Clif : Clifton	*Kimb* : Kimberley	*Rad T* : Radcliffe-on-Trent	*Wilf* : Wilford
Clip : Clipston	*Lamb* : Lambley	*R'hd* : Ravenshead	*Woll* : Wollaton
Cols B : Colston Bassett	*Lan M* : Langley Mill	*Red* : Redhill	*Wdbgh* : Woodborough
Colw : Colwick	*Lent* : Lenton	*Ris* : Risley	*Wd'p* : Woodthorpe
Colw I : Colwick Ind. Est.	*Lent L* : Lenton Lane Ind. Est.	*Rud* : Ruddington	

INDEX

Aaron Clo. *Nott* —4F **57**
Abba Clo. *Kimb* —6H **17**
Abbey Bri. *Nott* —1C **56**
Abbey Cir. *W Bri* —4C **58**
Abbey Clo. *Huck* —4E **7**
Abbey Ct. *Bees* —3F **55**
Abbey Ct. *Nott* —5D **44**
Abbeyfield Rd. *Nott* —3D **56**
Abbey Gro. *Nott* —2B **46**
Abbey Rd. *Bees* —3F **55**
Abbey Rd. *Bing* —4G **51**

Abbey Rd. *Eastw* —3D **16**
Abbey Rd. *W Bri* —4C **58**
Abbey St. *Ilk* —5B **28**
Abbey St. *Nott* —1C **56**
Abbot Clo. *Keyw* —3G **79**
Abbot Rd. *Ilk* —3G **39**
Abbotsbury Clo. *Day* —1H **33**
Abbots Clo. *Huck* —5E **7**
Abbotsford Dri. *Nott* —3H **45** (1F **5**)
Abbotsford M. *Ilk* —4H **27**
Abbots Rd. *Huck* —5E **7**

Abbot St. *Aws* —3E **29**
Abbots Wlk. *Huck* —5E **7**
Abbots Way. *Nott* —5H **43**
Abbott St. *Hean* —4C **14**
Abbott St. *Long E* —1F **73**
Abercarn Clo. *Nott* —6H **19**
Aberdeen St. *Nott* —4A **46** (3H **5**)
Aberford Av. *Nott* —1B **44**
Abingdon Dri. *Rud* —5H **67**
Abingdon Gdns. *Bees* —1D **64**
Abingdon Gdns. *Wd'p* —2C **34**
Abingdon Rd. *W Bri* —4C **58**

Abingdon Sq. *Nott* —6H **31**
Ablard Gdns. *Bees* —3C **64**
Acacia Clo. *Huck* —6H **7**
Acacia Ct. *Nott* —3H **45** (1G **5**)
Acacia Cres. *Cltn* —1H **47**
Acacia Gdns. *Watn* —5H **17**
Acacia Wlk. *Bees* —5F **55**
Academy Clo. *Nott* —4B **32**
Acaster Clo. *Bees* —1H **65**
Acle Gdns. *Nott* —4H **19**
Acorn Av. *Gilt* —5D **16**
Acorn Bank. *W Bri* —1F **67**

Acorn Dri. *Ged* —4A **36**
Acorn Pk. *Lent L* —3C **56**
Acourt St. *Nott* —3D **44**
Acton Av. *Long E* —1G **73**
Acton Av. *Nott* —3B **32**
Acton Clo. *Long E* —1G **73**
Acton Rd. *Arn* —5H **21**
Acton Rd. *Long E* —6G **63**
Acton Rd. Ind. Est. *Long E*
　　　　　　　　　　　　—1G **73**
Acton St. *Long E* —1G **73**
Adale Rd. *Smal* —5A **14**
Adams Clo. *Hean* —5B **14**
Adams Ct. *Ilk* —4A **28**
Adams Hill. *Keyw* —4H **79**
Adams Hill. *Nott* —1H **55**
Adam St. *Ilk* —3C **40**
Adbolton Av. *Ged* —6G **35**
Adbolton Gro. *W Bri* —1D **58**
Adbolton La. *W Bri & Hol P*
　　　　　　　　　　　　—2D **58**
Adbolton Lodge. *Cltn* —2D **58**
Adderley Clo. *Nott* —1E **33**
Addington Ct. *Rad T* —5G **49**
Addington Rd. *Nott* —3D **44**
Addison Dri. *Huck* —3E **7**
Addison Rd. *Cltn* —1D **46**
Addison Vs. *Nott* —2F **45** (1C **4**)
Addison Vs. *Eastw* —4A **16**
(in two parts)
Adelaide Clo. *S'fd* —2H **53**
Adelaide Gro. *Nott* —5C **20**
Adel Dri. *Ged* —5G **35**
Adenburgh Dri. *Bees* —4D **64**
Admiral Clo. *Hean* —3C **14**
Adrian Clo. *Bees* —4H **63**
Aeneas Ct. *Nott* —1F **45**
Agnes Vs. *Nott* —5A **34**
Aidan Gdns. *Nott* —3E **21**
Ainsdale Cres. *Nott* —4G **31**
Ainsley Rd. *Nott* —3B **44**
Ainsworth Dri. *Nott* —2F **57**
Aintree Clo. *Kimb* —6G **17**
Aira Clo. *Gam* —5F **59**
Airedale Clo. *Long E* —1C **72**
Airedale Ct. *Bees* —1A **64**
Airedale Wlk. *Nott* —6C **42**
Aitchison Av. *Huck* —4F **7**
Alandene Av. *Nuth* —6A **18**
Albany Clo. *Arn* —6A **22**
Albany Clo. *Huck* —6C **6**
Albany Ct. *S'fd* —2G **53**
Albany Rd. *Nott* —1E **45**
Albany St. *Ilk* —3C **40**
Albemarle Rd. *Wd'p* —3H **33**
Alberta Ter. *Nott* —1E **45**
Albert Av. *Cltn* —2D **46**
Albert Av. *Nott* —1B **44**
Albert Av. *Nut* —6C **18**
Albert Av. *S'fd* —4F **53**
Albert Ball Clo. *Nott* —5D **20**
Albert Gro. *Nott* —4D **44**
Albert Hall. —4C **4**
Albert Rd. *Bees* —3G **55**
Albert Rd. *Bun* —6A **78**
Albert Rd. *Lent* —6D **44**
Albert Rd. *Long E* —5F **63**
Albert Rd. *Nott* —6H **33**
Albert Rd. *Sand* —5D **52**
Albert Rd. *W Bri* —3B **58**
Albert Sq. Nott —6C **44**
(off Church St.)
Albert St. *Eastw* —2B **16**
(in two parts)
Albert St. *Ged* —6H **35**
Albert St. *Huck* —4H **7**
Albert St. *Ilk* —1A **40**
Albert St. *Nott* —5G **45** (4E **5**)
Albert St. *Rad T* —6F **49**
Albert St. *S'fd* —4F **53**
Albion Cen., The. *Ilk* —1B **40**
Albion Leisure Cen. —1B **40**
Albion Ri. *Arn* —4B **22**
Albion Rd. *Long E* —5H **63**
Albion St. *Bees* —4F **55**
Albion St. *Ilk* —6B **28**
Albion St. *Nott* —6G **45** (6D **4**)

Albury Dri. *Nott* —6H **31**
Albury Sq. *Nott* —5E **45** (4A **4**)
Alcester St. *Nott* —3C **56**
Aldene Ct. *Bees* —6D **54**
Aldene Way. *Wdbgh* —1C **24**
Aldercar La. *Lan M* —1F **15**
Alder Gdns. *Nott* —6G **19**
Aldermens Clo. *Nott* —1G **57**
Alderney St. *Nott* —6D **44**
Alderton Rd. *Nott* —1G **33**
Alder Way. *Keyw* —5A **80**
Aldgate Clo. *Nott* —5G **19**
Aldred's La. *Hean & Lan M* —4E **15**
Aldridge Clo. *Bees* —3G **63**
Aldrin Clo. *Nott* —2F **31**
Aldworth Clo. *Nott* —1F **33**
Aldwych Clo. *Arn* —4E **21**
Aldwych Clo. *Nut* —5D **30**
Alexander Clo. *Huck* —2H **7**
Alexander Fleming Building. *Nott*
　　　　　　　　　　　　—3B **56**
Alexander Rd. *Nott* —5E **45** (5A **4**)
Alexandra Cres. *Bees* —5G **55**
Alexandra Gdns. *Nott* —6F **33**
Alexandra M. *Nott* —1F **45**
Alexandra Rd. *Long E* —5F **63**
Alexandra St. *Eastw* —3B **16**
Alexandra St. *Nott* —1F **45**
Alexandra St. *S'fd* —5F **53**
Alford Clo. *Bees* —6G **55**
(in two parts)
Alford Rd. *W Bri & Edw* —5D **58**
Alfred Av. *Nott* —5C **34**
Alfred Clo. *Nott* —3G **45**
Alfred St. Central. *Nott* —3G **45**
Alfred St. N. *Nott* —3G **45**
Alfred St. S. *Nott* —4A **46** (2H **5**)
Alfreton Rd. *Nott* —2C **44** (2A **4**)
Alison Av. *Huck* —2A **8**
Alison Wlk. *Nott* —3H **45** (1F **5**)
Allandale Rd. *Hean* —3B **14**
Allen Av. *Nott* —6C **34**
(in two parts)
Allendale. *Ilk* —2A **40**
Allendale Av. *Bees* —3D **64**
Allendale Av. *Nott* —6F **31**
Allen Fld. Ct. *Nott* —6D **44**
Allen St. *Huck* —3G **7**
Allen's Wlk. *Arn* —4B **22**
All Hallows Dri. *Ged* —5H **35**
Allington Av. *Nott* —6D **44**
Allison Gdns. *Bees* —1D **64**
Allison Gdns. *Ilk* —6C **28**
All Saints St. *Nott* —3E **45** (1A **4**)
All Saints Ter. *Nott* —3E **45** (1A **4**)
Allwood Dri. *Cltn* —1G **47**
Allwood Gdns. *Huck* —5H **7**
Alma Clo. *Ged* —5A **36**
Alma Clo. *Nott* —3G **45** (1D **4**)
Alma Hill. *Kimb* —5G **17**
Alma Rd. *Nott* —3B **46**
Alma St. *Nott* —1E **45**
Almond Clo. *Huck* —6H **7**
Almond Clo. *Kimb* —6G **17**
Almond Ct. *Nott* —1G **57**
Almond Wlk. *Ged* —5A **36**
Alnwick Clo. *Nott* —1B **32**
Alpha Ter. *Nott* —3F **45**
Alpine Cres. *Cltn* —1G **47**
Alpine St. *Nott* —5C **32**
Althorpe St. *Nott* —4E **45**
Alton Av. *Nott* —1F **67**
Alton Clo. *W Bri* —2G **67**
Alton Dri. *Gilt* —5D **16**
Alum Ct. *Nott* —5D **20**
Alvenor St. *Ilk* —6B **28**
Alverstone Rd. *Nott* —6G **33**
Alvey Ter. *Nott* —4C **44**
Alwood Gro. *Nott* —2B **66**
Alwyn Ct. *Bees* —6F **55**
Alwyn Rd. *Nott* —5F **31**
Alyth Ct. *Nott* —4D **32**
Amber Ct. *Hean* —4C **14**
Amber Dri. *Lan M* —3F **15**
Ambergate Rd. *Nott* —2G **43**
(in two parts)
Amber Hill. *Nott* —6F **21**
Amberley Clo. *Ilk* —3B **40**
Amber Trad. Cen. *Kimb* —6F **17**

Ambleside. *Gam* —4E **59**
Ambleside Dri. *Eastw* —2H **15**
Ambleside Rd. *Nott* —6G **31**
Ambleside Way. *Ged* —1B **48**
American Adventure Theme Pk.
　　　　　　　　　　　　—2G **27**
Amersham Ri. *Nott* —6H **31**
Amesbury Cir. *Nott* —4G **31**
Amilda Av. *Ilk* —1B **40**
Ampthill Ri. *Nott* —3F **33**
Ancaster Gdns. *Nott* —4G **43**
Anchor Clo. *Nott* —5H **31**
Anchor Ct. *Nott* —6F **21**
Anchor Rd. *Eastw* —2G **15**
Anchor Row. *Ilk* —1B **40**
Anders Dri. *Nott* —2F **31**
Anderson Ct. *Nott* —5E **21**
Anderson Cres. *Bees* —3E **55**
Andover Clo. *Nott* —3H **43**
Andover Rd. *Nott* —1C **32**
Andrew Av. *Ilk* —2D **40**
Andrew Av. *Nott* —5C **34**
Andrews Ct. *Bees* —5C **54**
Andrews Dri. *Lan M* —1E **15**
Anfield Clo. *Bees* —3A **64**
Anford Clo. *Nott* —2H **31**
Angear Vis. Cen. —2B **56**
Angela Clo. *Arn* —3A **22**
Angela Ct. *Bees* —3B **64**
Angel All. *Nott* —5H **45** (4F **5**)
Angelica Ct. *Bing* —5C **50**
Angel Row. *Nott* —5G **45 (4D **4**)**
Angel Row Gallery. —4D **4**
Angletarn Clo. *W Bri* —5E **59**
Angrave Clo. *Nott* —2A **46**
Angus Clo. *Arn* —4D **22**
Angus Clo. *Kimb* —2A **30**
Anmer Clo. *Nott* —2F **57**
Annan Ct. *Nott* —1H **43**
Anne's Clo. *Nott* —5C **34**
Annesley Gro. *Nott* —3F **45** (1C **4**)
Annesley Rd. *Ann* —1D **6**
Annesley Rd. *Huck* —1D **6**
Annesley Rd. *W Bri* —4B **58**
Anslow Av. *Bees* —3G **55**
Anson Ter. *Nott* —2D **44**
Anson Wlk. *Ilk* —4B **28**
Anstee Rd. *Long E* —2E **73**
Anstey Ri. *Nott* —4B **46**
Anthony Wharton Ct. *Nott* —2C **66**
Antill St. *S'fd* —5F **53**
Apollo Dri. *Nott* —2F **31**
Appleby Clo. *Ilk* —3B **40**
Appledore Av. *Nott* —1D **54**
Appledorne Way. *Arn* —4A **22**
Appleton Clo. *Nott* —5A **66**
Appleton Ct. *Bees* —1H **65**
Appleton Rd. *Bees* —1H **65**
Apple Tree Clo. *Edw* —1C **68**
Appletree La. *Ged* —5H **35**
Apple Wlk. *Nott* —1C **46**
Applewood Gro. *Nott* —4H **33**
Arboretum St. *Nott* —3F **45** (1B **4**)
Arbour Hill. *Dal A* —6C **38**
Arbrook Dri. *Nott* —3B **44**
Arbutus Clo. *Nott* —4A **66**
Archdale Rd. *Nott* —1G **33**
Archer Cres. *Nott* —4F **43**
Archer Rd. *S'fd* —6G **53**
Archer St. *Ilk* —4A **28**
Arch Hill. *Red* —2A **22**
Archway Ct. Nott —3D **44**
(off Limpenny St.)
Arden Clo. *Bees* —3G **55**
Arden Clo. *Huck* —6A **8**
Arden Gro. *Bing* —4C **50**
Ardleigh Clo. *Nott* —4B **20**
Ardmore Clo. *Nott* —6B **46**
Ardsley Clo. *Hean* —3E **15**
Argyle Ct. *Nott* —4D **44**
Argyle St. *Lan M* —1F **15**
Argyle St. *Nott* —4D **44**
Ariel Clo. *Nott* —2D **32**
Arkers Clo. *Nott* —4B **32**
Arklow Clo. *Nott* —5G **31**
Arkwright St. *Nott* —1H **57**
(in two parts)
Arkwright St. N. *Nott* —6G **45**
Arkwright St. S. *Nott* —2H **57**

Arkwright Wlk. *Nott* —1G **57**
(in two parts)
Arleston Dri. *Nott* —6D **42**
Arlington Clo. *Huck* —6G **19**
Arlington Dri. *Nott* —6G **33**
Armadale Clo. *Arn* —5E **23**
Armfield Rd. *Arn* —1E **35**
Armitage Dri. *Long E* —6A **64**
Armstrong Rd. *Nott* —2F **31**
Arncliffe Clo. *Nott* —5C **42**
Arndale Rd. *Nott* —2G **33**
Arne Ct. *Nott* —2G **57**
Arnesby Rd. *Nott* —6B **44**
Arno Av. *Nott* —1F **45**
Arnold Av. *Long E* —3C **72**
Arnold Cres. *Long E* —3C **72**
Arnold La. *Ged* —2D **34**
Arnold Rd. *Nott* —3C **32**
Arnos Gro. *Nut* —4D **30**
Arnot Hill Rd. Arn —6A **22**
Arnot Ho. Cltn —1G **47**
(off Foxhill Rd. E.)
Arno Va. Gdns. *Wd'p* —2B **34**
Arno Va. Rd. *Wd'p* —2A **34**
Arnside. *S'fd* —6G **53**
Arnside Clo. *Nott* —2F **33**
Arnside Rd. *Nott* —2E **33**
A Rd. *Lent* —5A **56**
Arran Clo. *S'fd* —1G **53**
Arthur Av. *Nott* —5D **44**
Arthur Av. *S'fd* —3H **53**
Arthur Cres. *Cltn* —2E **47**
Arthur Mee Rd. *S'fd* —6G **53**
Arthur St. *N'fld* —3A **48**
Arthur St. *Nott* —3E **45** (1A **4**)
Artic Way. *Kimb* —6F **17**
Arts Cen. —4F **5**
Arundel Clo. *Sand* —1D **62**
Arundel Dri. *Bees* —1B **54**
Arundel St. *Nott* —4E **45**
Ascot Av. *Kimb* —6G **17**
Ascot Clo. *W Hal* —2B **38**
Ascot Dri. *Huck* —6D **6**
Ascot Dri. *Red* —5H **21**
Ascot Ind. Est. *Sand* —4E **53**
Ascot Pl. *Ilk* —4G **39**
Ascot Rd. *Nott* —2B **44**
Ascott Gdns. *W Bri* —6F **57**
Ashbourne Clo. *Bees* —2A **54**
Ashbourne Ct. *Nott* —1F **31**
Ashbourne St. *Nott* —4E **45**
Ashburnham Av. *Nott* —5D **44**
Ashchurch Dri. *Nott* —1D **54**
Ash Clo. *Bing* —5G **51**
Ash Clo. *Bur J* —3E **37**
Ash Clo. *Huck* —6C **6**
Ash Clo. *Wdbgh* —1C **24**
Ash Ct. *Cltn* —2F **47**
Ash Cres. *Nut* —1B **30**
Ashdale Av. *Huck* —6G **7**
Ashdale Rd. *Arn* —5C **22**
Ashdale Rd. *Ilk* —3C **40**
Ashdale Rd. *Nott* —3D **46**
Ashdown Clo. *Wilf* —5F **57**
Ashdown Gro. *Bing* —5D **50**
Ashe Clo. *Arn* —6D **22**
Asher La. *Rud* —1G **77**
Ashfield Av. *Bees* —6H **55**
Ashfield Rd. *Nott* —5B **46**
Ashford Ct. *W Hal* —1B **38**
Ashford Pl. *Ilk* —2A **28**
Ashford Ri. *Nott* —1D **54**
Ash Forth Av. *Hean* —4E **15**
Ashforth St. *Nott* —3H **45**
Ashgate Rd. *Huck* —5H **7**
Ash Gro. *Keyw* —5H **79**
Ash Gro. *Long E* —1E **73**
Ash Gro. *Sand* —4C **52**
Ash Gro. *S'fd* —5F **53**
Ash Gro. *Wdbgh* —6C **12**
Ashiana. *Nott* —5A **46** (4H **5**)
Ashington Dri. *Arn* —3C **22**
Ash Lea Clo. *Cotg* —3F **71**
Ashley Clo. *Bees* —5D **54**
Ashley Ct. *Bees* —5E **55**
Ashley Cres. *Keyw* —4H **79**
Ashley Gro. *Huck* —4E **7**
Ashley Rd. *Keyw* —4G **79**
Ashley St. *Nott* —4A **46** (3H **5**)

Ashling Ct. *Nott* —1A **58**
Ashling St. *Nott* —1H **57**
Ash Mt. Rd. *Lan M* —2F **15**
Ashness Clo. *Gam* —5E **59**
Ashridge Way. *Edw* —1E **69**
Ash St. *Ilk* —3A **28**
Ashton Av. *Arn* —3B **22**
Ash Tree Sq. *Bees* —3B **54**
Ash Vw. *Nott* —3D **44**
Ashview Clo. *Long E* —5D **62**
Ash Vs. *Nott* —6F **33**
Ashville Clo. *Q Dri* —2E **57**
Ashwater Dri. *Nott* —1F **35**
Ashwell Ct. *Wd'p* —3A **34**
Ashwell Gdns. *Nott* —1C **44**
Ashwell St. *N'fld* —3H **47**
Ashwick Clo. *Nott* —6E **57**
Ashworth Av. *Rud* —5G **67**
Ashworth Clo. *Nott* —4E **47**
Ashworth Cres. *Nott* —5D **34**
Askeby Dri. *Nott* —6D **30**
Aslockton Dri. *Nott* —5B **32**
Aspen Clo. *Bing* —5G **51**
Aspen Rd. *Nott* —1F **31**
Asper St. *N'fld* —2A **48**
Aspinall Ct. *Nott* —4A **44**
Aspley La. *Nott* —6F **31**
Aspley Pk. Dri. *Nott* —1G **43**
Aspley Pl. *Nott* —3D **44**
Assarts Lodge. *Nut* —3D **30**
Assarts Rd. *Nut* —3E **31**
Astcote Clo. *Hean* —4E **15**
Aster Rd. *Nott* —2H **45**
Astle Ct. *Arn* —1E **35**
Astley Dri. *Nott* —6B **34**
Aston Av. *Bees* —3G **55**
Aston Ct. *Ilk* —6B **28**
Aston Ct. *Nott* —2C **56**
Aston Dri. *Nott* —3A **20**
Aston Grn. *Bees* —2G **63**
Astral Dri. *Huck* —1E **19**
Astral Gro. *Huck* —1D **18**
(in two parts)
Astrid Gdns. *Nott* —1D **32**
Astwood Clo. *Nott* —2E **43**
Atherfield Gdns. *Eastw* —2B **16**
Atherton Ri. *Nott* —4H **31**
Atherton Rd. *Ilk* —4G **27**
Athorpe Gro. *Nott* —4D **32**
Attenborough La. *Bees* —3D **64**
Attenborough La. N. *Bees* —2C **64**
Attenborough Nature Reserve.
—2F **65**
Attercliffe Ter. *Nott* —2G **57**
Attewell Rd. *Aws* —2D **28**
Aubrey Av. *Nott* —5A **46** (5H 5)
Aubrey Rd. *Nott* —5F **33**
Aubyn Clo. *Stan C* —1A **38**
Auckland Clo. *Nott* —4C **44**
Auckland Rd. *Huck* —6D **6**
Audley Clo. *Ilk* —4H **27**
Audley Dri. *Bees* —2F **55**
Audon Av. *Bees* —6E **55**
Augustine Gdns. *Nott* —4E **21**
Austen Av. *Long E* —2E **73**
Austen Av. *Nott* —2E **45**
Austins Dri. *Sand* —1D **62**
Austin St. *Nott* —6A **20**
Austrey Av. *Bees* —3G **55**
Autumn Ct. *Huck* —5G **7**
Avalon Clo. *Nott* —1C **32**
Avebury Clo. *Nott* —5B **66**
Avenue A. *Nott* —5H **45** (4G 5)
Avenue B. *Nott* —5H **45** (4G 5)
Avenue C. *Nott* —5A **46** (4G 5)
Avenue Clo. *Nott* —5D **20**
Avenue D. *Nott* —5A **46** (4H 5)
Avenue E. *Nott* —4A **46** (3H 5)
Avenue, The. *C'tn* —4H **11**
Avenue, The. *Rad T* —5F **49**
Avenue, The. *Rud* —2H **77**
Averton Sq. *Nott* —6B **44**
Aviemore Clo. *Arn* —4D **22**
Avis Av. *Hean* —6D **14**
Avocet Clo. *Bing* —6G **51**
Avocet Wharf. *Nott* —1E **57**
Avon Av. *Huck* —2E **19**
Avonbridge Clo. *Arn* —4E **23**

Avondale. *Cotg* —2G **71**
Avondale Clo. *Long E* —1C **72**
Avondale Rd. *Cltn* —3F **47**
Avondale Rd. *Ilk* —4G **39**
Avon Gdns. *W Bri* —4B **58**
Avonlea Clo. *Ilk* —3D **40**
Avon Pl. *Bees* —4G **55**
Avon Rd. *Ged* —5H **35**
Avon Rd. *Nott* —4D **46**
Awsworth & Cossall By-Pass. *Aws*
—3D **28**
Awsworth La. *Coss* —5E **29**
Awsworth La. *Kimb* —1F **29**
Awsworth Rd. *Ilk & Aws* —5B **28**
Axford Clo. *Ged* —5H **35**
Aylesham Av. *Arn* —1B **34**
Aylestone Dri. *Nott* —1H **43**
Ayr St. *Nott* —3E **45** (1A 4)
Ayscough Av. *Nut* —1C **30**
Ayton Clo. *Nott* —1F **57**
Ayton Gdns. *Bees* —3C **64**
Azalea Ct. *Gilt* —5E **17**

Babbacombe Dri. *Nott* —1F **33**
Babbacombe Way. *Huck* —5D **6**
Babbington Cres. *Ged* —5G **35**
Babbington La. *Kimb* —3H **29**
Babington Ct. *Bees* —6C **54**
Back La. *C But* —1A **80**
Back La. *Hean* —4C **14**
Back La. *Ilk* —5A **28**
Back La. *Nut* —1D **30**
Bacon Clo. *Gilt* —5C **16**
Bacton Av. *Nott* —5H **19**
Bacton Gdns. *Nott* —5H **19**
Baden Powell Rd. *Nott* —5C **46**
Bader Rd. *Nott* —4F **57**
Badger Clo. *Cltn* —1G **47**
Badger Clo. *Huck* —5C **6**
Bagnall Av. *Arn* —1G **33**
Bagnall Cotts. *Nott* —2H **31**
Bagnall Rd. *Nott* —3H **31**
Bagot St. *W Hal* —1A **38**
Bagthorpe Clo. *Nott* —4E **33**
Baildon Clo. *Nott* —6A **44**
Bailey Brook Cres. *Lan M* —1E **15**
Bailey Brook Dri. *Lan M* —2E **15**
Bailey Brook Ind. Est. *Lan M*
—3F **15**
Bailey Brook Wlk. *Lan M* —2E **15**
Bailey Clo. *Day* —6H **21**
Bailey Ct. *N'fld* —2A **48**
Bailey Ct. *Rad T* —1E **61**
Bailey Gro. Rd. *Eastw* —3H **15**
Bailey St. *N'fld* —2A **48**
Bailey St. *Nott* —5C **32**
Bailey St. *S'fd* —5E **53**
Bainbridge, The. *C'tn* —4A **12**
Bainton Gro. *Nott* —4D **66**
Baker Av. *Arn* —4C **22**
Baker Av. *Hean* —6D **14**
Baker Brook Ind. Est. *Huck* —5B **8**
Bakerdale Rd. *Nott* —3D **46**
Baker Rd. *Gilt & Newt* —5E **17**
Bakers Clo. *Nott* —5C **44**
Baker's Hollow. *Cotg* —2E **71**
Baker St. *Huck* —4C **7**
Baker St. *Ilk* —6B **28**
Baker St. *Nott* —2F **45**
Bakewell Av. *Cltn* —6G **35**
Bakewell Dri. *Nott* —6C **20**
Bakewell Rd. *Long E* —2G **73**
Bala Dri. *Nott* —6E **21**
Baldwin Ct. *Nott* —4D **44**
Baldwin St. *Newt* —4E **17**
Baldwin St. *Nott* —4D **44**
Balfour Rd. *Nott* —4D **44**
Balfour Rd. *S'fd* —5F **53**
Balfron Gdns. *Nott* —1F **57**
Ballantrae Clo. *Arn* —5D **22**
Ballerat Cres. *Nott* —5C **20**
Ballon Wood N. *Nott* —5C **42**
Ball St. *Nott* —2B **46**
Balmoral Av. *W Bri* —3A **58**
Balmoral Clo. *Hean* —4A **14**
Balmoral Clo. *Sand* —2D **62**
Balmoral Cres. *Nott* —4C **42**

Balmoral Dri. *Bees* —1B **54**
Balmoral Gro. *Colw* —3H **47**
Balmoral Gro. *Huck* —3H **7**
Balmoral Rd. *Bing* —5C **50**
Balmoral Rd. *Colw* —3H **47**
Balmoral Rd. *Ilk* —4H **39**
Balmoral Rd. *Nott* —3F **45**
Bamkin Clo. *Huck* —5H **7**
Bampton Ct. *Gam* —4E **59**
Banbury Av. *Bees* —2H **63**
Bancroft St. *Nott* —6A **20**
Banes Rd. *Bing* —5H **51**
Bangor Wlk. *Nott* —2G **45**
Bankfield Dri. *Bees* —2C **54**
Bankfield Dri. *Ilk* —3F **39**
Bank Hill. *Wdbgh* —2H **23**
Bank Pl. *Nott* —5G **45** (4E 5)
Banksburn Clo. *Hean* —4A **14**
Banks Clo. *Arn* —1D **34**
Banks Cres. *Bing* —5E **51**
Banks Paddock. *Bing* —5F **51**
Banks Rd. *Bees* —2G **63**
Banks, The. *Bing* —5F **51**
Bank St. *Lan M* —1G **15**
Bank St. *Long E* —6G **63**
Bankwood Clo. *Nott* —6G **31**
Bank Yd. *Bulw* —6H **19**
(off Main St.)
Bannerman Rd. *Nott* —1A **32**
Barbara Sq. *Huck* —2F **7**
Barber Clo. *Ilk* —4A **28**
Barber St. *Eastw* —3C **16**
Barbrook Clo. *Nott* —4H **43**
Barbury Dri. *Nott* —6B **66**
Barclay Ct. *Ilk* —4H **27**
Barden Rd. *Nott* —3C **34**
Bardfield Gdns. *Nott* —3B **20**
Bardney Dri. *Nott* —5G **19**
Bardsey Gdns. *Nott* —6E **21**
Barent Clo. *Nott* —1D **32**
(in two parts)
Barent Wlk. *Nott* —1D **32**
Barker Av. E. *Sand* —5D **52**
Barker Av. N. *Sand* —5C **52**
Barker Ga. *Huck* —4H **7**
Barker Ga. *Ilk* —5B **28**
Barker Ga. *Nott* —5H **45** (4F 5)
Barker's La. *Bees* —1F **65**
Barkla Clo. *Nott* —5A **66**
Bar La. *Nott* —5A **32**
Bar La. Ind. Pk. *Nott* —5B **32**
Barley Cft. *W Bri* —1G **67**
Barleydale Dri. *Trow* —1F **53**
Barleylands. *Rud* —1G **77**
Barling Dri. *Ilk* —5G **27**
Barlock Rd. *Nott* —3C **32**
Barlow Dri. N. *Aws* —3D **28**
Barlow Dri. S. *Aws* —3D **28**
Barlows Cotts. *Aws* —2E **29**
Barnby Wlk. *Nott* —2G **33**
Barn Clo. *Cotg* —3E **71**
Barn Clo. *Nott* —2F **31**
Barn Cft. *Bees* —5B **54**
Barndale Clo. *W Bri* —2G **67**
Barnes Cft. *Hean* —5A **14**
(Heanor Ga. Rd.)
Barnes Cft. *Hean* —3D **14**
(Johnson St.)
Barnes Rd. *Nott* —5D **20**
Barnet Rd. *Nott* —2D **46**
Barnett Ct. *Keyw* —4G **79**
Barnfield. *Nott* —1F **67**
Barnham Clo. *Ilk* —5B **28**
Barnsley Ter. *Nott* —2G **57**
Barnston Rd. *Nott* —4B **46**
Barnum Clo. *Nott* —4E **43**
Barons Clo. *Ged* —6G **35**
Barrack La. *Nott* —5D **44**
Barra M. *Nott* —1F **57**
Barratt Clo. *Bees* —4D **64**
Barratt Cres. *Bees* —3D **64**
Barratt La. *Bees* —3C **64**
Barrhead Clo. *Nott* —4C **20**
Barrington Clo. *Rad T* —1E **61**
Barrique Rd. *Nott* —2C **56**
Barrow Slade. *Keyw* —5G **79**
Barrydale Av. *Bees* —6F **55**
Barry St. *Nott* —6H **19**
Bartlow Rd. *Nott* —2D **42**

Barton Clo. *Rud* —1F **77**
Barton La. *Bar F* —1G **75**
Barton La. *Bees* —4C **64**
Barton La. *Nott* —5H **65**
Barton La. *Thrum* —6C **74**
Barton Rd. *Long E* —1A **74**
Bartons Clo. *Newt* —3E **17**
Barton St. *Bees* —6G **55**
Barwell Dri. *Nott* —6D **30**
Basa Cres. *Nott* —5D **20**
Basford Rd. *Nott* —6B **32**
Baskin La. *Bees* —1C **64**
Baslow Av. *Cltn* —6F **35**
Baslow Clo. *Long E* —2C **72**
Baslow Dri. *Bees* —2G **55**
Bassett Clo. *Ilk* —4G **27**
Bassett Clo. *Kimb* —6G **17**
Bassford Av. *Hean* —3D **14**
Bassingfield La. *Gam & Rad T*
—5F **59**
Bastion St. *Nott* —4C **44**
Bateman Gdns. *Nott* —2D **44**
Bathley St. *Nott* —2G **57**
Baths. —1D **44**
Baths La. *Huck* —4H **7**
Bath St. *Ilk* —6A **28**
Bath St. *Nott* —4H **45** (2F 5)
Bathurst Dri. *Nott* —3D **43**
Baulk La. *S'fd* —3H **53**
Bawtry Wlk. *Nott* —3B **46**
Bayard Ct. *Nott* —4A **44**
Bayliss Rd. *Ged* —4F **35**
Bayswater Rd. *Kimb* —6H **17**
Baythorn Rd. *Nott* —3D **42**
Beacon Flatts. *Bees* —5H **55**
Beacon Hill Dri. *Huck* —6C **6**
Beacon Hill Ri. *Nott* —4A **46** (2H 5)
Beacon Rd. *Bees* —5H **55**
Beaconsfield St. *Long E* —6G **63**
Beaconsfield St. *Nott* —1D **44**
Bean Clo. *Nott* —2F **31**
Beanford La. *Oxt* —1G **11**
Beardall St. *Huck* —4H **7**
Beardsley Gdns. *Nott* —1F **57**
(in two parts)
Beardsmore Gro. *Huck* —2F **7**
Beastmarket Hill. *Nott*
—5G **45** (4D 4)
Beatty Wlk. *Ilk* —4B **28**
Beauclerk Dri. *Nott* —5C **20**
Beaufort Ct. *W Bri* —2G **67**
Beaufort Dri. *Bees* —6C **54**
Beaulieu Gdns. *W Bri* —6G **57**
Beaumaris Dri. *Bees* —1B **64**
Beaumaris Dri. *Ged* —6B **36**
Beaumont Clo. *Keyw* —3G **79**
Beaumont Clo. *S'fd* —2G **53**
Beaumont Gdns. *W Bri* —1H **67**
Beaumont St. *Nott* —5A **46** (5H 5)
Beauvale. *Newt* —3E **17**
Beauvale Ct. *Huck* —5E **7**
Beauvale Cres. *Huck* —5D **6**
Beauvale Dri. *Ilk* —2H **27**
Beauvale Ri. *Eastw* —2D **16**
Beauvale Rd. *Huck* —5D **6**
Beauvale Rd. *Nott* —2G **57**
Beaver Grn. *W Bri* —4H **57**
Beck Av. *C'tn* —3H **11**
Beckenham Rd. *Nott* —3C **44**
Beckett Ct. *Ged* —4F **35**
Beckford Rd. *Nott* —6B **46**
Beckhampton Rd. *Nott* —5F **21**
Beckley Rd. *Nott* —5F **31**
Beckside. *Gam* —1E **69**
Beck St. *Cltn* —1F **47**
Beck St. *Nott* —4H **45** (3F 5)
Bedale Ct. *Bees* —1A **64**
Bedale Rd. *Nott* —2G **33**
Bedarra Gro. *Lent* —5C **44**
Bede Clo. *Nott* —4E **21**
Bede Ling. *W Bri* —5G **57**
Bedford Ct. *Nott* —1D **44**
Bedford Ct. *S'fd* —2G **53**
Bedford Gro. *Nott* —2B **32**
Bedford Row. *Nott* —4H **45** (3G 5)
Bedlington Gdns. *Nott* —5A **34**
Beecham Av. *Nott* —3B **46**
Beech Av. *Bees* —6H **55**
Beech Av. *Bing* —5G **51**

Beech Av. *Breas* —5B **62**
Beech Av. *Huck* —4G **7**
Beech Av. *Keyw* —5H **79**
Beech Av. *Long E* —4G **63**
Beech Av. *Map* —3B **34**
Beech Av. *N'fld* —3H **47**
Beech Av. *New B* —1E **45**
Beech Av. *Nut* —1B **30**
Beech Av. *Sand* —4D **52**
Beech Clo. *Edw* —1D **68**
Beech Clo. *Nott* —3A **32**
Beech Clo. *Rad T* —1F **61**
Beech Ct. *Map* —3C **34**
Beechcroft. *W Hal* —2C **38**
Beechdale Rd. *Nott* —1F **43**
Beechdale Swimming Pool.
—3A **44**
Beeches, The. *Long E* —5G **63**
Beeches, The. *Nott* —1C **46**
Beeches, The. *Smal* —3A **14**
Beech La. *W Hal* —2B **38**
Beech Lodge. *Bing* —5G **51**
Beechwood Rd. *Arn* —5C **22**
Beeston Clo. *B Vil* —1C **20**
Beeston Ct. *Nott* —6B **20**
Beeston Fields Dri. *Bees* —3C **54**
Beeston Fields Golf Course.
—4D **54**
Beeston La. *Nott* —3H **55**
Beeston Rd. *Nott* —2B **56**
Beethan Clo. *Bing* —5F **51**
Belconnen Rd. *Nott* —2D **32**
Belfield Ct. *Los* —1A **14**
Belfield Gdns. *Long E* —6G **63**
Belfield St. *Ilk* —5B **28**
Belford Clo. *Nott* —5F **19**
Belfry Way. *Edw* —1E **69**
Belgrave M. *W Bri* —2G **67**
Belgrave Rd. *Nott* —6G **19**
Belgrave Sq. *Nott* —4F **45** (3C **4**)
Bellar Ga. *Nott* —5H **45** (4G **5**)
Belle-Isle Rd. *Huck* —5G **7**
Belleville Dri. *Nott* —6F **21**
Bellevue Ct. *Nott* —3A **46** (1H **5**)
Bell Ho. *Nott* —3C **56**
Bell La. *Smal & Ship* —2A **26**
Bell La. *Wilf* —4F **57**
Bellmore Gdns. *Nott* —4D **42**
Bells La. *Nott* —5G **31**
Bell St. *Cltn* —1F **47**
Bell Ter. *Nott* —3C **32**
Belmont Av. *Breas* —5A **62**
Belmont Av. *Nott* —6A **20**
Belmont Clo. *Bees* —1B **64**
Belmont Clo. *Huck* —1G **19**
Belper Av. *Cltn* —6F **35**
Belper Cres. *Cltn* —6F **35**
Belper Rd. *Nott* —6F **35**
Belper Rd. *Stan C & W Hal* —6A **26**
Belper St. *Ilk* —2B **40**
Belsay Rd. *Nott* —6E **21**
Belsford Ct. *Watn* —5A **18**
Belton Clo. *Sand* —1D **62**
Belton Dri. *W Bri* —1F **67**
Belton St. *Nott* —1D **44**
Belvedere Av. *Nott* —1D **44**
Belvedere Clo. *Keyw* —3G **79**
Belvoir Clo. *Ilk* —3H **39**
Belvoir Clo. *Long E* —2G **73**
Belvoir Hill. *Nott* —5B **46**
Belvoir Lodge. *Cltn* —3G **47**
Belvoir Rd. *N'fld* —2A **48**
Belvoir Rd. *W Bri* —2C **58**
Belvoir St. *Huck* —3F **7**
Belvoir St. *Nott* —5B **34**
Belvoir Ter. *Nott* —5B **46**
Belward St. *Nott* —5H **45** (4G **5**)
Belwood Clo. *Nott* —3D **66**
Bembridge Ct. *Bees* —3A **54**
Bembridge Dri. *Nott* —1F **33**
(in two parts)
Bendigo La. *Nott* —6C **46**
Benedict Ct. *Nott* —4E **21**
Ben Mayo Ct. *Nott* —3D **44**
Benner Av. *Ilk* —4C **40**
Bennerley Av. *Ilk* —3B **28**
Bennerley Ct. *Nott* —5F **19**
Bennerley Rd. *Blen I* —5F **19**
Bennett Rd. *Nott* —4C **34**

Bennett St. *Long E* —2E **63**
Bennett St. *Nott* —5B **34**
Bennett St. *Sand* —6D **52**
Benneworth Clo. *Huck* —6F **7**
Bennington Dri. *Nott* —6C **42**
Ben St. *Nott* —3D **44**
Bentinck Av. *Toll* —4F **69**
Bentinck Ct. *Nott* —5A **46** (4H **5**)
Bentinck Rd. *Cltn* —5E **35**
Bentinck Rd. *Nott* —3D **44**
Bentinck St. *Huck* —3F **7**
Bentley Av. *Nott* —3C **46**
Bentwell Av. *Arn* —6C **22**
Beresford Dri. *Ilk* —2A **28**
Beresford Ho. *Long E* —2B **72**
Beresford Rd. *Long E* —2C **72**
Beresford St. *Nott* —4C **44**
Berkeley Av. *Long E* —1E **73**
Berkeley Av. *Nott* —1G **45**
Berkeley Ct. *Nott* —6G **33**
Berle Av. *Hean* —2C **14**
Bernard Av. *Huck* —2H **7**
Bernard St. *Nott* —6F **33**
Bernard Ter. *Carr* —6F **33**
Bernisdale Clo. *Nott* —4D **20**
Berridge Rd. Central. *Nott* —1H **45**
Berridge Rd. E. *Nott* —1E **45**
Berridge Rd. W. *Nott* —2C **44**
Berriedale Clo. *Arn* —5E **23**
Berrydown Clo. *Nott* —6A **32**
Berry Hill Gro. *Ged* —5G **35**
Berwick Clo. *Nott* —1G **33**
Berwin Clo. *Long E* —4C **62**
Beryldene Av. *Watn* —6A **18**
Besecar Av. *Ged* —5G **35**
Besecar Clo. *Ged* —5G **35**
Bessell La. *S'fd* —6E **53**
Bestwick Av. *Hean* —4F **15**
Bestwick Clo. *Ilk* —5C **40**
Bestwood Av. *Arn* —5A **22**
Bestwood Clo. *Arn* —5A **22**
Bestwood Country Pk. —2D **20**
Bestwood Footpath. *Huck & B Vil*
—6B **8**
Bestwood Lodge Dri. *Arn* —4G **21**
Bestwood Pk. Dri. *Nott* —4F **21**
Bestwood Pk. Dri. W. *Nott* —4B **20**
Bestwood Pk. Vw. *Arn* —4A **22**
Bestwood Rd. *Huck* —5A **8**
Bestwood Rd. *Nott* —3H **31**
Bestwood Swimming Pool.
—1F **33**
Bestwood Ter. *Nott* —5A **20**
Bethel Gdns. *Huck* —6C **6**
Bethnal Wlk. *Nott* —6H **19**
Betony Clo. *Bing* —6C **50**
Betula Clo. *Nott* —4A **66**
Bevel St. *Nott* —2D **44**
Beverley Clo. *Nott* —5B **42**
Beverley Dri. *Kimb* —6G **17**
Beverley Gdns. *Ged* —6H **35**
Beverley Sq. *Nott* —2A **46**
Bewcastle Rd. *Nott* —4E **21**
Bewick Dri. *Nott* —4E **47**
Bexhill Ct. *Bees* —2E **55**
Bexleigh Gdns. *Nott* —1G **43**
Bexwell Clo. *Nott* —5C **66**
Biant Clo. *Nott* —4H **31**
Bible Wlk. *Nott* —4F **45** (2C **4**)
Bidford Rd. *Nott* —6F **31**
Bidwell Cres. *Got* —5H **75**
Biggart Clo. *Bees* —3C **64**
Biko Sq. *Nott* —1D **44**
Bilberry Wlk. *Nott* —3A **46**
Bilborough Rd. *Nott* —4B **42**
Bilby Gdns. *Nott* —4B **46**
Billesdon Dri. *Nott* —3D **32**
Bingham By-Pass. *Bing* —5B **50**
Bingham Ind. Pk. *Bing* —4E **51**
Bingham Leisure Cen. —5F **51**
Bingham Rd. *Cotg* —2F **71**
(in two parts)
Bingham Rd. *Nott* —5G **33**
Bingham Rd. *Rad T* —6F **49**
Bingley Clo. *Nott* —3H **43**
Birch Av. *Bees* —1H **65**
Birch Av. *Cltn* —2F **47**
Birch Av. *Ilk* —2C **40**
Birch Av. *Nut* —1B **30**

Birch Clo. *Nut* —1B **30**
Birchdale Av. *Huck* —6G **7**
Birchfield Pk. *Hean* —6D **14**
Birchfield Rd. *Arn* —5C **22**
Birch Lea. *Red* —5H **21**
Birchover Pl. *Ilk* —2A **28**
Birchover Rd. *Nott* —4C **42**
Birch Pas. *Nott* —4E **45** (2A **4**)
Birch Ri. *Wdbgh* —6C **12**
Birchwood. *Los* —1A **14**
Birchwood Av. *Breas* —6B **62**
Birchwood Av. *Long E* —1E **73**
Birchwood Rd. *Nott* —5C **42**
Bircumshaw Rd. *Hean* —3C **14**
Birdcroft La. *Ilk* —4B **40**
Birdsall Av. *Nott* —5E **43**
Birkdale Clo. *Edw* —2C **68**
Birkdale Clo. *Man I* —6H **27**
Birkdale Way. *Nott* —5D **20**
Birkin Av. *Bees* —3A **64**
Birkin Av. *Nott* —2D **44**
Birkin Av. *Rad T* —5G **49**
Birkin Av. *Rud* —5G **67**
Birkland Av. *Map* —2C **34**
Birkland Av. *Nott* —3G **45** (1D **4**)
Birley St. *S'fd* —6F **53**
Birling Clo. *Nott* —6F **19**
Birrell Rd. *Nott* —1E **45**
Bisham Dri. *W Bri* —4D **58**
Bishopdale Clo. *Long E* —1C **72**
Bishopdale Dri. *Watn* —6A **18**
Bishops Clo. *Keyw* —3G **79**
Bishops Rd. *Bing* —4D **50**
Bishop St. *Eastw* —3B **16**
Bishops Way. *Huck* —2H **7**
Bispham Dri. *Bees* —2H **63**
Blackacre. *Bur J* —2E **37**
Blackburn Pl. *Ilk* —4A **28**
Blackcliffe Farm M. *Bradm* —4A **78**
Blackett's Wlk. *Nott* —5A **66**
Blackfriars Clo. *Nut* —5D **30**
Blackhill Dri. *Cltn* —1H **47**
Black Hills Dri. *Ilk* —3A **40**
Blackrod Clo. *Bees* —3A **64**
Blacksmith Ct. *Cotg* —1E **71**
Blackstone Wlk. *Nott* —1G **57**
Black Swan Clo. *Wd'p* —3H **33**
Blackthorn Clo. *Bing* —5G **51**
Blackthorn Dri. *Eastw* —3A **16**
Blackthorn Dri. *Nott* —3H **31**
Bladon Clo. *Nott* —5A **34**
Bladon Rd. *Rud* —6F **67**
Blair Clo. *Nott* —2D **57**
Blair Gro. *Sand* —1C **62**
Blaise Clo. *Nott* —5C **66**
Blake Clo. *Arn* —6C **22**
Blake Ct. *Long E* —2D **72**
Blakeney Rd. *Rad T* —6H **49**
Blakeney Wlk. *Arn* —2B **34**
Blake Rd. *S'fd* —5G **53**
Blake Rd. *W Bri* —4B **58**
Blake St. *Ilk* —6B **28**
Blandford Av. *Long E* —1D **72**
Blandford Rd. *Bees* —6C **54**
Bland La. *Epp* —6G **13**
Blanford Gdns. *W Bri* —6G **57**
Blankney St. *Nott* —3C **32**
Blantyre Av. *Nott* —4C **20**
Blatherwick's Yd. *Arn* —5B **22**
Bleaberry Clo. *W Bri* —6E **59**
Bleachers Yd. *Nott* —6D **32**
Bleasby St. *Nott* —5B **46**
Bleasdale Clo. *Ged* —5A **36**
Blencathra Clo. *W Bri* —6E **59**
Blenheim Av. *Nott* —5E **35**
Blenheim Clo. *Rud* —6F **67**
Blenheim Ct. *Sand* —1D **62**
Blenheim Dri. *Bees* —6C **54**
Blenheim Ind. Est. *Nott* —5F **19**
Blenheim La. *Nott* —3D **18**
Blidworth Clo. *Strel* —5E **31**
Blind La. *Breas* —5A **62**
Bloomsbury Dri. *Nut* —4E **31**
Bloomsgrove Ind. Est. *Nott*
—4D **44**
Bloomsgrove Rd. *Ilk* —5B **28**
Bloomsgrove St. *Nott* —4E **44**
Bluebell Bank. *Bing* —6D **50**
Bluebell Clo. *Huck* —5C **6**

Blue Bell Hill Rd. *Nott* —3A **46**
Bluebell Way. *Hean* —4F **15**
Bluecoat Clo. *Nott* —3G **45** (1D **4**)
Bluecoat St. *Nott* —3G **45** (1D **4**)
Blundell Clo. *Nott* —1B **46**
Blyth Gdns. *Nott* —5A **34**
Blyth St. *Nott* —6A **34**
Blyton Wlk. *Nott* —6F **21**
Boatmans Clo. *Ilk* —5B **28**
Bobbers Mill Bri. *Nott* —2B **44**
Bobbers Mill Rd. *Nott* —2C **44**
Boden Dri. *Nut* —1C **30**
Boden St. *Nott* —4D **44**
Bodmin Av. *Huck* —6C **6**
Bodmin Dri. *Nott* —5A **32**
Body Rd. *Bees* —2B **64**
Bohem Rd. *Long E* —2E **63**
Bolcote Ho. Cltn —1G 47
(off Foxhill Rd. E.)
Bold Clo. *Nott* —5H **19**
Bolero Clo. *Nott* —4E **43**
Bolingey Way. *Huck* —5C **6**
Bolsover St. *Huck* —4H **7**
Bolton Av. *Bees* —1C **64**
Bolton Clo. *W Bri* —5C **58**
Bolton Ter. *Rad T* —6F **49**
Bond St. *Arn* —5A **22**
Bond St. *Nott* —5A **46** (4H **5**)
Bonetti Clo. *Arn* —2D **34**
Boniface Gdns. *Nott* —4E **21**
Bonington Dri. *Arn* —6B **22**
Bonington Gallery, The. —1C **4**
Bonington Rd. *Nott* —3B **34**
Bonner Hill. *C'tn* —5H **11**
Bonner La. *C'tn* —4A **12**
Bonner's Rd. *Aws* —3E **29**
Bonnington Clo. *Nott* —1G **31**
(in three parts)
Bonnington Cres. *Nott* —3G **33**
Bonny Mead. *Cotg* —3E **71**
Bonsall Ct. *Long E* —5G **63**
Bonsall St. *Long E* —5G **63**
Bonser Clo. *Cltn* —2G **47**
Booth Clo. *Nott* —4H **45** (2F **5**)
Borlace Cres. *S'fd* —5G **53**
Borman Clo. *Nott* —2F **31**
Borrowdale Clo. *Gam* —5F **59**
Borrowdale Ct. *Bees* —1B **64**
Borrowdale Dri. *Long E* —1C **72**
Boscawen Ct. *Ilk* —4B **28**
Bosden Clo. *Nott* —3C **42**
Bosley Sq. *Bees* —3G **55**
Bostock's La. *Ris* —1B **62**
Bostock's La. *Sand* —2C **62**
Boston M. *Nott* —4D **32**
Boston St. *Nott* —4H **45** (3G **5**)
Bosworth Clo. *Shelf* —1H **49**
Bosworth Dri. *Newt* —2D **16**
Bosworth Wlk. *Nott* —2F **57**
Bosworth Way. *Long E* —2G **73**
Botany Av. *Nott* —2B **46**
Botany Clo. *W Bri* —2G **67**
Botany Dri. *Ilk* —2B **28**
Bothe Clo. *Long E* —1E **73**
Bottle La. *Nott* —5G **45** (4E **5**)
Boundary Cres. *Bees* —2F **55**
Boundary La. *Lan M* —2G **15**
Boundary Rd. *Bees* —2F **55**
Boundary Rd. *W Bri* —1A **68**
Bourne Clo. *Bees* —2F **55**
Bourne M. *N'fld* —3A **48**
Bourne Sq. *Breas* —5A **62**
Bourne St. *N'fld* —3A **48**
Bournmoor Av. *Nott* —4C **66**
Bovill St. *Nott* —3D **44**
Bowden Clo. *Nott* —4G **33**
Bowden Dri. *Bees* —5H **55**
Bowers Av. *Nott* —2H **45**
Bowes Well Rd. *Ilk* —5A **28**
Bowland Clo. *Nott* —2C **46**
Bowland Rd. *Bing* —5C **50**
Bowling Clo. *Stan D* —3A **52**
Bowlwell Av. *Nott* —5D **20**
Bowness Av. *Nott* —5A **32**
Bowness Clo. *Gam* —4E **59**
Bowscale Clo. *W Bri* —6E **59**
Boxley Dri. *W Bri* —1G **67**
Boyce Gdns. *Nott* —6B **34**
Boycroft Av. *Nott* —1B **46**

Boyd Clo. *Arn* —4D **22**
Boynton Dri. *Nott* —6B **34**
Bracadale Rd. *Nott* —4D **20**
Bracebridge Dri. *Nott* —3D **42**
Bracey Ri. *W Bri* —2A **68**
Bracken Clo. *Cltn* —5F **35**
Bracken Clo. *Long E* —4D **62**
Bracken Clo. *Nott* —6F **31**
Brackendale Av. *Arn* —5B **22**
Brackenfield Dri. *Gilt* —6D **16**
Bracken Rd. *Long E* —4D **62**
Bracknell Cres. *Nott* —6B **32**
Bracton Dri. *Nott* —3B **46**
Bradbourne Av. *Nott* —5E **67**
Bradbury St. *Nott* —5C **46**
Braddock Clo. *Lent* —5C **44**
Braddon Av. *S'fd* —2G **53**
Bradfield Rd. *Nott* —6F **31**
Bradford Ct. *Nott* —1L **14**
Bradgate Clo. *Sand* —1D **62**
Bradgate Rd. *Nott* —1E **45**
Bradley Ct. *Bees* —5G **55**
Bradley St. *Sand* —6E **53**
Bradleys Yd. *Plum* —6G **69**
Bradley Wlk. *Nott* —5D **66**
Bradman Gdns. *Arn* —1D **34**
Bradmore Av. *Rud* —5G **67**
Bradmore La. *Keyw* —3E **79**
Bradmore Ri. *Nott* —3G **33**
Bradshaw St. *Long E* —2D **72**
Bradwell Clo. *Gilt* —5E **17**
Bradwell Dri. *Nott* —5D **20**
Braefell Clo. *W Bri* —6F **59**
Braefield Clo. *Ilk* —4G **39**
Braemar Av. *Eastw* —5B **16**
Braemar Dri. *Ged* —6B **36**
Braemar Rd. *Nott* —6A **20**
Braidwood Ct. *Nott* —2D **44**
Brailsford Rd. *Nott* —2C **56**
Brailsford Way. *Bees* —4C **64**
Bramber Gro. *Nott* —6C **66**
Bramble Clo. *Bees* —3D **64**
Bramble Clo. *Long E* —4D **62**
Bramble Clo. *Nott* —4B **32**
Bramble Ct. *Ged* —6H **35**
Bramble Dri. *Nott* —2C **46**
Brambleway. *Cotg* —3G **71**
Bramcote Av. *Bees* —5C **54**
Bramcote Dri. *Bees* —4E **55**
Bramcote Dri. *Nott* —6D **42**
Bramcote Dri. W. *Bees* —5D **54**
Bramcote La. *Bees* —5C **54**
Bramcote La. *Nott* —1D **54**
Bramcote Leisure Cen. —2B **54**
Bramcote Rd. *Bees* —4E **55**
Bramcote St. *Nott* —4C **44**
Bramcote Wlk. *Nott* —4C **44**
Bramerton Rd. *Nott* —3C **42**
Bramhall Rd. *Nott* —3C **42**
Bramley Ct. *Kimb* —1H **29**
Bramley Grn. *Nott* —6E **31**
Bramley Rd. *Nott* —6E **31**
Brampton Av. *Hean* —3E **15**
Brampton Dri. *S'fd* —6H **53**
Brancaster Clo. *Nott* —3H **31**
Brandish Cres. *Nott* —4B **66**
Brandreth Av. *Nott* —1B **46**
Brandreth Dri. *Gilt* —5C **16**
Brand St. *Nott* —1B **58**
Branklene Clo. *Kimb* —6G **17**
Branksome Wlk. *Nott* —1G **57**
Bransdale Clo. *Long E* —1D **72**
Bransdale Rd. *Nott* —4B **66**
Branston Gdns. *W Bri* —1H **67**
Branston Wlk. *Nott* —3G **33**
Brantford Av. *Nott* —4D **66**
Brassington Clo. *Gilt* —6D **16**
Brassington Clo. *W Hal* —1C **38**
Braunton Clo. *Huck* —5D **6**
Brayton Cres. *Nott* —2B **32**
Breach Rd. *Hean* —5E **15**
Breadsall Ct. *Ilk* —4B **28**
Breaston Clo. Nott —5E **21**
(off Erewash Gdns.)
Breaston La. *Ris* —2A **62**
Brechin Clo. *Arn* —3D **22**
Breckhill Rd. *Wd'p & Map* —2A **34**
Breckwood Dri. *Nott* —6C **66**

Brecon Clo. *Long E* —5C **62**
Brecon Clo. *Nott* —3G **31**
Bredon Clo. *Long E* —5C **62**
Breedon St. *Long E* —2D **62**
Brendon Ct. *Bees* —3B **54**
Brendon Dri. *Kimb* —6H **17**
Brendon Dri. *Nott* —4G **43**
Brendon Gdns. *Nott* —4G **43**
Brendon Gro. *Bing* —4C **50**
Brendon Rd. *Nott* —4G **43**
Brendon Way. *Long E* —3C **62**
Brentcliffe Av. *Nott* —2C **46**
Brentnall Ct. *Bees* —2D **64**
Bressingham Dri. *W Bri* —2G **67**
Brett Clo. *Huck* —6E **7**
Brewery St. *Kimb* —1H **29**
Brewhouse Mus. —6D **4**
Brewhouse Yd. *Nott* —6F **45** (6C **4**)
Brewsters Clo. *Bing* —5E **51**
Brewsters Rd. *Nott* —1A **46**
Breydon Ind. Cen. *Long E* —6H **63**
Briar Av. *Sand* —2D **62**
Briarbank Av. *Nott* —1C **46**
Briarbank Wlk. *Nott* —2C **46**
Briar Clo. *Bees* —2E **55**
Briar Clo. *Huck* —6D **6**
Briar Clo. *Keyw* —3H **79**
Briar Ct. *Nott* —2F **57**
Briar Gdns. *C'tn* —3E **11**
Briar Ga. *Cotg* —3G **71**
Briar Ga. *Long E* —3C **62**
Briar Rd. *Newt* —5D **16**
Briarwood Av. *Nott* —2C **46**
Briarwood Ct. *Sher* —4A **34**
Brickenell Rd. *C'tn* —5H **11**
Brickyard. *Huck* —5A **8**
Brickyard Cotts. *Nott* —2F **67**
Brickyard Dri. *Huck* —6A **8**
Brickyard La. *Rad T* —6H **49**
Brickyard Plantation Nature
Reserve. —1G **41**
Brickyard, The. *Stan C* —6A **26**
Bridge Av. *Bees* —6E **55**
Bridge Ct. *Bees* —4H **55**
Bridge Ct. *Huck* —6G **7**
Bri. Farm La. *Nott* —3C **66**
Bridge Grn. Wlk. *Nott* —6E **31**
Bridge Gro. *W Bri* —3A **58**
Bridgend Clo. *S'fd* —6F **53**
Bridge Rd. *Nott* —4D **42**
Bridge St. *Ilk* —3B **28**
Bridge St. *Lan M* —2G **15**
Bridge St. *Long E* —4F **63**
Bridge St. *Sand* —6E **53**
Bridgeway Cen. *Nott* —1G **57**
Bridgeway Ct. *Nott* —1H **57**
Bridgford Rd. *W Bri* —2A **58**
Bridgnorth Dri. *Nott* —3C **66**
Bridgnorth Way. *Bees* —2G **63**
Bridle Rd. *Bees* —2B **54**
Bridle Rd. *Bur J* —1D **36**
Bridlesmith Ga. *Nott*
—5G **45** (4E **5**)
Bridlington St. *Nott* —2C **44**
Bridport Av. *Nott* —4B **44**
Brielen Ct. *Rad T* —6G **49**
Brielen Rd. *Rad T* —6G **49**
Brierfield Av. *Nott* —1F **67**
Brierley Grn. *N'fld* —2A **48**
Brightmoor Ct. *Nott* —5H **45** (4F **5**)
Brightmoor St. *Nott* —5H **45** (4F **5**)
Bright St. *Ilk* —4A **28**
Bright St. *Nott* —4C **44**
Brindley Rd. *Nott* —4C **42**
Brinkhill Cres. *Nott* —6D **66**
Brinsley Clo. *Nott* —6G **31**
Brisbane Dri. *Nott* —5C **20**
Brisbane Dri. *S'fd* —2H **53**
Bristol Rd. *Ilk* —6A **28**
Britannia Av. *Nott* —3C **32**
Britannia Ct. *N'fld* —3A **48**
Britannia Rd. *Long E* —4F **63**
Britten Gdns. *Nott* —3B **46**
Brixham Rd. *Huck* —6D **6**
Brixton Rd. *Nott* —4C **44**
B Rd. *Lent* —5B **56**
Broad Clo. *Wdbgh* —1B **24**
Broad Eadow Rd. *Nott* —6F **19**
Broadfields. *C'tn* —3H **11**

Broadgate. *Bees* —4G **55**
Broadgate Av. *Bees* —4G **55**
Broadgate Pk. *Bees* —3G **55**
Broadholme St. *Nott* —6D **44**
Broadhurst Av. *Nott* —5B **32**
Broadlands. *Sand* —2D **62**
Broadleigh Clo. *W Bri* —2G **67**
Broad Marsh Shop. Cen. *Nott*
—5G **45** (5E **5**)
Broadmead. *Bur J* —2F **37**
Broad Meer. *Cotg* —2E **71**
Broadmere Ct. *Arn* —4D **22**
Broad Oak Clo. *Nott* —2A **46**
Broad Oak Dri. *S'fd* —5F **53**
Broadstairs Rd. *Bees* —3H **63**
Broadstone Clo. *W Bri* —6G **57**
Broad St. *Long E* —6F **63**
Broad St. *Nott* —4H **45** (3F **5**)
Broad Valley Dri. *B Vil* —1C **20**
Broad Wlk. *Nott* —4A **32**
Broadway. *Hean* —4C **14**
Broadway. *Ilk* —4A **28**
Broadway. *Nott* —5H **45** (5F **5**)
Broadway E. *Cltn* —3F **47**
Broadway Media Cen. —3F **5**
Broadwood Ct. *Bees* —3G **55**
Broadwood Rd. *Nott* —5F **21**
Brockdale Gdns. *Keyw* —3G **79**
Brockenhurst Gdns. *Nott* —3B **46**
Brockhall Ri. *Hean* —4E **15**
Brockhole Clo. *W Bri* —2G **67**
Brockley Rd. *W Bri* —4D **58**
Brockwood Cres. *Keyw* —3G **79**
Bromfield Clo. *Nott* —2E **47**
Bromley Clo. *Nott* —1H **31**
Bromley Pl. *Nott* —5F **45** (4C **4**)
Bromley Rd. *W Bri* —5A **58**
Brompton Clo. *Arn* —3E **21**
Brompton Way. *W Bri* —2G **67**
Bronte Clo. *Long E* —6C **62**
Bronte Ct. *Nott* —3E **45**
Brook Av. *Arn* —5D **22**
Brook Clo. *Long E* —2G **73**
Brook Clo. *Newt* —4D **16**
Brook Clo. *Nott* —1H **31**
Brook Cotts. *Ilk* —4B **28**
Brook Ct. *Lan M* —3F **15**
Brookdale Ct. *Nott* —2H **33**
Brooke St. *Ilk* —3D **40**
Brooke St. *Sand* —6D **52**
Brookfield Av. *Huck* —6F **7**
Brookfield Clo. *Rad T* —6F **49**
Brookfield Ct. *Arn* —6C **22**
Brookfield Ct. *Nott* —1G **57**
Brookfield Gdns. *Arn* —6C **22**
Brookfield Rd. *Arn* —6B **22**
Brookfield Way. *Hean* —4F **15**
Brook Gdns. *Arn* —5C **22**
Brookhill Cres. *Nott* —6E **43**
Brookhill Dri. *Nott* —6E **43**
Brookhill Leys Rd. *Eastw* —4A **16**
Brookhill St. *S'fd* —6E **53**
Brookland Dri. *Bees* —6D **54**
Brooklands Av. *Hean* —3D **14**
Brooklands Cres. *Ged* —6A **36**
Brooklands Dri. *Ged* —6A **36**
Brooklands Rd. *Nott* —2D **46**
Brook La. *Gam* —4E **59**
Brooklyn Av. *Bur J* —3E **37**
Brooklyn Clo. *Nott* —2B **32**
Brooklyn Rd. *Nott* —1B **32**
Brook Rd. *Bees* —3F **55**
Brooksby La. *Nott* —1D **66**
Brookside. *Eastw* —1B **16**
Brookside. *Huck* —6H **7**
Brookside Av. *Nott* —1D **54**
Brookside Clo. *Long E* —5D **62**
Brookside Gdns. *Rud* —5F **67**
Brookside Rd. *Rud* —5F **67**
Brook St. *Huck* —3G **7**
Brook St. *Los* —1A **14**
Brook St. *Nott* —4H **45** (3F **5**)
Brookthorpe Way. *Nott* —1E **67**
Brook Va. Rd. *Lan M* —3G **15**
Brook Vw. Ct. *Keyw* —5G **79**
Brook Vw. Dri. *Keyw* —5G **79**
Brookwood Cres. *Cltn* —2E **47**
Broom Clo. *C'tn* —3H **11**
Broomfield Clo. *Sand* —6C **52**

Broomhill Av. *Ilk* —3C **40**
(in two parts)
Broomhill Pk. Vw. *Huck* —6A **8**
Broomhill Rd. *Huck* —6G **7**
Broomhill Rd. *Kimb* —1A **30**
Broomhill Rd. *Nott* —1A **32**
Broom Rd. *C'tn* —4H **11**
Broom Wlk. *Nott* —1C **46**
Brora Rd. *Nott* —6B **20**
Broughton Clo. *Ilk* —4A **28**
Broughton Dri. *Nott* —5A **44**
Broughton St. *Bees* —4F **55**
Brownes Rd. *Bing* —4G **51**
Browning Clo. *Day* —6H **21**
Browning Ct. *Nott* —4F **33**
Brown La. *Bar F* —1E **75**
Brownlow Dri. *Nott* —4B **20**
Browns Cft. *Nott* —4B **32**
Brown's Flat. *Kimb* —6H **17**
Browns La. *Keyw* —6B **80**
Brown's Rd. *Long E* —5G **63**
Brown St. *Nott* —2D **44**
Broxtowe Av. *Kimb* —1F **29**
Broxtowe Av. *Nott* —5A **32**
Broxtowe Dri. *Huck* —2G **7**
Broxtowe Hall Clo. *Nott* —5G **31**
Broxtowe Ho. *Nott* —6D **30**
Broxtowe La. *Nott* —6F **31**
Broxtowe Pk. —5E **31**
Broxtowe Ri. *Nott* —4H **31**
Broxtowe St. *Nott* —5G **33**
Bruce Clo. *Nott* —1H **57**
Bruce Dri. *W Bri* —4H **57**
Brunel Av. *Newt* —1D **16**
Brunel Ter. *Nott* —4E **45**
Brunswick Dri. *S'fd* —6G **53**
Brushfield St. *Nott* —2C **44**
Brussells Ter. *Ilk* —6A **28**
(off Bath St.)
Brusty Pl. *Bur J* —2E **37**
Bryan Ct. *Nott* —1A **56**
Buckfast Way. *W Bri* —4C **58**
Buckingham Av. *Huck* —3H **7**
Buckingham Clo. *Hean* —3A **14**
Buckingham Ct. *Sand* —2C **62**
Buckingham Rd. *Sand* —2C **62**
Buckingham Rd. *Wd'p* —2A **34**
Buckingham Way. *Watn* —6B **18**
Buckland Dri. *Wdbgh* —1C **24**
Bucklee Dri. *C'tn* —4G **11**
Bucklow Clo. *Nott* —6B **32**
Buckminster Rd. *Ilk* —5G **39**
Budby Ri. *Huck* —3H **7**
Bulcote Dri. *Bur J* —4D **36**
Bulcote Rd. *Nott* —2D **66**
Bullace Rd. *Nott* —2B **46**
Bull Clo. Rd. *Lent* —3C **56**
Buller St. *Ilk* —3C **40**
Buller Ter. *Nott* —4H **33**
Bullfinch Rd. *Nott* —3B **32**
Bullins Clo. *Arn* —4G **21**
Bullivant St. *Nott* —3H **45** (1F **5**)
Bulwell Bus. Cen. *Nott* —6E **19**
Bulwell Forest Golf Course.
—5B **20**
Bulwell High Rd. *Nott* —6H **19**
Bulwell La. *Nott* —3B **32**
Bulwer Rd. *Nott* —4D **44**
Bunbury St. *Nott* —2H **57**
Bunny La. *Keyw* —5E **79**
Bunting Clo. *Ilk* —3G **39**
Buntings La. *Cltn* —2E **47**
Bunting St. *Nott* —2C **56**
Burcot Clo. *W Hal* —1C **38**
Burford Rd. *Nott* —1D **44**
Burford St. *Arn* —5A **22**
Burgass Rd. *Nott* —2C **46**
Burge Clo. *Nott* —1G **57**
Burghill. *Cotg* —3G **71**
Burke St. *Nott* —4E **45** (2A **4**)
Burleigh Clo. *Cltn* —2H **47**
Burleigh Rd. *W Bri* —5B **58**
Burleigh Sq. *Bees* —1C **64**
Burleigh St. *Ilk* —6B **28**
Burlington Av. *Nott* —4F **33**
Burlington Ct. *Nott* —4G **33**
Burlington Rd. *Cltn* —1G **47**
Burlington Rd. *Nott* —4G **33**

Burnaby St. *Nott* —3B **32**
Burnbank Clo. *W Bri* —6F **59**
Burnbreck Gdns. *Nott* —5E **43**
Burncroft. *W Hal* —2C **38**
Burndale Wlk. *Nott* —5C **20**
Burnham Av. *Bees* —1F **65**
Burnham Clo. *W Hal* —1B **38**
Burnham Lodge. *Nott* —4C **20**
Burnham St. *Nott* —5G **33**
Burnham Way. *Nott* —6A **20**
Burnor Pool. *C'tn* —4H **11**
Burns Av. *Nott* —3E **45** (1A **4**)
Burns Ct. *Nott* —4F **33**
Burnside Dri. *Bees* —1C **54**
Burnside Grn. *Nott* —2E **43**
Burnside Gro. *Toll* —4E **69**
Burnside Rd. *Nott* —3D **42**
Burnside Rd. *W Bri* —6A **58**
Burns St. *Hean* —3B **14**
Burns St. *Ilk* —1A **40**
Burns St. *Nott* —3E **45** (1A **4**)
Burnstump Hill. *Arn & C'tn* —1G **9**
Burnt Ho. *Hean* —4B **14**
Burnt Oak Clo. *Nut* —4D **30**
Burntstump Country Pk. —1H **9**
(Woodland Walks)
Burnwood Dri. *Nott* —4D **42**
Burr La. *Ilk* —6B **28**
Burrows Av. *Bees* —2F **55**
Burrows Ct. *Nott* —4B **46**
Burrows Cres. *Bees* —2F **55**
Burtness Rd. *Nott* —4C **66**
Burton Av. *Cltn* —1D **46**
Burton Clo. *Cltn* —6A **36**
Burton Dri. *Bees* —1C **64**
Burton Manderfield Ct. *Nott*
—1G **57**
Burton Rd. *Cltn* —1H **47**
Burton St. *Hean* —3C **14**
Burton St. *Nott* —4G **45** (3D **4**)
Burwell St. *Nott* —3D **44**
Bush Clo. *Nott* —5D **20**
Bushy Clo. *Long E* —1D **72**
Bute Av. *Nott* —5D **44**
Butler Av. *Rad T* —5G **49**
Butlers Clo. *Huck* —6A **8**
Butler St. *Nott* —5C **44**
Butterfield Ct. *Watn* —6A **18**
Buttermead Clo. *Trow* —1F **53**
Buttermere Clo. *Gam* —4F **59**
Buttermere Clo. *Long E* —2C **62**
Buttermere Ct. *Nott* —5G **33**
Buttermere Dri. *Bees* —3D **54**
Butterton Clo. *Ilk* —2C **40**
Butt Houses. *Nott* —5C **44**
Buttrey Gdns. *Rud* —1G **77**
Butt Rd. *Bing* —5G **51**
Butts Clo. *Ilk* —5B **40**
Butt St. *Sand* —6D **52**
Buxton Av. *Cltn* —6F **35**
Buxton Av. *Hean* —5D **14**
Buxton Ct. *Ilk* —5H **27**
Buxton Grn. *Hean* —6B **14**
Byard La. *Nott* —5G **45** (5E **5**)
Bye Pass Rd. *Bees* —3D **64**
Byfield Clo. *Nott* —3D **44**
Byford Clo. *Nott* —5A **34**
Byley Rd. *Nott* —4B **42**
Byrne Ct. *Arn* —2D **34**
Byron Av. *Long E* —2D **62**
Byron Ct. *Nott* —5A **46** (4H **5**)
Byron Ct. *S'fd* —2G **53**
Byron Cres. *Aws* —3E **29**
Byron Gro. *Nott* —4G **33**
Byron Rd. *W Bri* —4B **58**
Byron St. *Day* —6H **21**
Byron St. *Huck* —5G **7**
Byron St. *Ilk* —6B **28**

Caddaw Av. *Huck* —5G **7**
Cadlan Clo. *Nott* —6E **21**
Cadlan Ct. *Nott* —6E **21**
Caernarvon Pl. *Bees* —1B **64**
Caincross Rd. *Nott* —2D **42**
Cairngorm Dri. *Arn* —3F **21**
Cairns Clo. *Nott* —2E **33**
Cairnsmore Clo. *Long E* —4C **62**
Cairns St. *Nott* —4G **45** (2E **5**)

Cairo St. *Nott* —6D **32**
Caister Rd. *Nott* —5C **66**
Caithness Ct. *Nott* —6F **33**
Calcroft Clo. *Nott* —5A **32**
Caldbeck Ct. *Gam* —4E **59**
Caldbeck Ct. *Bees* —1B **64**
Caldbeck Wlk. *Nott* —6F **21**
Calderdale. *Nott* —8B **42**
Calderdale Dri. *Long E* —1C **72**
Calderhall Gdns. *Nott* —5G **21**
Calder Wlk. *Nott* —6H **19**
Caldon Grn. *Nott* —3A **20**
Caledon Rd. *Nott* —4F **33**
Calladine Ct. *Nott* —1G **31**
Calladine Rd. *Hean* —3B **14**
Callaway Clo. *Nott* —4E **43**
Calstock Rd. *Wd'p* —2A **34**
Calveley Rd. *Nott* —1E **43**
Calver Clo. *Nott* —5A **44**
Calvert Clo. *Bees* —1D **64**
Calverton Av. *Cltn* —6D **34**
Calverton Clo. *Bees* —3A **64**
Calverton Dri. *Strel* —5D **30**
Calverton Rd. *Arn* —4B **22**
Calverton Sports & Leisure Cen.
—3G **11**
Camberley Ct. *Nott* —5G **19**
Camberley Rd. *Nott* —5G **19**
Camborne Dri. *Nott* —5A **32**
Cambria M. *Nott* —2G **45**
Cambridge Ct. *Nott* —3D **44**
Cambridge Cres. *S'fd* —1F **53**
Cambridge Gdns. *Wd'p* —2D **34**
Cambridge Rd. *Nott* —5G **43**
Cambridge Rd. *W Bri* —4C **58**
Cambridge St. *Cltn* —6G **35**
Camdale Clo. *Bees* —5B **54**
Camden Clo. *Nott* —5A **46** (4H **5**)
Camelia Av. *Nott* —4A **66**
Camelot Av. *Nott* —5E **33**
Camelot Cres. *Rud* —5F **67**
Camelot St. *Rud* —5F **67**
Cameo Clo. *Colw* —3H **47**
Cameron St. *Nott* —6C **20**
Camomile Clo. *Nott* —6C **20**
Camomile Gdns. *Nott* —2C **44**
Campbell Dri. *Cltn* —1E **47**
Campbell Gdns. *Arn* —4E **23**
Campbell Gro. *Nott* —4H **45** (2G **5**)
Campbell St. *Lan M* —1G **15**
Campbell St. *Nott* —4H **45** (2H **5**)
Campden Grn. *Nott* —3C **66**
Campion St. *Arn* —5A **22**
Campion Way. *Bing* —5D **50**
Camrose Clo. *Nott* —1F **43**
Canal Mus., The. —6E **5**
Canal Side. *Bees* —2H **65**
Canalside. *Nott* —6G **45** (6E **5**)
Canalside Wlk. *Nott* —6G **45**
Canal St. *Ilk* —6C **28**
Canal St. *Long E* —4D **62**
Canal St. *Nott* —6G **45** (6D **4**)
Canal St. *Sand* —6D **52**
Canberra Clo. *S'fd* —2G **53**
Canberra Cres. *W Bri* —1H **67**
Canberra Gdns. *W Bri* —2H **67**
Candleby Clo. *Cotg* —2F **71**
Candleby Ct. *Cotg* —2F **71**
Candleby La. *Cotg* —2F **71**
Candle Mdw. *Colw P* —4F **47**
Canning Cir. *Nott* —4E **45** (3A **4**)
Canning Ter. *Nott* —4E **45** (3A **4**)
Cannock Way. *Long E* —6H **63**
Cannon St. *Nott* —4G **33**
Canonbie Clo. *Arn* —4E **23**
Canon Clo. *Ilk* —2A **28**
Cantabury Av. *Nott* —1D **44**
Cantelupe Rd. *Ilk* —1B **40**
Canterbury Clo. *Nott* —3F **45** (1C **4**)
Canterbury Rd. *Nott* —4B **44**
Cantley Av. *Ged* —5G **35**
Cantrell Rd. *Nott* —1A **32**
Canver Clo. *Nott* —3C **42**
Canwick Clo. *Nott* —4C **42**
Capenwray Gdns. *Nott* —5G **21**
Capitol Ct. *Nott* —4G **43**
Caporn Clo. *Nott* —2A **32**
Cardale Rd. *Nott* —3C **46**

Cardiff St. *Nott* —4B **46**
Cardinal Clo. *Nott* —3A **46**
Cardington Clo. *Nott* —4C **20**
Cardwell St. *Nott* —1D **44**
Carew Rd. *Nott* —3C **66**
Carey Rd. *Nott* —5A **20**
Carisbrooke Av. *Bees* —3G **55**
Carisbrooke Av. *Ged* —6B **36**
Carisbrooke Av. *Nott* —6G **33**
Carisbrooke Dri. *Nott* —6G **33**
Carlight Cvn. Site. *W Bri* —2D **58**
Carlin Clo. *Breas* —5A **62**
Carlingford Rd. *Huck* —4G **7**
Carlin St. *Nott* —6H **19**
Carlisle Av. *Nott* —6A **20**
Carlisle Rd. *Cltn* —1G **47**
Carlswark Gdns. *Nott* —4D **20**
Carlton Bus. Cen. *Cltn* —2H **47**
Carlton Clo. *Hean* —2E **15**
Carlton Fold. *Nott* —6B **46**
Carlton Forum Leisure Cen. S.
—1E **47**
Carlton Grange. *Cltn* —2E **47**
Carlton Hill. *Cltn* —2D **46**
Carlton M. *Cltn* —2E **47**
Carlton Rd. *Long E* —2D **72**
Carlton Rd. *Nott* —5A **46** (4H **5**)
Carlton Sq. *Cltn* —2G **47**
Carlton St. *Nott* —5H **45** (4F **5**)
Carlton Va. Clo. *Nott* —6F **35**
Carlyle Pl. *Hean* —2B **14**
Carlyle Rd. *W Bri* —4A **58**
Carlyle St. *Hean* —2B **14**
Carman Clo. *Watn* —5A **18**
Carmel Gdns. *Arn* —1B **34**
Carnarvon Clo. *Bing* —4E **51**
Carnarvon Dri. *Bur J* —2F **37**
Carnarvon Gro. *Cltn* —1F **47**
Carnarvon Gro. *Ged* —6H **35**
Carnarvon Pl. *Bing* —5D **50**
Carnarvon Rd. *W Bri* —5B **58**
Carnarvon St. *N'fld* —3A **48**
Carnforth Clo. *S'fd* —6F **53**
Carnforth Ct. *Nott* —5G **21**
Carnwood Rd. *Nott* —1E **33**
Caroline Clo. *Ilk* —3C **40**
Caroline Wlk. *Nott* —2H **45**
Carradale Clo. *Arn* —5E **23**
Carrfield Av. *Bees* —3H **63**
Carrfield Av. *Long E* —4H **63**
Carrington Ct. *Nott* —6G **33**
Carrington La. *C'tn* —2H **11**
Carrington St. *Nott* —6G **45** (6E **5**)
(in three parts)
Carrock Av. *Hean* —4F **15**
Carroll Gdns. *Nott* —2G **57**
Carr Rd. *Bing* —4H **51**
Cartbridge. *Cotg* —3F **71**
Carter Av. *Rad T* —6H **49**
Carter Clo. *Long E* —6D **62**
Carter Dri. *Sand* —5E **53**
Carter Ga. *Nott* —5H **45** (5G **5**)
Carter Rd. *Bees* —2A **64**
(Readman Rd.)
Carter Rd. *Bees* —3A **64**
(Swiney Way)
Carterswood Dri. *Nut* —4F **31**
Carver St. *Nott* —1D **44**
Carwood Rd. *Bees* —2D **54**
Casper Ct. *Nott* —5E **21**
(off Birkdale Way)
Castellan Ri. *Nott* —5G **21**
Casterton Rd. *Nott* —5F **21**
Castle Boulevd. *Nott* —6D **44** (6A **4**)
Castlebridge Office Village.
—1E **57**
Castle Bri. Rd. *Nott* —6E **45**
Castle Clo. *C'tn* —4F **11**
Castle Ct. *Nott* —6F **45** (6C **4**)
Castlefields. *Nott* —1G **57**
Castle Gdns. *Nott* —6D **44**
Castle Ga. *Nott* —5G **45** (5D **4**)
(in three parts)
Castle Gro. *Nott* —5F **45** (5C **4**)
Castle Marina Pk. *Nott* —6E **45**
Castle Marina Rd. *Nott* —1E **57**
Castle Mdw. Rd. *Nott* —1F **57**
(in two parts)

Castle M. *Nott* —6E **45**
Castle Mus. & Art Gallery. —6C **4**
Castle Pk. Ind. Est. *Nott* —1F **57**
Castle Pl. *Nott* —5F **45** (5C **4**)
Castle Quay. *Nott* —6F **45** (6B **4**)
Castle Retail Pk. *Nott* —3C **44**
Castlerigg Clo. *W Bri* —6E **59**
Castle Rd. *Nott* —5G **45** (5C **4**)
Castle Rock. *Nott* —6F **45** (6C **4**)
Castle St. *Eastw* —4C **16**
Castle St. *Nott* —5B **46**
Castleton Av. *Arn* —6B **22**
Castleton Av. *Cltn* —6G **35**
Castleton Av. *Ilk* —2A **28**
Castleton Clo. *Huck* —5D **6**
Castleton Clo. *Nott* —1F **57**
Castleton Ct. *Nott* —1F **31**
Castle Vw. *Lan M* —1E **15**
Castle Vw. *W Bri* —5H **57**
Castle Vw. Cotts. *Bees* —3A **56**
Castle Vs. *Nott* —5B **46**
Castle Wlk. *Nott* —2D **44**
Cat & Fiddle La. *W Hal* —3B **38**
Caterham Clo. *Nott* —2D **42**
Catfoot La. *Lamb* —5F **23**
Catherine Av. *Ilk* —3B **40**
Catherine Clo. *Nott* —6G **19**
Catherine St. *Nott* —6G **19**
Catkin Dri. *Gilt* —5E **17**
Catlow Wlk. *Nott* —5G **21**
Cator Clo. *Ged* —4F **35**
Cator La. *Bees* —5D **54**
Cator La. N. *Bees* —5D **54**
Catriona Cres. *Arn* —3C **22**
Catterley Hill Rd. *Nott* —2C **46**
Cattle Mkt. Rd. *Nott* —1H **57**
Catton Rd. *Arn* —5C **22**
Caulton St. *Nott* —3D **44**
Caunton Av. *Nott* —6A **34**
Causeway M. *Nott* —1F **57**
Cavan Ct. *Nott* —2G **57**
Cavell Clo. *Nott* —3B **66**
Cavell Ct. *Nott* —1B **56**
Cavendish Av. *Ged* —5H **35**
Cavendish Av. *Nott* —4H **33**
Cavendish Clo. *Huck* —6A **8**
Cavendish Ct. *Nott* —4B **34**
Cavendish Ct. *Park T*
—5E **45** (4A **4**)
Cavendish Cres. *Cltn* —5E **35**
Cavendish Cres. *S'fd* —1F **53**
Cavendish Cres. N. *Nott*
—5E **45** (4A **4**)
Cavendish Cres. S. *Nott*
—6E **45** (6A **4**)
Cavendish Dri. *Cltn* —5E **35**
Cavendish Ho. *Cltn* —1G **47**
(off Foxhill Rd. E.)
Cavendish M. *Nott* —5E **45** (4A **4**)
Cavendish Pl. *Bees* —5F **55**
Cavendish Pl. *Nott* —6E **45** (6A **4**)
Cavendish Rd. *Cltn* —5E **35**
Cavendish Rd. *Ilk* —3B **40**
Cavendish Rd. *Long E* —3E **63**
Cavendish Rd. E. *Nott*
—5E **45** (4A **4**)
Cavendish Rd. W. *Nott* —5E **45**
Cavendish St. *Arn* —5A **22**
Cavendish St. *Lent L* —2C **56**
Cavendish Va. *Nott* —4H **33**
Caversham Way. *W Hal* —1B **38**
Caves of Nottingham, The. —5E **5**
Cawdron Wlk. *Nott* —3C **66**
Cawston Gdns. *Nott* —5H **19**
Caxmere Dri. *Nott* —4F **43**
Caxton Clo. *N'fld* —2A **48**
Caythorpe Cres. *Nott* —3G **33**
Caythorpe Ri. *Nott* —3G **33**
Cecil St. *Nott* —6D **44**
Cedar Av. *Bees* —4G **55**
Cedar Av. *Long E* —2E **73**
Cedar Av. *Nut* —3F **31**
Cedar Clo. *Bing* —5G **51**
Cedar Clo. *Sand* —4D **52**
Cedar Ct. *Bees* —4G **55**
Cedar Dri. *Keyw* —5G **79**
Cedar Gro. *Arn* —5D **22**
Cedar Gro. *Huck* —6H **7**
Cedar Gro. *Nott* —4H **31**

Cedarland Cres. *Nut* —3F **31**
Cedar Lodge. *Nott* —5E **45** (4A **4**)
Cedar Pk. *Ilk* —1A **40**
Cedar Rd. *Bees* —6E **55**
Cedar Rd. *Nott* —1G **45**
Cedars, The. *Nott* —3H **33**
Cedar Tree Rd. *Arn* —4F **21**
Celandine Clo. *Nott* —6C **20**
Celandine Gdns. *Bing* —5C **50**
Celia Dri. *Cltn* —2F **47**
Cemetery Rd. *S'fd* —4G **53**
Central Av. *Arn* —6B **22**
Central Av. *Bees* —5D **54**
  (Bramcote Av.)
Central Av. *Bees* —2E **55**
  (Derby Rd.)
Central Av. *Huck* —5G **7**
Central Av. *Map* —3D **34**
Central Av. *New B* —6E **33**
Central Av. *Sand* —5D **52**
Central Av. *S'fd* —3G **53**
Central Av. *W Bri* —3B **58**
Central Av. S. *Arn* —6B **22**
Central Ct. *Nott* —2D **56**
Central St. *Nott* —3A **46**
Centre Way. *Rad T* —5E **49**
Centurion Way. *Nott* —3D **56**
Cernan Ct. *Nott* —2F **31**
Cerne Clo. *Nott* —5D **66**
Chaceley Way. *Nott* —2E **67**
Chadborn Av. *Got* —6H **75**
Chaddesden, The. *Nott* —2G **45**
Chad Gdns. *Nott* —3E **21**
Chadwick Rd. *Nott* —2C **44**
Chainfield Clo. *Nott* —4B **66**
Chalfont Dri. *Nott* —3A **44**
Challond Ct. *Nott* —5F **21**
Chalons Clo. *Ilk* —6B **28**
Chalons Way. *Ilk* —6B **28**
Chamberlain Clo. *Nott* —4A **66**
Chambers Av. *Ilk* —2D **40**
Champion Av. *Ilk* —4G **27**
Chancery Ct. *Wilf* —5E **57**
Chancery, The. *Bees* —4C **54**
Chandos Av. *N'fld* —1A **48**
Chandos St. *N'fld* —2A **48**
Chandos St. *Nott* —2A **46**
Chantrey Rd. *W Bri* —4A **58**
Chantry Clo. *Bees* —1D **64**
Chantry Clo. *Kimb* —2A **30**
Chantry Clo. *Long E* —3C **72**
Chapel Bar. *Nott* —5F **45** (4C **4**)
Chapel Ct. *Ilk* —3B **28**
Chapel La. *Arn* —5A **22**
Chapel La. *Bing* —2D **50**
Chapel La. *Cotg* —2F **71**
Chapel La. *Epp* —5G **13**
Chapel La. *Lamb* —6B **24**
Chapel M. Ct. *Bramc* —3B **54**
Chapel Pl. *Kimb* —1H **29**
Chapel St. *Bees* —3B **54**
Chapel St. *Eastw* —4B **16**
Chapel St. *Hean* —5E **15**
Chapel St. *Huck* —4G **7**
Chapel St. *Ilk* —6B **28**
  (in two parts)
Chapel St. *Kimb* —1H **29**
  (in two parts)
Chapel St. *Long E* —6G **63**
Chapel St. *Nott* —4E **45**
Chapel St. *Rud* —1G **77**
Chapel St. Pl. *Ilk* —6B **28**
Chapman Ct. *Nott* —2H **43**
Chapmans Wlk. *B Vil* —5F **9**
Chapter Dri. *Kimb* —2A **30**
Chard St. *Nott* —5D **32**
Chard Ter. *Nott* —5D **32**
Charlbury Ct. *Bees* —5B **42**
Charlbury Rd. *Nott* —3G **43**
Charlecote Dri. *Nott* —6C **42**
Charlecote Pk. Dri. *W Bri* —1G **67**
Charles Av. *Bees* —2G **55**
  (Derby Rd.)
Charles Av. *Bees* —2C **64**
  (High Rd.)
Charles Av. *Eastw* —3D **16**
Charles Av. *Sand* —5D **52**

Charles Av. *S'fd* —3H **53**
Charles Clo. *Ged* —5H **35**
Charles Clo. *Ilk* —3D **40**
Charles St. *Arn* —6A **22**
Charles St. *Huck* —4G **7**
Charles St. *Long E* —1F **73**
Charles St. *Nott* —6G **67**
Charles Way. *Bulw* —2H **31**
Charles Way Bus. Pk. *Bulw*
  —2A **32**
Charlesworth Av. *Nott* —1C **44**
Charlock Clo. *Nott* —6C **20**
Charlock Gdns. *Bing* —6D **50**
Charlotte Clo. *Arn* —3A **22**
Charlotte Ct. *Eastw* —2B **16**
Charlotte Gro. *Bees* —2D **54**
Charlotte St. *Ilk* —4A **28**
Charlton Av. *Long E* —4H **63**
Charlton Gro. *Bees* —1F **65**
Charnock Av. *Nott* —6B **44**
Charnwood Av. *Bees* —5D **54**
Charnwood Av. *Keyw* —5G **79**
Charnwood Av. *Long E* —3D **72**
Charnwood Av. *Sand* —1C **62**
Charnwood Gdns. *Nott* —6F **33**
Charnwood Gro. *Bing* —5D **50**
Charnwood Gro. *Huck* —4D **6**
Charnwood Gro. *W Bri* —4A **58**
Charnwood La. *Arn* —1C **34**
Charnwood Way. *Wdbgh* —1C **24**
Charter Pk. *Ilk* —2A **40**
Chartwell Av. *Rud* —6F **67**
Chartwell Gro. *Nott* —2E **35**
Chase Pk. *Nott* —6C **46**
Chatham Ct. *Nott* —1A **32**
Chatham St. *Nott* —3G **45**
Chatsworth Av. *Bees* —3C **64**
Chatsworth Av. *Cltn* —1G **47**
Chatsworth Av. *Long E* —1A **74**
Chatsworth Av. *Nott* —5D **32**
Chatsworth Av. *Rad T* —5G **49**
Chatsworth Clo. *Sand* —1D **62**
Chatsworth Ct. *Huck* —5G **7**
Chatsworth Ct. *W Hal* —1B **38**
Chatsworth Dri. *Huck* —5G **7**
Chatsworth Pl. *Ilk* —4F **39**
Chatsworth Rd. *W Bri* —3D **58**
Chaucer St. *Ilk* —6B **28**
Chaucer St. *Nott* —4F **45** (2B **4**)
Chaworth Av. *Watn* —4A **18**
Chaworth Rd. *Bing* —5D **50**
Chaworth Rd. *Colw* —3H **47**
Chaworth Rd. *W Bri* —5A **58**
Cheadle Clo. *Bilb* —1D **42**
Cheadle Clo. *Map* —5D **34**
Cheapside. *Nott* —5G **45** (4E **5**)
Cheddar Rd. *Nott* —5C **66**
Chedington Av. *Nott* —1F **35**
Chediston Va. *Nott* —5F **21**
Chedworth Clo. *Nott* —4B **46**
Chelmsford Rd. *Nott* —5D **32**
Chelmsford Ter. *Nott* —5D **32**
  (off Chelmsford Rd.)
Chelsbury Ct. *Arn* —6A **22**
Chelsea Clo. *Nut* —4E **31**
Chelsea St. *Nott* —6D **32**
Cheltenham Clo. *Bees* —3H **63**
Cheltenham St. *Nott* —3C **32**
Chennel Nook. *Cotg* —3G **71**
Chepstow Rd. *Nott* —5C **66**
Cherhill Clo. *Nott* —6B **66**
Cheriton Dri. *Ilk* —4G **27**
Cherry Av. *Huck* —6H **7**
Cherry Clo. *Arn* —5A **22**
Cherry Clo. *Breas* —5A **62**
Cherry Hill. *Keyw* —4H **79**
Cherry Orchard. *Cotg* —2E **71**
Cherry Orchard Mt. *Nott* —1F **33**
Cherry St. *Bing* —5F **51**
Cherry Tree Clo. *Ilk* —3H **39**
Cherry Tree Clo. *Rad T* —1F **61**
Cherry Tree Clo. *Ris* —1B **62**
Cherry Tree La. *Edw* —2D **68**
Cherry Wood Dri. *Nott* —2H **43**
Cherrywood Gdns. *Nott* —1C **46**
Chertsey Clo. *Nott* —6B **34**
Chertsey Ct. *W Hal* —1B **38**
Cherwell Ct. *Nott* —1F **31**
Chesham Clo. *Nut* —4D **30**

Chesham Dri. *Bees* —6B **42**
Chesham Dri. *Nott* —5F **33**
Cheshire Ct. *W Bri* —6H **57**
Chesil Av. *Nott* —4B **44**
Chesil Cotts. *Nott* —4B **44**
Cheslyn Dri. *Nott* —1A **44**
Chesnuts, The. *Ged* —6B **36**
Chesterfield Av. *Long E* —5E **51**
Chesterfield Av. *Ged* —4F **35**
Chesterfield Av. *Long E* —6H **63**
Chesterfield Ct. *Ged* —4F **35**
Chesterfield Dri. *Bur J* —2G **37**
Chesterfield St. *Cltn* —2F **47**
Chester Grn. *Bees* —3G **63**
Chesterman Dri. *Aws* —3D **28**
Chester Rd. *Nott* —4E **47**
Chestnut Av. *Bees* —5F **55**
Chestnut Av. *Bing* —5E **51**
Chestnut Av. *Nott* —5D **34**
Chestnut Bank. *Hean* —4B **15**
Chestnut Dri. *Nut* —6B **18**
Chestnut Gro. *Arn* —4C **22**
Chestnut Gro. *Bur J* —3F **37**
Chestnut Gro. *Ged* —6H **35**
Chestnut Gro. *Huck* —1H **19**
Chestnut Gro. *Nott* —2G **45**
Chestnut Gro. *Rad T* —4F **49**
Chestnut Gro. *Sand* —4C **52**
Chestnut Gro. *W Bri* —4H **57**
Chestnut La. *Bar F* —1E **75**
Chestnut Rd. *Lan M* —2E **15**
Chestnuts, The. *Long E* —5C **62**
Chestnuts, The. *Nott* —6B **34**
Chestnut, The. *Rad T* —6E **49**
Chettles Ind. Est. *Nott* —4B **44**
Chetwin Rd. *Nott* —4C **42**
Chetwynd Rd. *Bees* —2B **64**
  (Highfield Rd.)
Chetwynd Rd. *Bees* —3A **64**
  (High Rd.)
Cheverton Ct. *Nott* —2G **45**
Chevin Gdns. *Nott* —5E **21**
Cheviot Clo. *Arn* —3F **21**
Cheviot Ct. *Bees* —2C **64**
Cheviot Dri. *Nott* —5F **19**
Cheviot Rd. *Long E* —4C **62**
Chewton Av. *Eastw* —4C **16**
Chewton St. *Eastw* —4B **16**
Cheyny Clo. *Nott* —2G **57**
Chichester Clo. *Ilk* —1C **40**
Chichester Clo. *Nott* —6C **20**
Chichester Dri. *Cotg* —1E **71**
Chidlow Rd. *Nott* —2D **42**
Chigwell Clo. *Nott* —5D **30**
Chillon Way. *Huck* —5D **6**
Chiltern Clo. *Arn* —3F **21**
Chiltern Dri. *W Hal* —1C **38**
Chiltern Gdns. *Long E* —4C **62**
Chiltern Way. *Nott* —1F **33**
Chilton Dri. *Watn* —6A **18**
Chilvers Clo. *Nott* —6E **21**
Chilwell Ct. *Nott* —6B **20**
Chilwell La. *Bees* —4B **54**
Chilwell Manor Golf Course.
  —1E **65**
Chilwell Meadows Nature
  Reserve. —1D **64**
Chilwell Retail Pk. *Bees* —4B **64**
  (in two parts)
Chilwell Rd. *Bees* —6F **55**
  (in two parts)
Chilwell St. *Nott* —6D **44**
Chine Gdns. *W Bri* —6G **57**
Chingford Rd. *Nott* —1E **43**
Chippendale St. *Nott* —6D **44**
Chippenham Rd. *Nott* —1F **33**
Chisbury Grn. *Nott* —6B **66**
Chisholm Way. *Nott* —1E **33**
Chiswick Ct. *Nott* —4G **33**
Christchurch Rd. *Huck* —1D **18**
Christina Av. *Nott* —3A **32**
Christina Cres. *Nott* —3A **32**
Christine Clo. *Huck* —2A **8**
Christine Ct. *Nott* —2C **46**
Christopher Clo. *Nott* —3F **43**
Chrysalis Way. *Eastw* —2G **15**
Church Av. *Day* —6A **22**
Church Av. *Long E* —3C **72**
Church Av. *Nott* —6D **44**

Church Clo. *Bing* —4F **51**
Church Clo. *Day* —6A **22**
Church Clo. *Nott* —3G **45** (1E **5**)
Church Clo. *Trow* —5E **41**
Church Ct. *Cotg* —6E **49**
Church Cres. *Bees* —1A **64**
Church Cres. *Day* —6H **21**
Church Cft. *W Bri* —3B **58**
Churchdale Av. *S'fd* —2G **53**
Church Dri. *Day* —6H **21**
Church Dri. *Huck* —4G **7**
Church Dri. *Ilk* —2H **27**
Church Dri. *Keyw* —4G **79**
Church Dri. *Nott* —6F **33**
Church Dri. *Sand* —4D **52**
Church Dri. *W Bri* —4B **58**
Church Dri. E. *Day* —6A **22**
Churchfield Ct. *Nott* —4E **21**
Churchfield La. *Nott* —2C **44**
Churchfield Ter. *Nott* —5C **32**
Churchfield Way. *Nott* —4E **21**
Church Ga. *Cols B* —5C **70**
Church Gro. *Nott* —6C **44**
Church Hill. *Kimb* —1H **29**
Church Hill. *Plum* —1G **79**
Churchill Av. *Ilk* —1D **40**
Churchill Clo. *Arn* —1B **34**
Churchill Dri. *Rud* —6F **67**
Churchill Dri. *S'fd* —3G **53**
Churchill Pk. *Colw* —4H **47**
Church La. *Arn* —4A **22**
Church La. *Bar F* —1E **75**
Church La. *Bees* —4D **64**
Church La. *Bing* —5F **51**
Church La. *Bulw* —6A **20**
Church La. *Coss* —5E **29**
Church La. *Cotg* —2E **71**
Church La. *Epp* —5G **13**
Church La. *L'by & Huck* —1G **7**
Church La. *Plum* —6G **69**
Church La. *S'fd* —4F **53**
Church La. *Thrum* —4B **74**
Church Mdw. *C'tn* —5H **11**
Church M. *Nott* —2H **57**
Churchmoor Ct. *Arn* —4A **22**
Churchmoor La. *Arn* —4A **22**
Church Rd. *B Vil* —1C **20**
Church Rd. *Bur J* —3F **37**
Church Rd. *Greas* —3G **17**
Church Rd. *Newt* —1F **17**
Church Rd. *Nott* —2H **45**
Churchside Gdns. *Nott* —1C **44**
Church Sq. *Hean* —4D **14**
Church Sq. *Nott* —6D **44**
Church St. *Arn* —5B **22**
Church St. *Bees* —3B **54**
  (Derby Rd.)
Church St. *Bees* —5F **55**
  (Middle St.)
Church St. *Bing* —5F **51**
Church St. *Cltn* —2G **47**
Church St. *Eastw* —4A **16**
Church St. *Got* —6H **75**
Church St. *Hean* —4D **14**
Church St. *Ilk* —3H **27**
Church St. *Lamb* —5C **24**
Church St. *Lent* —6C **44**
  (in two parts)
Church St. *Old B* —5C **32**
Church St. *Rud* —6G **67**
Church St. *Sand* —4D **52**
Church St. *Shelf* —6H **37**
Church St. *S'fd* —4F **53**
Church Vw. *Breas* —6A **62**
Church Vw. *Ged* —6H **35**
Church Vw. *Ilk* —4B **40**
Church Vw. *Los* —1A **14**
Church Vw. Clo. *Arn* —4F **21**
Church Wlk. *Cltn* —2G **47**
Church Wlk. *Eastw* —3B **16**
Church Wlk. *S'fd* —4F **53**
Church Wlk. *Wdbgh* —1C **24**
Church Way. *Ilk* —2H **27**
Church Wilne Water Sports Club.
  —2A **72**
Churnet Clo. *Nott* —1C **66**
Churston Ct. *Bees* —5G **55**
Cinderhill Footway. *Nott* —3B **32**
Cinderhill Gro. *Ged* —5G **35**

Cottam Dri. *Nott* —5D **20**
Cottam Gdns. *Nott* —5E **21**
Cottesmore Rd. *Nott* —5D **44**
County Bus. Pk. *Nott* —6A **46**
County Clo. *Bees* —6G **55**
County House. —5F **5**
County Rd. *Ged* —4E **35**
County Rd. *Nott* —1A **58**
Court Cres. *Nott* —5F **43**
Courtenay Gdns. *Nott* —2H **45**
Court Gdns. *W Bri* —1F **67**
Courtleet Way. *Nott* —2H **31**
Courtney Clo. *Nott* —4E **43**
Court St. *Nott* —2D **44**
Court, The. *Bees* —3A **64**
Court Vw. *Nott* —5E **45** (4A **4**)
Court Yd. *Bees* —3B **54**
Covedale Rd. *Nott* —2G **33**
Coventry Ct. *Nott* —2H **31**
Coventry La. *Bees* —2H **53**
Coventry Rd. *Bees* —4G **55**
Coventry Rd. *Nott* —6H **19**
(in two parts)
Covert Clo. *Bur J* —2E **37**
Covert Clo. *Huck* —5A **8**
Covert Clo. *Keyw* —3H **79**
Covert Cres. *Rad T* —4H **49**
Covert Rd. *W Bri* —5D **58**
Cowdrey Gdns. *Arn* —1D **34**
Cowen St. *Nott* —4H **45** (3F **5**)
Cowlairs. *Nott* —6C **20**
Cow La. *Bees* —3B **54**
Cowley St. *Old B* —4B **32**
Cowper Rd. *Newt* —5C **16**
Cowper Rd. *Wd'p* —3A **34**
Cowslip Clo. *Bing* —5C **50**
Coxmoor Clo. *Edw* —1E **69**
Coxmoor Ct. *Nott* —4E **21**
Crabtree Fld. *Colw P* —5F **47**
Crabtree Rd. *Nott* —1G **31**
Cragdale Rd. *Nott* —2G **33**
Cragmoor Rd. *Bur J* —4E **37**
Craig Moray. *Rad T* —5G **49**
Craig St. *Long E* —6G **63**
Crammond Clo. *Nott* —1F **57**
Crampton Ct. *Nott* —5E **21**
Cramworth Gro. *Nott* —4H **33**
Cranberry Clo. *W Bri* —5F **57**
Cranborne Clo. *Trow* —1F **53**
Cranbourne Gro. *Huck* —4E **7**
Cranbrook St. *Nott* —4H **45** (3F **5**)
Cranfield Wlk. *Nott* —3D **66**
Cranfleet Way. *Long E* —6C **62**
Cranford Gdns. *W Bri* —1G **67**
Cranmer Gro. *Nott* —2G **45**
Cranmer St. *Ilk* —6B **28**
Cranmer St. *Long E* —5F **63**
Cranmer St. *Nott* —2G **45**
Cranmer Wlk. *Nott* —2G **45**
Cranmore Clo. *Arn* —3C **22**
Cransley Av. *Nott* —1D **54**
Cranston Av. *Arn* —4B **22**
Cranston Rd. *Bees* —2C **54**
Cranthorne Dri. *Nott* —3E **47**
Crantock Gdns. *Keyw* —4H **79**
Cranwell Ct. *Nott* —1F **31**
Cranwell Rd. *Nott* —6D **30**
Craster Dri. *Arn* —3C **22**
Craster Dri. *Nott* —5F **19**
Craven Rd. *Nott* —2C **44**
Crawford Av. *S'fd* —3F **53**
Crawford Clo. *Nott* —4E **43**
Crawford Ri. *Arn* —5E **23**
Creeton Grn. *Nott* —5D **66**
Crescent Av. *Cltn* —6G **35**
Crescent, The. *Bees* —2C **64**
(Attenborough La. N.)
Crescent, The. *Bees* —3A **64**
(Chetwynd Rd.)
Crescent, The. *Eastw* —3C **16**
Crescent, The. *Nott* —1H **45**
Crescent, The. *Rad T* —6G **49**
Crescent, The. *Ris* —2E **45**
Crescent, The. *Stan C* —1A **38**
Crescent, The. *S'fd* —2G **53**
Crescent, The. *Wd'p* —3A **34**
Cresswell Rd. *Bees* —6B **54**
Cressy Rd. *Nott* —3D **66**
Cresta Gdns. *Nott* —5H **33**

Crest Vw. *Nott* —4F **33**
Crewe Clo. *Nott* —3D **44**
Cribb Clo. *Nott* —4F **57**
Crich Vw. *Nott* —5G **33**
Cricketers Ct. *W Bri* —2B **58**
Criftin Rd. *Bur J* —3G **37**
Cripps Hill. *Nott* —1A **56**
Critchley St. *Ilk* —6B **28**
Critch's Flat. *Kimb* —1H **29**
Crocus Pl. *Nott* —6H **45**
Crocus St. *Nott* —1G **57**
Croft Av. *Huck* —6G **7**
Croft Cres. *Aws* —2E **29**
Crofton Clo. *Bees* —2D **64**
Crofton Clo. *Nott* —3H **43**
Crofton Rd. *Bees* —3D **64**
Croft Rd. *Arn* —5B **22**
Croft Rd. *Edw* —1C **68**
Croft Rd. *Keyw* —4F **79**
Crofts, The. *Bing* —5E **51**
Cromarty Ct. *Nott* —1F **57**
Cromdale Clo. *Arn* —4E **23**
Cromer Rd. *Nott* —2A **46**
Cromford Av. *Cltn* —1F **47**
Cromford Clo. *Lan M* —1F **15**
Cromford Clo. *Long E* —2C **72**
Cromford Rd. *Lan M* —1D **14**
Cromford Rd. *W Bri* —5B **58**
Cromford Rd. Ind. Est. *Lan M*
—1F **15**
Crompton Rd. *Ilk* —1D **52**
Crompton Rd. Ind. Est. *Ilk* —6D **40**
Cromwell Av. *Ilk* —4C **40**
Cromwell Cres. *Lamb* —6B **24**
Cromwell Rd. *Bees* —4E **55**
Cromwell St. *Cltn* —2G **47**
Cromwell St. *Gilt* —5D **16**
Cromwell St. *Nott* —4E **45** (2A **4**)
Cromwell Ter. *Ilk* —4B **28**
Crookdole La. *C'tn* —4H **11**
Cropston Clo. *W Bri* —1A **68**
Cropton Cres. *Nott* —3H **43**
Cropton Gro. *Bing* —5C **50**
Cropwell Gdns. *Rad T* —1G **61**
Cropwell Grn. *Nott* —3B **46**
Cropwell Rd. *Rad T* —6F **49**
Crosby Rd. *W Bri* —2B **58**
Crossdale Dri. *Keyw* —3G **79**
Crossdale Wlk. *Nott* —5C **20**
Crossfield Ct. *Nott* —5E **21**
Crossfield Dri. *Nott* —5E **21**
Crossgate Dri. *Q Dri & Nott* —3E **57**
Crosshill. *Cotg* —2G **71**
Crosshill Dri. *Ilk* —4G **39**
Crosslands Mdw. *Colw* —5H **47**
Cross Lea. *Dal A* —6D **38**
Crossley St. *Nott* —5F **33**
Crossman St. *Nott* —5F **33**
Cross St. *Arn* —5H **21**
Cross St. *Bees* —4F **55**
Cross St. *Cltn* —1F **47**
Cross St. *Eastw* —3C **16**
Cross St. *Long E* —5G **63**
Cross St. *N'fld* —2A **48**
Cross St. *Sand* —5E **53**
Cross, The. *Cotg* —2E **71**
Crowborough Av. *Nott* —1E **55**
Crow Ct. *Bing* —5G **51**
Crowcroft Way. *Long E* —3D **62**
Crow Hill Rd. *Cltn* —2H **47**
Crowley Clo. *Nott* —3C **42**
Crown Clo. *Long E* —6C **62**
Crown Hill Way. *Stan C* —1A **38**
Crow Pk. Dri. *Bur J* —4E **37**
Crowthorne Clo. *Nott* —4C **20**
Crowthorne Gdns. *Nott* —4C **20**
Croxall Clo. *Nott* —1C **66**
Croxley Gdns. *Nut* —4D **30**
Croydon Rd. *Nott* —4C **44**
Crummock Clo. *Bees* —3C **54**
Crusader Ct. *Nott* —4A **66**
Cuillin Clo. *Long E* —4C **62**
Cuillin Clo. *Nott* —3D **20**
Culbert Lodge. *Nott* —6D **32**
Culbert Pl. *Nott* —6D **32**
Culdrose Wlk. *Nott* —6A **34**
Cullens Ct. *Nott* —5G **33**
Cumberland Av. *Bees* —5D **54**
Cumberland Clo. *Rud* —6G **67**

Cumberland Pl. *Nott* —5F **45** (4C **4**)
Cumbria Grange. *Gam* —4E **59**
Curie Ct. *Nott* —1C **56**
Curlew Clo. *Nott* —4E **47**
Curlew Wharf. *Nott* —1E **57**
Cursley Way. *Bees* —3C **64**
Curtis St. *Huck* —5G **7**
Curzon Av. *Cltn* —2D **46**
Curzon Ct. *Nott* —3H **45** (1G **5**)
Curzon Gdns. *Nott* —3H **45** (1G **5**)
Curzon Pl. *Nott* —4H **45** (2F **5**)
Curzon St. *Got* —6H **75**
Curzon St. *Long E* —3D **62**
Curzon St. *N'fld* —2A **48**
Curzon St. *Nott* —4H **45** (2F **5**)
Cutthrough La. *Nott* —3H **55**
Cuxton Clo. *Nott* —6D **30**
Cycle Rd. *Nott* —5C **44**
Cypress Ct. *Huck* —6C **6**
Cyprus Av. *Bees* —4F **55**
Cyprus Ct. *Nott* —1G **45**
Cyprus Dri. *Bees* —4F **55**
Cyprus Rd. *Nott* —1G **45**
Cyril Av. *Bees* —4E **55**
Cyril Av. *Nott* —1B **44**
Cyril Av. *S'fd* —4F **53**
Cyril Rd. *W Bri* —3C **58**

Dabell Av. *Nott* —5E **19**
Dagmar Gro. *Bees* —5G **55**
Dagmar Gro. *Nott* —6H **33**
Daisy Clo. *Cotg* —3E **71**
Daisy Farm Rd. *Newt* —4D **16**
Daisy Rd. *Nott* —6C **34**
Dakeyne St. *Nott* —4A **46** (3H **5**)
Dalby Sq. *Nott* —6A **44**
Dale Av. *Cltn* —2E **47**
Dale Av. *Long E* —4F **63**
Dale Av. *Map* —5C **34**
Dalebrook Cres. *Huck* —5C **6**
Dale Clo. *Breas* —5A **62**
Dale Clo. *Huck* —5C **6**
Dale Clo. *W Bri* —4D **58**
Dale Farm Av. *Nott* —4C **46**
Dale Gro. *Nott* —5B **46**
Dale La. *Bees* —5E **55**
Dalehead Rd. *Nott* —3B **66**
Dalemoor Gdns. *Nott* —1H **43**
Dale Rd. *Cltn* —2E **47**
Dale Rd. *Keyw* —4G **79**
Dale Rd. *Kimb* —2H **29**
Dale Rd. *Stan* —4A **38**
Dale Rd. *Stan D* —2A **52**
Daleside. *Cotg* —3E **71**
Daleside Rd. *Nott* —6B **46**
Daleside Rd. E. *Nott* —5D **46**
Dales Shop. Cen. *W Hal* —2C **38**
Dale St. *Ilk* —2B **40**
Dale St. *Nott* —5A **46**
Dale Ter. *Nott* —5B **46**
Dale Vw. *Ilk* —3A **40**
Dale Vw. Rd. *Nott* —2D **46**
Dalkeith Ter. *Nott* —2D **44**
Dallas-York Rd. *Bees* —5H **55**
Dalley Clo. *S'fd* —4G **53**
Dallimore Rd. *Ilk* —5H **39**
Dalton Clo. *S'fd* —6G **53**
Daltons Clo. *Lan M* —1E **15**
Damson Wlk. *Nott* —1D **46**
Danbury Mt. *Nott* —5H **33**
Dane Clo. *Nott* —3H **45** (1F **5**)
Dane Ct. *Nott* —3H **45** (1F **5**)
Danes Clo. *Arn* —5H **21**
Danethorpe Va. *Nott* —3G **33**
Daniels Way. *Huck* —1E **19**
Darfield Dri. *Hean* —3E **15**
Darkey La. *S'fd* —6G **53**
(in two parts)
Dark La. *Bing* —5G **51**
Dark La. *C'tn* —5G **11**
Darley Av. *Bees* —2G **63**
Darley Av. *Cltn* —6G **35**
Darley Av. *Nott* —2D **44**
Darley Dri. *Long E* —2C **72**
Darley Dri. *W Hal* —1C **38**
Darley Rd. *Nott* —2C **44**
Darley Sq. *Ilk* —2A **28**

Darlton Dri. *Arn* —6C **22**
Darnall Clo. *Nott* —6C **20**
Darnhall Cres. *Nott* —2D **42**
Daron Gdns. *Nott* —6E **21**
Dartmeet Ct. *Nott* —2B **44**
Darvel Clo. *Nott* —3H **43**
Darwin Av. *Ilk* —2A **40**
Darwin Clo. *Nott* —5C **20**
Darwin Rd. *Long E* —2D **72**
David Gro. *Bees* —2E **55**
David La. *Nott* —4B **32**
Davidson Clo. *Arn* —6E **23**
Davidson St. *Nott* —6B **46**
Davies Rd. *W Bri* —4B **58**
Davy Clo. *L'by* —1H **7**
Dawlish Clo. *Huck* —5D **6**
Dawlish Ct. *Eastw* —2H **15**
Dawlish Dri. *Nott* —2F **33**
Dawn Clo. *Huck* —2A **8**
Dawn Vw. *Trow* —1F **53**
Dawson Clo. *Newt* —4C **16**
Dawver Rd. *Kimb* —2H **29**
Daybrook Av. *Nott* —4G **33**
Daybrook Bus. Cen. *Nott* —1H **33**
Daybrook St. *Nott* —4G **33**
Deabill St. *N'fld* —3A **48**
Dead La. *Coss* —6F **29**
Deakins Pl. *Nott* —4C **44**
Deal Gdns. *Nott* —6F **19**
Dean Av. *Nott* —4D **34**
Dean Clo. *Nott* —4D **42**
Dean Rd. *Wd'p* —2A **34**
Deanscourt. *Cotg* —2G **71**
Deans Cft. *Bees* —2E **63**
Dean St. *Lan M* —2G **15**
Dean St. *Nott* —5H **45** (5G **5**)
Debdale La. *Keyw* —4F **79**
Deddington La. *Bees* —1B **54**
(in two parts)
Deepdale Av. *Ilk* —4H **39**
Deepdale Av. *S'fd* —5F **53**
Deepdale Clo. *Gam* —4D **58**
Deepdale Ct. *Hean* —4C **14**
Deepdale Rd. *Long E* —1C **72**
Deepdale Rd. *Nott* —5D **42**
Deepdene Clo. *Nott* —5G **31**
Deepdene Way. *Nott* —5G **31**
Deep Furrow Av. *Cltn* —1F **47**
Deering Ct. *Nott* —1F **57**
Deerleap Dri. *Arn* —6G **21**
Deer Pk. *Nott* —5E **43**
Deer Pk. *Arn* —5F **21**
Delia Av. *Huck* —2A **8**
Dell Way. *Nott* —3D **66**
Dellwood Clo. *Cltn* —5D **34**
Delta Ct. *Nott* —3F **45**
Delta St. *Nott* —6D **32**
Delves Ct. *Hean* —5C **14**
Delves Rd. *Hean* —5B **14**
Delville Av. *Keyw* —3G **79**
Denacre Av. *Long E* —4H **63**
Denehurst Av. *Nott* —6A **32**
Denewood Av. *Bees* —1C **54**
Denewood Cres. *Nott* —1E **43**
Denholme Rd. *Nott* —4D **42**
Denison St. *Bees* —4E **55**
Denison St. *Nott* —3D **44**
Denman St. *Nott* —4D **44**
Denman St. Central. *Nott* —4C **44**
(in three parts)
Denmark Gro. *Nott* —6H **33**
Dennett Clo. *Nott* —3A **46** (1H **5**)
Dennis Av. *Bees* —3E **55**
Dennis St. *N'fld* —2A **48**
Denstone Rd. *Nott* —4A **46**
Dentdale Dri. *Nott* —5B **42**
Denton Av. *Sand* —5C **52**
Denton Dri. *W Bri* —1H **67**
Denton Grn. *Nott* —5F **31**
Denver Ct. *S'fd* —1G **53**
(Crescent, The)
Denver Ct. *S'fd* —2G **53**
(Melbourne Rd.)
Deptford Cres. *Nott* —1A **32**
(in two parts)
Derby Gro. *Nott* —4D **44**
Derby Rd. *Bees & Nott*
—3A **54** (3A **4**)
Derby Rd. *Hean* —4B **14**

Elgar Dri. *Long E* —2D **72**
Elgar Gdns. *Nott* —3B **46**
Eliot Clo. *Long E* —2D **72**
Eliot Dri. *Ilk* —4H **39**
Eliot Wlk. *Nott* —5A **66**
Elizabeth Clo. *Huck* —6E **7**
Elizabeth Clo. *W Hal* —1B **38**
Elizabeth Ct. *Ilk* —6H **27**
Elizabeth Gro. *Ged* —5G **35**
Ella Bank Rd. *Hean* —4D **14**
Ella Rd. *W Bri* —2B **58**
Ellastone Av. *Nott* —5G **21**
Ellerby Av. *Nott* —3C **66**
Ellerslie Gro. *Sand* —6C **52**
Ellesmere Bus. Pk. *Nott* —5E **33**
Ellesmere Clo. *Arn* —6D **22**
Ellesmere Dri. *Trow* —4E **41**
Ellesmere Rd. *W Bri* —1B **68**
Ellington Rd. *Arn* —3C **22**
Elliot Durham Swimming Pool.
  —6A **34**
Elliot St. *Nott* —4E **45** (3A **4**)
Ellis Av. *Huck* —6E **7**
Ellis Clo. *Long E* —1E **73**
Ellis Ct. *Nott* —3H **45**
Ellis Gro. *Bees* —6F **55**
Ellsworth Ri. *Nott* —1D **32**
Ellwood Cres. *Nott* —4G **43**
Elm Av. *Bees* —3D **64**
  (Long La.)
Elm Av. *Bees* —5E **55**
  (Newcastle Av.)
Elm Av. *Bing* —5G **51**
Elm Av. *Cltn* —2H **47**
Elm Av. *Huck* —6E **7**
Elm Av. *Keyw* —5H **79**
Elm Av. *Long E* —4E **63**
Elm Av. *Nott* —2G **45**
Elm Av. *Nut* —1B **30**
Elm Av. *Sand* —4D **52**
Elm Bank. *Nott* —1G **45**
Elm Bank Dri. *Nott* —1G **45**
Elmbridge. *Nott* —6F **21**
Elm Clo. *Keyw* —5H **79**
Elm Clo. *Nott* —2G **45**
Elmdale Gdns. *Nott* —1H **43**
Elm Dri. *Cltn* —2H **47**
Elm Gro. *Arn* —4C **22**
Elmhurst Av. *Nott* —5E **35**
Elmore Ct. *Nott* —3E **45**
Elms Clo. *Rud* —1H **77**
Elmsdale Gdns. *Bur J* —3F **37**
Elmsfield Av. *Hean* —3E **15**
Elms Gdns. *Rud* —1G **77**
Elmsham Av. *Nott* —4C **20**
Elms Pk. *Rud* —1H **77**
Elms, The. *Colw* —3H **47**
Elms, The. *Watn* —6H **17**
Elmsthorpe Av. *Nott* —5C **44**
Elmswood Gdns. *Nott* —4H **33**
Elm Tree Av. *W Bri* —4H **57**
Elmtree Rd. *C'tn* —4F **11**
Elm Vw. *Nott* —3D **44**
Elnor St. *Lan M* —3G **15**
Elson St. *Nott* —1D **44**
Elston Gdns. *Nott* —1C **66**
Elston M. *Nott* —2D **46**
Elstree Dri. *Nott* —3G **43**
Elswick Clo. *Nott* —5F **21**
Elswick Dri. *Bees* —1H **65**
Elterwater Dri. *Gam* —4E **59**
Eltham Clo. *Nott* —4F **31**
Eltham Dri. *Nott* —4F **31**
Eltham Rd. *W Bri* —4B **58**
Elton Clo. *S'fd* —3G **53**
Elton M. *Nott* —6F **33**
Elton Rd. N. *Nott* —6F **33**
Elton Ter. *Nott* —2D **44**
Elvaston Ct. *Nott* —2D **32**
Elvaston Dri. *Long E* —3B **72**
Elvaston Rd. *Nott* —4G **43**
Elveden Dri. *Ilk* —4G **27**
Elwes Lodge. *Cltn* —3H **47**
Emerys Rd. *Ged* —1B **48**
  (in four parts)
Emmanuel Av. *Arn* —4E **21**
Emmanuel Av. *Nott* —6C **34**
Emneth Clo. *Nott* —1B **46**
Empingham Clo. *Bees* —3B **64**

Emsworth Clo. *Ilk* —4H **27**
Ena Av. *Nott* —4B **46**
Enderby Gdns. *Red* —4A **22**
Enderby Sq. *Bees* —3F **55**
Endsleigh Gdns. *Bees* —4F **55**
Endsleigh Gdns. *Edw* —1C **68**
Enfield Chambers. *Nott*
  —5G **45** (5E **5**)
Enfield St. *Bees* —5E **55**
Engine La. *Newt* —1D **16**
England Cres. *Hean* —3E **15**
Ennerdale Clo. *Gam* —4E **59**
Ennerdale Rd. *Long E* —3D **62**
Ennerdale Rd. *Nott* —2H **33**
Ennismore Gdns. *Nott* —3A **44**
Ennismore M. *W Bri* —2G **67**
Enthorpe St. *Nott* —3H **43**
Epperstone By Pass. *Wdbgh*
  —5E **13**
Epperstone Ct. *W Bri* —3A **58**
Epperstone Pk. —2D **12**
Epperstone Rd. *Epp* —1B **12**
Epperstone Rd. *W Bri* —3A **58**
Epsom Rd. *Bees* —2G **63**
Erdington Way. *Bees* —2G **63**
Erewash Ct. *Long E* —4F **63**
Erewash Ct. *Man I* —6H **27**
Erewash Dri. *Ilk* —3C **40**
Erewash Gdns. *Nott* —5E **21**
Erewash Gro. *Bees* —3H **63**
  (in two parts)
Erewash Mus. —1B **40**
Erewash Sq. *Ilk* —3D **40**
Erewash St. *Long E* —5G **63**
Erewash Valley Golf Course.
  —3C **52**
Eric Av. *Huck* —2F **7**
Erith Clo. *Nott* —6D **30**
Ernest Rd. *Cltn* —1D **46**
Ernhale Ct. *Arn* —5A **22**
Erskine Rd. *Nott* —6F **33**
Esher Gro. *Nott* —6G **33**
Eskdale Clo. *Long E* —2D **72**
Eskdale Ct. *Gam* —4E **59**
Eskdale Dri. *Bees* —6A **54**
Eskdale Dri. *Nott* —1H **43**
Esk Ho. Clo. *Edw* —1E **69**
Essex St. *Eastw* —3B **16**
Essex St. *Ilk* —6B **28**
Estwic Av. *Eastw* —2B **16**
Ethel Av. *Nott* —2F **7**
Ethel Av. *Nott* —6C **34**
Ethel Rd. *W Bri* —4B **58**
Ethel Ter. *Nott* —6E **33**
Eton Ct. *W Hal* —1B **38**
Eton Gro. *Nott* —5H **43**
Eton Rd. *W Bri* —3A **58**
Eucalyptus Av. *Nott* —4A **66**
Eugene Gdns. *Nott* —1H **57**
Eugene St. *Nott* —6H **45**
Europa Way. *Nott* —2G **67**
Evans Rd. *Nott* —4B **32**
Evedon Wlk. *Nott* —4F **21**
Evelyn St. *Bees* —4H **55**
Evelyn St. *Nott* —5A **46** (5H **5**)
Eversley Wlk. *Nott* —5F **21**
Evesham Ct. *Bees* —4A **64**
Ewart Rd. *Nott* —1D **44**
Ewe Lamb Clo. *Bees* —2H **53**
Ewe Lamb La. *Bees* —2H **53**
Ewell Rd. *Nott* —4E **43**
Exbourne Rd. *Nott* —6F **31**
Exbury Gdns. *W Bri* —1F **67**
Exchange Arc. *Nott* —4E **5**
Exchange Rd. *W Bri* —4B **58**
Exchange Wlk. *Nott* —5G **45** (4E **5**)
Excise Chambers. *Nott* —4F **5**
Exeter Clo. *Ged* —5H **35**
Exeter Rd. *Nott* —1E **45**
Exeter Rd. *W Bri* —5B **58**
Extension St. *Ilk* —1B **40**
Exton Rd. *Nott* —4E **33**
Eyam Clo. *Bees* —6C **42**
Eyre's Gdns. *Ilk* —5B **28**
Eyre St. *Nott* —5A **46** (4H **5**)

Fabis Dri. *Nott* —1C **66**
Factory La. *Bees* —6E **55**

Factory La. *Ilk* —5A **28**
Failsworth Clo. *Nott* —2C **66**
Fairbank Cres. *Nott* —5H **33**
Fairburn Clo. *Bramc* —4B **54**
Fairburn Clo. *Nott* —5C **42**
Faircroft Av. *Sand* —6D **52**
Fairdale Dri. *Newt* —3D **16**
Fairfax Clo. *Nott* —5D **32**
Fairfield Clo. *Nott* —6F **57**
Fairfield Cres. *Long E* —3C **72**
Fairfield St. *Bing* —5E **51**
Fairham Av. *Got* —6H **75**
Fairham Brook Nature Reserve.
  —5E **67**
Fairham Clo. *Rud* —5F **67**
Fairham Ct. *Nott* —2E **67**
Fairham Dri. *Nott* —5B **44**
Fairham Rd. *Keyw* —4F **79**
Fairholm Ct. *Nott* —3A **46** (1H **5**)
Fairisle Clo. *Nott* —4E **67**
Fairland Cres. *W Bri* —1H **67**
Fairlawn Pl. *Sher* —5H **33**
Fair Lea Clo. *Long E* —1F **73**
Fairlight Way. *Nott* —6F **21**
Fairmaid Gro. *Nott* —3C **66**
Fairmead Clo. *Nott* —1C **46**
Fairnley Rd. *Nott* —1D **42**
Fairview Ct. *W Bri* —3H **67**
Fairview Rd. *Wd'p* —3A **34**
Fairway. *Keyw* —4H **79**
Fairway Cres. *Nwtn* —1B **50**
Fairway Dri. *Bees* —5D **54**
Fairway Dri. *Nott* —6B **20**
Fairway, The. *Ged* —4G **35**
Falcon Clo. *Lent* —5C **44**
Falcon Ct. *Ilk* —6H **27**
Falconers Wlk. *Arn* —5G **21**
Falcon Gro. *Nott* —6E **33**
Falcon St. *Nott* —6E **33**
Falconwood Gdns. *Nott* —4A **66**
Fallow Clo. *Nott* —3C **66**
Fall Rd. *Hean* —2C **14**
Falstaff M. *New B* —6E **33**
Falston Rd. *Nott* —3G **43**
Faraday Building. *Nott* —2B **56**
Faraday Ct. *S'fd* —2G **53**
Faraday Rd. *Nott* —4C **44**
Farfield Av. *Bees* —3E **55**
Farfield Gro. *Bees* —3E **55**
Farleys La. *Huck* —5G **7**
  (in two parts)
Farley St. *Nott* —6H **19**
Farm Av. *Huck* —1D **18**
Farm Clo. *Ilk* —1C **40**
Farm Clo. *Long E* —2G **73**
Farm Clo. *Nott* —3C **66**
Farmer St. *Bradm* —4A **78**
Farm Rd. *Arn* —6D **22**
Farm Rd. *Bees* —6C **54**
Farnborough Rd. *Nott* —5B **66**
Farndale Clo. *Long E* —2C **72**
Farndale Dri. *Nott* —5B **42**
Farndon Dri. *Bees* —2H **63**
Farndon Grn. *Nott* —5A **44**
Farndon M. *Nott* —1C **46**
Far New Clo. *Sand* —6D **52**
Farnham Wlk. *W Hal* —1B **38**
Farnsworth Clo. *Watn* —4A **18**
Far Pastures Clo. *Keyw* —5G **79**
Farriers Cft. *Ilk* —4G **27**
Farriers Grn. *Clif* —3A **66**
Farringdon Clo. *Nut* —4D **30**
Far Rye. *Nott* —3F **43**
Far St. *Bradm* —4A **78**
Farthing Ct. *Long E* —6D **62**
Farwells Clo. *Nott* —4A **32**
Faulconbridge Clo. *Nott* —1H **31**
Fearn Chase. *Cltn* —2G **47**
Fearn Clo. *Breas* —6C **62**
Fearnleigh Dri. *Nott* —5B **32**
Featherstone Clo. *Ged* —4F **35**
Feignies Ct. *Keyw* —4G **79**
Felen Clo. *Nott* —6E **21**
Fellbarrow Clo. *W Bri* —6E **59**
Felley Clo. *Huck* —6E **7**
Fellows Rd. *Bees* —4E **55**
Fellows Yd. *Plum* —6G **69**
Fell Side. *Wd'p* —2C **34**

Fellside Clo. *Gam* —5E **59**
Felstead Ct. *Bees* —2C **54**
Felstead Rd. *Nott* —3G **43**
Felton Clo. *Bees* —6B **54**
Felton Rd. *Nott* —2H **57**
Fenchurch Clo. *Arn* —4E **21**
Fenimore Ct. *Rad T* —5H **49**
Fenroth Clo. *Nott* —5F **19**
Fenton Ct. *Nott* —3D **32**
Fenton Dri. *Nott* —3A **20**
Fenton Rd. *Nott* —3D **32**
Fenwick Clo. *Nott* —5F **31**
Fenwick Rd. *Nott* —5F **31**
Fergus Clo. *Nott* —5D **66**
Ferguson Clo. *Bees* —3C **64**
Fern Av. *Nott* —6F **33**
Fern Clo. *Bees* —4B **54**
Fern Cres. *Eastw* —2A **16**
Ferndale Clo. *Bees* —3D **64**
Ferndale Gro. *Nott* —3D **46**
Ferndale Rd. *Nott* —3D **46**
Ferndene Dri. *Long E* —6C **62**
Ferngill Clo. *Nott* —2F **57**
Fernilee Clo. *W Hal* —1C **38**
Fern Lea Av. *Cotg* —3E **71**
Fernleigh Av. *Nott* —5D **34**
Fernwood Cres. *Nott* —5C **42**
Fernwood Dri. *Rad T* —5F **49**
Fernwood Dri. *Watn* —5A **18**
Ferny Hollow Clo. *Nott* —5C **20**
Ferrers Wlk. *Nott* —4A **46** (2H **5**)
Ferriby Ter. *Nott* —2G **57**
Ferry Lodge. *Cltn* —3G **47**
Festival Rd. *Ilk* —4G **39**
Festus Clo. *Nott* —3H **45**
Festus St. *N'fld* —2A **48**
Field Av. *Huck* —1D **18**
Field Clo. *Bees* —1A **64**
Field Clo. *Breas* —6B **62**
Field Clo. *Ged* —5H **35**
Field Ho. Clo. *Nott* —4D **42**
Field La. *Bees* —1A **64**
Field La. *Wdbgh* —1C **24**
Field Rd. *Ilk* —2B **40**
Fields Av. *Rud* —2G **77**
Fields Farm Rd. *Long E* —2E **73**
Field, The. *Hean* —2D **26**
  (in two parts)
Fieldway. *Nott* —1F **67**
Fiennes Cres. *Nott* —6E **45** (6A **4**)
Fifth Av. *Lent* —5A **56**
Filey St. *Nott* —5A **20**
Finch Clo. *Nott* —3D **56**
Finchley Clo. *Nott* —4A **66**
Findern Grn. *Nott* —3C **46**
Fingal Clo. *Nott* —4D **66**
Finsbury Av. *Nott* —5B **46**
Finsbury Pk. Clo. *W Bri* —6G **57**
Finsbury Rd. *Arn* —3E **21**
Finsbury Rd. *Bees* —6C **42**
Firbank Ct. *Bees* —6B **54**
Firbeck Rd. *Arn* —5C **22**
Firbeck Rd. *Nott* —5B **42**
Fir Clo. *Huck* —1H **19**
Fir Clo. *Nott* —6F **19**
Fircroft Av. *Nott* —1E **43**
Fircroft Dri. *Huck* —6C **6**
Fir Dale. *Cotg* —2G **71**
Firecrest Way. *Nott* —3B **32**
Firfield Av. *Breas* —5A **62**
Firs Av. *Bees* —4F **55**
Firsby Rd. *Nott* —5F **31**
Firs Rd. *Edw* —1C **68**
Firs St. *Long E* —3C **72**
First Av. *Bees* —3E **55**
First Av. *Cltn* —2E **47**
First Av. *Colw* —4G **47**
First Av. *Ged* —6H **35**
First Av. *Ilk* —2B **40**
First Av. *Lent* —5A **56**
First Av. *Nott* —1F **45**
First Av. *Ris* —6B **52**
Firs, The. *Nott* —4H **33**
Firth Clo. *Arn* —4E **23**
Firth Dri. *Bees* —3C **64**
Firth Way. *Nott* —5F **19**
Fir Wlk. *Nott* —2D **46**
Fisher Av. *Wd'p* —2B **34**
Fisher Ct. *Ilk* —3B **28**

Fisher Ga. *Nott* —5H **45** (5G **5**)
Fisher La. *Bing* —5E **51**
Fisher St. *Nott* —1D **44**
Fishpond Dri. *Nott* —6E **45** (6A **4**)
Five Acres. *Nott* —1E **67**
Flagholme. *Cotg* —3F **71**
Flake La. *Stan D* —2A **52**
Flamingo Ct. *Nott* —1E **57**
Flamstead Av. *Lamb* —6B **24**
Flamstead Av. *Los* —1A **14**
Flamstead Rd. *Ilk* —6B **28**
Flamsteed Rd. *Nott* —6D **30**
Flatts La. *C'tn* —3G **11**
Flatts, The. *Bees* —6B **54**
Flawborough Ri. *W Bri* —2F **67**
Flawforth Av. *Rud* —6H **67**
Flawforth La. *Rud* —6H **67**
Flaxendale. *Cotg* —5G **71**
Flaxton Way. *Nott* —6D **20**
Fleam Rd. *Nott* —1C **66**
Fleeman Gro. *W Bri* —2C **58**
Fleet Clo. *Nott* —3B **44**
Fleetway Clo. *Newt* —4D **16**
Fleetwith Clo. *W Bri* —6E **59**
Fleming Clo. *Watn* —5A **18**
Fleming Dri. *Cltn* —2E **47**
Fleming Gdns. *Nott* —4A **66**
Fletcher Ga. *Nott* —5G **45** (4E **5**)
Fletcher Rd. *Bees* —4G **55**
Fletcher St. *Hean* —3C **14**
Fletcher St. *Long E* —5F **63**
Fletcher Ter. *Nott* —5A **34**
Flewitt Gdns. *Nott* —3A **46** (1H **5**)
Flintham Dri. *Nott* —3F **33**
Flixton Rd. *Kimb* —6H **17**
Florence Av. *Long E* —4H **63**
Florence Ct. *Ilk* —6B **28**
Florence Cres. *Ged* —1B **48**
Florence Gro. *Nott* —2C **46**
Florence Rd. *Ged* —6B **36**
Florence Rd. *Nott* —6C **34**
Florence Rd. *W Bri* —3B **58**
Florence St. *Huck* —6G **7**
Florey Ct. *Nott* —1C **56**
Florey Wlk. *Nott* —5A **66**
Florin Gdns. *Long E* —6D **62**
Flowers Clo. *Arn* —1D **34**
Flying Horse Wlk. *Nott*
—5G **45** (4E **5**)
Foljambe Ter. *Nott* —4H **45** (2G **5**)
Folkton Gdns. *Nott* —6B **34**
Forbes Clo. *Long E* —2G **73**
Forbes Hole Local Nature
Reserve. —2H 73
Ford Av. *Los* —1A **14**
Fordham Grn. *Nott* —5C **66**
Ford St. *Nott* —6E **33**
Ford St. N. *Nott* —6E **33**
Foredrift Clo. *Got* —6H **75**
Forest Clo. *Cotg* —2E **71**
Forest Cotts. *Nott* —4B **20**
Forest Ct. *Nott* —3E **45**
 (Gamble St.)
Forest Ct. *Nott* —2F **45**
 (N. Sherwood St.)
Forester Ga. *Bees* —1C **64**
Forester Gro. *Cltn* —2F **47**
Forester Rd. *Nott* —1C **46**
Forester St. *N'fld* —2A **48**
Forest Gro. *Nott* —2F **45**
 (Colville St.)
Forest Gro. *Nott* —3E **45**
 (Mt. Hooton Rd.)
Forest La. *Pap* —1B **8**
Forest Rd. *Bing* —5C **50**
Forest Rd. *C'tn* —3F **11**
Forest Rd. E. *Nott* —3E **45**
Forest Rd. W. *Nott* —3E **45** (1A **4**)
Forest Vw. Dri. *Huck* —4E **7**
Forest Vw. Ind. & Retail Est. *Nott*
—4A **20**
Forge Av. *C'tn* —3H **11**
Forge Hill. *Bees* —1D **64**
Forge Mill Gro. *Huck* —6B **8**
Forge, The. *Trow* —4D **40**
Forman St. *Nott* —4G **45** (3D **4**)
Forster St. *Nott* —3C **44**
 (in two parts)

Forsythia Gdns. *Nott* —1C **56**
Fosbrooke Dri. *Long E* —2F **73**
Fosse Rd. *Bing* —5B **50**
Fosse, The. *Cotg* —6H **71**
Fosse Wlk. *Cotg* —3G **71**
Foss Way. *Bing* —6A **50**
Foster Av. *Bees* —5F **55**
Foster Dri. *Nott* —3H **33**
Fosters La. *Bing* —5F **51**
Fothergill Ct. *Nott* —2G **45**
Fountaindale Ct. *Nott* —2H **45**
Fountains Clo. *W Bri* —5D **58**
Fountains Ct. *Bees* —5G **55**
Fourth Av. *Cltn* —1D **46**
Fourth Av. *Lent* —5A **56**
Fourth Av. *Nott* —1F **45**
Fowler St. *Nott* —1H **45**
Fox Clo. *Long E* —2F **73**
Fox Covert. *Colw* —5H **47**
Fox Covert La. *Nott* —5H **65**
Fox Covert Local Nature Reserve.
—6F **63**
Foxearth Av. *Nott* —3E **67**
Foxes Clo. *Nott* —6A **4**
Foxglove Rd. *Newt* —5D **16**
Foxgloves, The. *Bing* —6D **50**
Fox Gro. *Nott* —4C **32**
Fox Gro. Ct. *Nott* —4C **32**
Foxhall Rd. *Nott* —1E **45**
Fox Hill. *Cotg* —3E **71**
Foxhill Rd. *Cltn* —1G **47**
Foxhill Rd. *Bur J* —2E **37**
Foxhill Rd. *Cltn* —1E **47**
Foxhill Rd. Central. *Cltn* —1D **46**
Foxhill Rd. E. *Cltn* —1F **47**
Foxhill Rd. W. *Cltn* —1C **46**
Foxhollies Gro. *Nott* —4F **33**
Fox Mdw. *Huck* —6F **7**
Fox Rd. *Nott & W Bri* —2B **58**
Foxton Clo. *Ilk* —4G **27**
Foxton Clo. *Nott* —5F **19**
Foxton Gdns. *Nott* —2G **43**
Foxwood Gro. *C'tn* —4H **11**
Foxwood La. *Wdbgh* —5H **11**
Fradley Clo. *Nott* —3A **20**
Frampton Rd. *Nott* —2G **43**
Frances Gro. *Huck* —2H **7**
Francis Gro. *Nott* —4C **32**
Francis Rd. *Cltn* —1H **47**
Francis St. *Nott* —3E **45** (1A **4**)
 (in two parts)
Franklin Clo. *Nott* —5G **21**
Franklin Dri. *Toll* —4F **69**
Franklyn Gdns. *Keyw* —3G **79**
Franklyn Gdns. *Nott* —4A **66**
Fraser Cres. *Cltn* —6D **34**
Fraser Rd. *Cltn* —5D **34**
Fraser Rd. *Nott* —3H **57**
Fraser Sq. *Cltn* —6D **34**
Frearson Farm Ct. *Eastw* —4B **16**
Freckingham St. *Nott*
—4H **45** (3H **5**)
Freda Av. *Ged* —5F **35**
Freda Clo. *Ged* —4F **35**
Frederic Av. *Hean* —6D **14**
Frederick Av. *Cltn* —2D **46**
Frederick Av. *Ilk* —4C **40**
Frederick Gro. *Nott* —6D **44**
Frederick Rd. *S'fd* —4F **53**
Frederick St. *Long E* —6H **63**
Freeland Clo. *Bees* —2H **63**
Freemans Rd. *Cltn* —1A **48**
Freemans Ter. *Cltn* —1H **47**
Freemantle Wlk. *Nott* —5C **20**
Freeston Dri. *Nott* —5F **19**
Freeth Ct. *Nott* —1B **58**
Freeth St. *Nott* —1A **58**
Freiston St. *Nott* —2C **44**
Fremount Dri. *Nott* —3F **43**
French St. *Ilk* —3C **40**
Fretwell St. *Nott* —2C **44**
Friar La. *Nott* —5F **45** (5C **4**)
Friars Ct. *Ilk* —3G **39**
Friars Ct. *Nott* —6E **45** (6A **4**)
Friar St. *Long E* —6F **63**
Friar St. *Nott* —1C **56**
Friar Wlk. *Nwtn* —1C **50**
Friary Clo. *Nott* —1C **56**
Friary, The. *Nott* —1C **56**

Friday La. *Ged* —5H **35**
Friends Meeting House. —2B 4
Friesland Dri. *Sand* —6B **52**
Frinton Rd. *Nott* —6E **31**
Frisby Av. *Long E* —1G **73**
Frobisher Gdns. *Nott* —1H **33**
Frogmore St. *Nott* —3G **45** (1D **4**)
Front St. *Arn* —6B **22**
Frost Av. *Lan M* —1E **15**
Fryar Rd. *Eastw* —1B **16**
Fulforth St. *Nott* —3G **45** (1D **4**)
Fuller St. *Rud* —1G **77**
Fullwood Av. *Ilk* —6A **28**
Fullwood St. *Ilk* —6A **28**
Fulwood Clo. *Bees* —1C **64**
Fulwood Cres. *Nott* —6G **31**
Fulwood Dri. *Long E* —6C **62**
Furlong Av. *Arn* —6A **22**
Furlong Clo. *S'fd* —3F **53**
Furlong St. *Arn* —6A **22**
 (in two parts)
Furnace La. *Los* —1A **14**
Furnace Rd. *Ilk* —2D **40**
Furness Clo. *W Bri* —4D **58**
Furness Rd. *Nott* —4A **32**
Furzebrook Rd. *Colw* —4G **47**
Furze Gdns. *Nott* —2H **45**
Fylde Clo. *Bees* —3G **63**
Fylingdale Way. *Nott* —6B **42**

Gables, The. *Nott* —6E **33**
Gabor Clo. *Nott* —4A **66**
Gabor Ct. *Nott* —4A **66**
Gabrielle Clo. *Nott* —3B **32**
Gadd St. *Nott* —3D **44**
Gadsby Clo. *Ilk* —5C **40**
Gadwall Cres. *Nott* —1E **57**
Gainsborough Clo. *Long E* —2G **73**
Gainsborough Clo. *S'fd* —5G **53**
Gainsborough Ct. *Bees* —4G **55**
Gainsford Clo. *Nott* —2D **32**
Gainsford Cres. *Nott* —2D **32**
Gala Way. *Nott* —1C **32**
Gale Clo. *Bees* —5H **55**
Galena Dri. *Nott* —2C **46**
Galen Ct. *Nott* —1C **56**
Gallows Inn Clo. *Ilk* —4C **40**
Gallows Inn Ind. Est. *Ilk* —3D **40**
Galway Rd. *Arn* —5H **21**
Galway Rd. *Nott* —6D **44**
Gamble St. *Nott* —3E **45** (1A **4**)
Gamston Cres. *Nott* —4G **33**
Gamston Lodge. *Cltn* —3G **47**
Ganton Clo. *Nott* —6B **34**
Garden Av. *Cltn* —2F **47**
Garden Av. *Ilk* —4B **40**
Garden City. *Cltn* —1G **47**
Gardendale Av. *Nott* —4B **66**
Gardenia Clo. *Bees* —3A **64**
Gardenia Cres. *Nott* —5D **34**
Gardenia Gro. *Nott* —5D **34**
Garden Rd. *Bing* —5D **50**
Garden Rd. *Eastw* —2B **16**
Garden Rd. *Huck* —4F **7**
Garden Rd. *S'fd* —5F **53**
Gardens Ct. *W Bri* —4C **58**
Gardens, The. *Los* —1A **14**
Garden St. *Nott* —4D **44**
Garfield Clo. *S'fd* —2G **53**
Garfield Ct. *Nott* —4D **44**
Garfield Rd. *Nott* —3D **44**
Garforth Clo. *Nott* —1C **44**
Garners Hill. *Nott* —5H **45** (5E **5**)
Garnet Ct. *Nott* —4A **46** (2H **5**)
Garnet St. *N'fld* —2H **47**
Garnett Av. *Hean* —3D **14**
Garrett Gro. *Nott* —3A **66**
Garsdale Clo. *Gam* —5E **59**
Garsdale Dri. *Nott* —2E **67**
Garton Clo. *Bees* —6B **54**
Garton Clo. *Nott* —2H **31**
Gas St. *Sand* —5E **53**
Gatcombe Clo. *Rad T* —6G **49**
Gatcombe Gro. *Sand* —2C **62**
Gateford Clo. *Bees* —1B **54**
Gatehouse Ct. *Bees* —6D **54**
Gate Ind. Est. *Ilk* —5B **28**
Gateside Rd. *Q Dri* —2E **57**

Gatling St. *Nott* —4C **44**
Gaul St. *Nott* —6H **19**
Gauntley Ct. *Nott* —1D **44**
Gauntley St. *Nott* —1C **44**
Gautries Clo. *Nott* —5E **21**
Gavin M. *Nott* —1D **44**
Gawthorne St. *Nott* —6D **32**
Gayhurst Grn. *Nott* —2C **32**
Gayhurst Rd. *Nott* —2C **32**
Gaynor Ct. *Nott* —3H **43**
Gayrigg Ct. *Bees* —6B **54**
Gayton Clo. *Nott* —1D **42**
Gaywood Clo. *Nott* —5D **66**
Gedling. *Arn* —6B **22**
Gedling Gro. *Nott* —3E **45** (1A **4**)
Gedling Rd. *Arn* —6B **22**
Gedling Rd. *Cltn* —1H **47**
Gedling St. *Nott* —5H **45** (4G **5**)
Gedney Av. *Nott* —1B **46**
Geldling Rd. *Arn* —1D **34**
Gell Rd. *Bees* —1A **64**
George Av. *Bees* —6F **55**
George Av. *Long E* —4H **63**
George Ct. *Long E* —5G **63**
George Grn. Ct. Snei —5B **46**
 (off Sneinton Boulevd.)
George Rd. *Cltn* —2G **47**
George Rd. *W Bri* —4B **58**
George's La. *C'tn* —6E **11**
George St. *Arn* —1A **34**
George St. *Huck* —3G **7**
George St. *Lan M* —2F **15**
George St. *Nott* —4H **45** (3F **5**)
Georgia Dri. *Arn* —3A **22**
Georgina Rd. *Bees* —6F **55**
Gerrard Clo. *Arn* —3E **21**
Gertrude Rd. *W Bri* —3C **58**
Gervase Gdns. *Nott* —3A **66**
Ghost Ho. La. *Bees* —6B **54**
Gibbons Av. *S'fd* —5F **53**
Gibbons St. *Nott* —3C **56**
Gibb St. *Long E* —6G **63**
Gibson Rd. *Nott* —1E **45**
Gifford Gdns. *Nott* —1G **57**
Gilbert Av. *Got* —6H **75**
Gilbert Gdns. *Nott* —3C **46**
Gilbert St. *Huck* —4G **7**
Gilead St. *Nott* —6H **19**
Giles Av. *W Bri* —5H **57**
Gillercomb Clo. *Edw* —1E **69**
Gillian Ct. *S'fd* —5G **53**
Gilliver La. *Clip* —4C **70**
Gillotts Clo. *Bing* —5B **50**
Gillott St. *Hean* —5E **15**
Gill St. *Nott* —3F **45** (1C **4**)
Gilpet Av. *Nott* —1B **46**
Giltbrook Cres. *Gilt* —5E **17**
Giltbrook Ind. Est. *Gilt* —6E **17**
Gilt Hill. *Kimb* —6F **17**
Giltway. *Gilt* —6E **17**
Gimson Clo. *Ilk* —4G **27**
Gin Clo. Way. *Aws* —1E **29**
Gipsy La. *Nott* —3A **66**
Girton Rd. *Nott* —4E **33**
Gisburn Clo. *Nott* —1E **67**
Gladehill Rd. *Nott & Arn* —6G **21**
Glade, The. *Nott* —6C **66**
Gladstone Av. *Got* —6H **75**
Gladstone Av. *Hean* —3C **14**
Gladstone St. *Bees* —6E **55**
Gladstone St. *Cltn* —2F **47**
Gladstone St. *Hean* —3C **14**
Gladstone St. *Ilk* —2B **40**
 (in two parts)
Gladstone St. *Lan M* —2G **15**
Gladstone St. *Long E* —1F **73**
Gladstone St. *Nott* —1D **44**
Gladstone St. E. *Ilk* —1B **40**
Gladys St. *Nott* —6E **33**
Glaisdale Dri. E. *Nott* —3D **42**
Glaisdale Dri. W. *Nott* —4D **42**
Glaisdale Pk. Ind. Est. *Nott* —3D **42**
Glaisdale Parkway. *Nott* —4D **42**
Glamis Rd. *Nott* —5E **33**
Glanton Way. *Arn* —3C **22**
Glapton La. *Nott* —3B **66**
Glapton Rd. *Nott* —2G **57**
Glaramara Clo. *Nott* —2F **57**

Glasshouse St. *Nott* —4G **45** (2E **5**)
Glebe Cotts. *Nott* —3F **57**
Glebe Cres. *Ilk* —2C **40**
Glebe Cres. *Stan* —3A **38**
Glebe Dri. *Bur J* —4D **36**
Glebe Farm Clo. *W Bri* —1G **67**
Glebe Farm Vw. *Ged* —4H **35**
Glebe La. *Rad T* —6F **49**
Glebe Rd. *Cltn* —5E **35**
Glebe Rd. *Nut* —1C **30**
Glebe Rd. *W Bri* —4B **58**
Glebe St. *Bees* —5E **55**
Glebe St. *Huck* —3G **7**
Glebe, The. *Coss* —3D **28**
Glen Av. *Eastw* —4D **16**
Glenbrook. *Cotg* —2G **71**
Glenbrook Cres. *Nott* —2G **43**
Glencairn Dri. *Nott* —1G **43**
Glencairn M. *Nott* —1G **43**
Glencoe Rd. *Nott* —4E **67**
Glencoyne Rd. *Nott* —5C **66**
Glendale Clo. *Cltn* —5F **35**
Glendale Ct. *Bees* —2E **65**
Glendale Gdns. *Arn* —6C **22**
Glendoe Gro. *Bing* —5C **50**
Glendon Dri. *Huck* —6G **7**
Glendon Dri. *Nott* —4E **33**
Glendon Rd. *Ilk* —5G **39**
Gleneagles Ct. *Edw* —2D **68**
Gleneagles Dri. *Arn* —4D **22**
Glenfield Av. *Kimb* —6F **17**
Glenfield Rd. *Long E* —2F **73**
Glen Helen. *Colw* —3H **47**
Glenlivet Gdns. *Nott* —4D **66**
(in two parts)
Glenloch Dri. *Nott* —5D **66**
Glenmore Rd. *W Bri* —5D **58**
Glenorchy Cres. *Nott* —5C **20**
Glenparva Av. *Red* —4A **22**
Glenridding Clo. *W Bri* —6F **59**
Glen Rd. *Bur J* —2E **37**
Glensford Gdns. *Nott* —3C **20**
Glenside. *Wd'p* —2D **34**
Glenside Rd. *Bees* —2C **54**
Glenstone Ct. *Nott* —1D **44**
Glen, The. *Nott* —4C **66**
Glentworth Rd. *Nott* —3C **44**
Glenwood Av. *Nott* —5D **42**
Glins Rd. *Nott* —5D **20**
Gloucester Av. *Bees* —6F **55**
Gloucester Av. *Nott* —5C **44**
Gloucester Av. *Nut* —4F **31**
Gloucester Av. *Sand* —1C **62**
Glover Av. *Nott* —5D **42**
Glue La. *Los* —3A **14**
Goatchurch Ct. *Nott* —4E **21**
Goathland Clo. *Nott* —5F **21**
Godber Rd. *Huck* —6E **7**
Godfrey Dri. *Ilk* —4G **39**
Godfrey St. *Hean* —4C **14**
(in two parts)
Godfrey St. *N'fld* —3A **48**
Godkin Dri. *Lan M* —1E **15**
Goldcrest Clo. *Bing* —6G **51**
Goldcrest Rd. *Nott* —3H **31**
Goldham Rd. *Nott* —1D **42**
Goldsmith Sq. *Nott* —4F **45** (2C **4**)
Goldsmith St. *Nott* —4F **45** (2C **4**)
Goldswong Ter. *Nott* —2G **45**
Golf Club Rd. *Stan D* —2C **52**
Golf Course Rd. *Keyw* —5B **80**
Golf Rd. *Rad T* —6G **49**
Gonalston La. *Epp* —6H **13**
Goodall Cres. *Huck* —5A **8**
Goodall St. *Nott* —2D **44**
Goodliffe St. *Nott* —1D **44**
Goodman Clo. *Gilt* —5E **17**
Goodwin Clo. *Sand* —5C **52**
Goodwin Dri. *Kimb* —1G **29**
Goodwin St. *Nott* —3E **45** (1A **4**)
Goodwood Av. *Arn* —5A **22**
Goodwood Cres. *Ilk* —5H **39**
Goodwood Dri. *Bees* —3H **63**
Goodwood Rd. *Nott* —5D **42**
Goole Av. *Ilk* —4H **39**
Goosedale La. *B Vil* —4C **8**
Goose Fair. —2E **45**
(site of)
Goosegate. *Cotg* —2E **71**

Goose Ga. *Nott* —5H **45** (4F **5**)
Gordon Clo. *Bees* —3D **64**
Gordon Gro. *Nott* —6D **32**
Gordon Ri. *Nott* —5A **34**
Gordon Rd. *Bur J* —2G **37**
Gordon Rd. *Nott* —3A **46**
Gordon Rd. *W Bri* —4B **58**
Gordon Sq. *W Bri* —4B **58**
Gordon St. *Ilk* —6B **28**
Gordon St. *Nott* —3B **32**
Gorman Ct. *Arn* —6D **22**
Gorse Clo. *C'tn* —4F **11**
Gorse Clo. *Long E* —3D **62**
Gorse Clo. *Newt* —4D **16**
Gorse Ct. *Nott* —2C **32**
Gorse Rd. *Keyw* —4F **79**
Gorse Wlk. *Nott* —2D **46**
Gorsey Rd. *Nott* —2H **45**
Gosforth Ct. *Nott* —2H **57**
Goshawk Rd. *Quar H* —6C **40**
Gothic Clo. *Nott* —3C **32**
Goverton Sq. *Nott* —2B **32**
Gowan Clo. *Bees* —3C **64**
Goyden Clo. *Nott* —5E **21**
G.P.T. Bus. Pk. *Bees* —6G **55**
Grace Av. *Bees* —6H **55**
Grace Cres. *Hean* —3D **14**
Grace Dri. *Nott* —1B **44**
Grafton Av. *Wd'p* —2A **34**
Grafton Ct. *Nott* —4E **45** (3A **4**)
Graham St. *Ilk* —2B **40**
Graham St. *Nott* —4D **44**
Grainger Av. *W Bri* —2A **68**
Graingers Ter. *Huck* —6H **7**
Grainger St. *Nott* —1A **58**
Grampian Dri. *Arn* —3F **21**
Grampian Way. *Long E* —5C **62**
Granby Ct. *Bing* —5D **50**
Granby St. *Ilk* —5B **28**
Granby Vs. *Nott* —5B **46**
Grandfield Av. *Rad T* —5F **49**
Grandfield Cres. *Rad T* —5F **49**
Grandfield St. *Los* —1A **14**
Grange Av. *Bees* —5F **55**
Grange Av. *Breas* —5A **62**
Grange Av. *Rud* —6F **67**
Grange Clo. *Lamb* —6C **24**
Grange Clo. *Nott* —3F **57**
Grange Cres. *Ged* —4H **35**
Grange Dri. *Long E* —5H **63**
Grange Farm. *Gam* —4E **59**
Grange Farm Clo. *Bees* —4A **64**
Grangelea Gdns. *Bees* —3B **54**
Grangemoor. *Pap* —2B **8**
Grange Pk. *Long E* —5H **63**
Grange Pk. *W Bri* —6D **58**
Grange Rd. *Edw* —1C **68**
Grange Rd. *Long E* —5H **63**
Grange Rd. *Stock* —4B **32**
Grange Rd. *Wd'p* —3A **34**
Grange, The. *Smal* —5A **14**
Grange Vw. *Eastw* —3B **16**
Grange Vw. Rd. *Ged* —5H **35**
Grangewood Av. *Ilk* —2B **40**
Grangewood Ct. *Nott* —6C **42**
Grangewood Rd. *Nott* —6C **42**
Grannis Dri. *Nott* —1G **43**
Grantham Clo. *Gilt* —6E **17**
Grantham Rd. *Bing* —5F **51**
Grantham Rd. *Rad T* —1D **60**
Grantleigh Clo. *Nott* —4F **43**
(in two parts)
Granton Av. *Nott* —5D **66**
Grant St. *Nott* —4D **44**
Granville Av. *Long E* —4F **63**
Granville Ct. *Nott* —4B **46**
Granville Cres. *Rad T* —1E **61**
Granville Gro. *Nott* —4B **46**
Grasby Wlk. *Nott* —3B **66**
Grasmere Av. *Nott* —5A **32**
Grasmere Clo. *Huck* —3F **7**
Grasmere Ct. *Long E* —3D **62**
Grasmere Gdns. *Got* —5H **75**
Grasmere Rd. *Bees* —3D **54**
Grasmere Rd. *Long E* —3D **62**
Grasmere St. *Sand* —6D **52**
Grassingdale Clo. *Cltn* —5F **35**
Grassington Rd. *Nott* —3B **44**
Grassmere. *Cotg* —2G **71**

Grass St. *Ilk* —4A **28**
Grassy La. *Bees* —6G **55**
Gravelly Hollow. *C'tn* —1B **10**
Graveney Gdns. *Arn* —1A **34**
Graylands Rd. *Nott* —2D **42**
Graystones Clo. *W Bri* —6E **59**
Grazingfield. *Nott* —1E **67**
Greasley Av. *Newt* —3E **17**
Greasley Castle. —3F **17**
(remains of)
Greasley Sports &
    Community Cen. —3D **16**
Greasley St. *Nott* —6H **19**
Gt. Freeman St. *Nott*
                 —3G **45** (1E **5**)
Gt. Hoggett Dri. *Bees* —5A **54**
Gt. Northern Clo., The. *Nott*
                 —6H **45** (6G **5**)
Gt. Northern Cotts. *Huck* —2H **7**
Gt. Northern Rd. *Eastw* —3H **15**
Gt. Northern Way. *N'fld* —3B **48**
Greaves Clo. *Arn* —2D **34**
Greaves Clo. *Nott* —6D **30**
Greek St. *Nott* —4E **45**
Greenacre. *Bur J* —2E **37**
Greenacre. *Edw* —1D **68**
Greenacre. *Nott* —4B **42**
Greenacre Av. *Hean* —2E **15**
Greenacres Cvn. Pk. *W Bri* —2E **59**
Greenacres Clo. *Newt* —3E **17**
Green Av. *N'fld* —2A **48**
Greenbank. *Cltn* —3F **47**
Greenbank Ct. *Nott* —5G **33**
Greenburn Clo. *Gam* —5E **59**
Green Clo. *Huck* —6A **8**
Green Clo. *Plum* —3H **79**
Greencroft. *Nott* —3D **66**
Greendale Gdns. *Nott* —1H **43**
Greendale Rd. *Arn* —1B **34**
Greendale Rd. *Nott* —3E **47**
Greenfield Gro. *Cltn* —1D **46**
Greenfields. *Lan M* —1E **15**
Greenfields Dri. *Cotg* —3F **71**
Greenfield St. *Nott* —2B **56**
Greenford Clo. *Nut* —4E **31**
Greengates Av. *Nott* —4B **34**
Greenhill Cres. *Cltn* —3G **47**
Greenhill Ri. *Cltn* —2G **47**
Greenhill Rd. *Cltn* —3G **47**
Greenhills Av. *Eastw* —2C **16**
Greenhills Rd. *Eastw* —2B **16**
Greenland Cres. *Bees* —1C **64**
Green La. *Ilk* —2C **40**
Green La. *Lamb* —4B **24**
Green La. *Nott* —3B **66**
Green Leys. *W Bri* —1G **67**
Green Platt. *Cotg* —2E **71**
Greens Ct. *Ilk* —6H **27**
Greens Farm La. *Ged* —5A **36**
Greenside Clo. *Long E* —6G **63**
Greenside Wlk. *Nott* —3E **47**
Greens La. *Kimb* —1H **29**
Green's Mill Mus. —5B **46**
Green St. *Bar F* —3E **75**
Green St. *Nott* —2D **57**
Green, The. *Bees* —1E **65**
Green, The. *Breas* —5A **62**
Green, The. *Low* —3F **25**
Green, The. *Rad T* —6E **49**
Green, The. *Rud* —1G **77**
Greenway Clo. *Rad T* —6E **49**
Greenway, The. *Sand* —5D **52**
Greenwich Av. *Nott* —3A **32**
Greenwich Pk. Clo. *W Bri* —6G **57**
Greenwood Av. *Huck* —3F **7**
Greenwood Av. *Ilk* —2C **40**
Greenwood Av. *Nott* —4F **47**
Greenwood Bonsai Studio.
                 —4A **10**
Greenwood Ct. *Bees* —6D **54**
Greenwood Cres. *Cltn* —3G **47**
Greenwood Gdns. *Rud* —2H **77**
Greenwood Rd. *Nott & C'tn*
                 —4C **46**
Greenwood Va. *Huck* —3E **7**
Greet Ct. *Nott* —2B **44**
Greetwell Clo. *Nott* —3G **43**
Gregg Av. *Hean* —3D **14**
Gregory Av. *Lan M* —2E **15**

Gregory Av. *Lent* —6D **44**
Gregory Av. *Map* —5C **34**
Gregory Boulevd. *Nott* —2C **44**
Gregory Clo. *S'fd* —3H **53**
Gregory Ct. *Bees* —1B **64**
Gregory Ct. *Nott* —6C **44**
    (Derby Rd.)
Gregory Ct. *Nott* —1D **44**
    (Noel St.)
Gregory St. *Ilk* —1A **40**
Gregory St. *Nott* —6C **44**
Gregson Gdns. *Bees* —4B **64**
Grenay Ct. *Rud* —5F **67**
Grenfell Ter. *Nott* —3C **32**
Grenville Dri. *Ilk* —4B **28**
Grenville Dri. *S'fd* —3G **53**
Grenville Ri. *Arn* —4B **22**
Grenville Rd. *Bees* —1H **65**
Gresham Clo. *W Bri* —4G **57**
Gresham Gdns. *W Bri* —4H **57**
Gresham Gdns. *Wd'p* —2C **34**
Gresley Dri. *Nott* —6B **46**
Gresley Rd. *Ilk* —6B **28**
Gretton Rd. *Nott* —3C **34**
Greyfriar Ga. *Nott* —6G **45** (6D **4**)
Greyhound St. *Nott* —5G **45** (3E **5**)
Greys Rd. *Wd'p* —3B **34**
Greystoke Dri. *Nott* —2C **42**
Grey St. *Newt* —4C **16**
Greythorn Dri. *W Bri* —1H **67**
Grierson Av. *Nott* —5F **21**
Griffon Rd. *Quar H* —5B **40**
Griffs Hollow. *Cltn* —2G **47**
Grimesmoor Rd. *C'tn* —3A **12**
Grimsby Ter. *Nott* —3G **45** (1E **5**)
Grimston Rd. *Nott* —3C **44**
Grindon Cres. *Nott* —3A **20**
Grindslow Av. *W Hal* —1C **38**
Grinsbrook. *Lent* —5C **44**
Gripps Comn. *Cotg* —3F **71**
Gripps, The. *Cotg* —3F **71**
Grisedale Ct. *Bees* —1A **64**
Gritley M. *Nott* —1F **57**
Grizedale Gro. *Bing* —5B **50**
Groome Av. *Los* —1A **14**
Grosvenor Av. *Breas* —5B **62**
Grosvenor Av. *Long E* —3C **72**
Grosvenor Av. *Nott* —6G **33**
Grosvenor Ct. *Nott* —1G **45**
    (off Elm Bank Dri.)
Grosvenor Rd. *Eastw* —2B **16**
Grouville Dri. *Wd'p* —2C **34**
Grove Av. *Bees* —5E **55**
Grove Av. *Nott* —3E **45**
Grove Clo. *Bur J* —2F **37**
Grove Ct. *Bees* —5D **54**
Grove M. *Eastw* —4A **16**
Grover Av. *Nott* —4C **34**
Grove Rd. *Bing* —4F **51**
Grove Rd. *Nott* —6D **44**
Groveside Cres. *Nott* —2A **66**
Grove St. *Bees* —6G **55**
Grove, The. *Breas* —5B **62**
Grove, The. *C'tn* —4A **12**
Grove, The. *Nott* —5F **33**
    (Haydn Av.)
Grove, The. *Nott* —3D **44**
    (Southey St.)
Grundy St. *Nott* —2C **44**
Guardian Ct. *Nott* —1A **44**
Guinea Clo. *Long E* —5C **62**
Gunn Clo. *Nott* —6G **19**
Gunnersbury Way. *Nut* —4D **30**
Gunthorpe Clo. *Nott* —4F **33**
Gunthorpe Dri. *Nott* —4F **33**
Gunthorpe Rd. *Ged* —4E **35**
Gutersloh Ct. *S'fd* —3H **53**
Guy Clo. *S'fd* —5G **53**
Gwenbrook Av. *Bees* —6E **55**
Gwenbrook Rd. *Bees* —6E **55**
Gwndy Gdns. *Nott* —6E **21**
GX Superbowl. —2C **56**
Gypsum La. *Got* —6G **75**

Hackworth Clo. *Newt* —2D **16**
Hadbury Rd. *Nott* —4D **32**
Hadden Ct. *Nott* —4D **42**

Henley Gdns. *S'fd* —2G **53**
Henley Ri. *Nott* —4E **33**
Henley Way. *W Hal* —1B **38**
Henning Gdns. *Nott* —5E **21**
Henrietta St. *Nott* —1A **32**
Henry Ct. *Nott* —1G **57**
Henry Rd. *Bees* —5G **55**
Henry Rd. *Nott* —6D **44**
Henry Rd. *W Bri* —3A **58**
Henry St. *Huck* —5H **7**
Henry St. *Red* —3A **22**
Henry St. *Snei* —5A **46** (4H **5**)
Henshaw Av. *Ilk* —4H **39**
Henshaw Pl. *Ilk* —3A **28**
Henson Sq. *Bees* —3B **54**
Hensons Row. *Nott* —5B **32**
Hepple Dri. *Nott* —6F **19**
Herald Clo. *Bees* —4H **55**
*Herbert Buzzard Ct. Huck —5A 8
(off Hankin St.)*
Herbert Rd. *Nott* —6F **33**
Hereford Rd. *Ged* —4H **35**
Hereford Rd. *Nott* —4D **46**
Hereford Rd. *Wd'p* —2A **34**
Hermitage Sq. *Nott* —5B **46**
Hermitage Wlk. *Ilk* —4B **40**
Hermitage Wlk. *Nott* —6E **45** (6A **4**)
Hermon St. *Nott* —4E **45**
Heron Dri. *Lent* —5C **44**
Herons Ct. *W Bri* —1E **69**
Heron Wharf. *Nott* —1D **56**
Herrywell La. *Cotg* —6H **71**
Hervey Grn. *Nott* —3C **66**
Heskey Clo. *Nott* —3G **45**
Heskey Wlk. *Nott* —3G **45** (1E **5**)
Heslington Av. *Nott* —1C **44**
Hethbeth Ct. *Nott* —1G **57**
Hethersett Gdns. *Nott* —5H **19**
Hetley Rd. *Bees* —3F **55**
Hexham Av. *Ilk* —5C **40**
Hexham Clo. *W Bri* —5C **58**
Hexham Gdns. *Nott* —3E **21**
Heyford Ct. *Hean* —4E **15**
Hey St. *Long E* —3D **72**
Hickings La. *S'fd* —3G **53**
Hickling Rd. *Nott* —5C **34**
Hickling Way. *Cotg* —4G **71**
Hickton Dri. *Bees* —4B **64**
Highbank Dri. *Nott* —5C **66**
Highbury Av. *Nott* —2A **32**
Highbury Clo. *Nut* —4D **30**
Highbury Rd. *Keyw* —3G **79**
Highbury Rd. *Nott* —6A **20**
Highbury Wlk. *Nott* —1A **32**
High Chu. St. *Nott* —6D **32**
  (in two parts)
Highclere Dri. *Cltn* —1H **47**
Highcliffe Rd. *Nott* —4C **46**
Highcroft. *Nott* —3B **34**
High Cft. Clo. *Long E* —2G **73**
Highcroft Dri. *Nott* —4B **42**
Highcross Ct. *Nott* —3D **44**
High Cross Leys. *Nott*
  —3G **45** (1E **5**)
Highcross St. *Nott* —4H **45** (3F **5**)
Highfield Ct. *Bees* —5F **55**
Highfield Dri. *Cltn* —2D **46**
Highfield Dri. *Ilk* —4F **39**
Highfield Dri. *Nut* —3F **31**
Highfield Gro. *W Bri* —4B **58**
Highfield Rd. *Bees* —1A **64**
Highfield Rd. *Keyw* —3G **79**
Highfield Rd. *Nott* —2B **56**
Highfield Rd. *Nut* —3E **31**
Highfield Rd. *W Bri* —4B **58**
Highfields Science Pk. *Nott* —2B **56**
Highfield St. *Long E* —3E **63**
Highgate Clo. *Cltn* —5E **35**
Highgate Dri. *Ilk* —4G **27**
Highgrove Av. *Bees* —5D **54**
Highgrove Clo. *Hean* —4A **14**
Highgrove Gdns. *Edw* —1C **68**
High Hazels Ct. *Newt* —1D **16**
High Hazels Dri. *Cotg* —1G **71**
High Hazles Clo. *Ged* —4G **35**
High Holborn. *Ilk* —4A **28**
High Hurst. *C'tn* —4G **11**
High La. Central. *W Hal* —6D **26**
High La. E. *W Hal* —6E **27**

High La. W. *W Hal* —1A **38**
High Leys Rd. *Huck* —6F **7**
High Mdw. *Toll* —4F **69**
High Pavement. *Nott*
  —5H **45** (5F **5**)
High Rd. *Bees* —5F **55**
  (Acacia Wlk.)
High Rd. *Bees* —6E **55**
  (Hall Dri.)
High Rd. *Bees* —3A **64**
  (Rutland Av.)
High Spannia. *Kimb* —6H **17**
High St. *Arn* —6B **22**
High St. *Hean* —3C **14**
High St. *Huck* —4G **7**
High St. *Ilk* —1B **40**
High St. *Kimb* —1H **29**
High St. *Long E* —5G **63**
High St. *Los* —1A **14**
High St. *Nott* —5G **45** (4E **5**)
High St. *Rud* —6G **67**
High St. *S'fd* —4G **53**
High St. Av. *Arn* —6A **22**
High St. Pl. *Nott* —5G **45** (4E **5**)
Highurst Ct. *Nott* —4E **45**
Highurst St. *Nott* —4E **45**
High Vw. Av. *Keyw* —4H **79**
High Vw. Ct. *Nott* —1H **45**
Highwood Av. *Nott* —1F **43**
Highwray Gro. *Nott* —4B **66**
Hilary Clo. *Nott* —6D **42**
Hilcot Dri. *Nott* —6H **31**
Hillary Pl. *Ilk* —4F **39**
Hillbeck Cres. *Nott* —5C **42**
Hill Clo. *Newt* —4E **17**
Hill Clo. *W Bri* —5D **58**
Hillcrest Clo. *Watn* —6A **18**
Hillcrest Dri. *Huck* —5D **6**
Hillcrest Gdns. *Bur J* —2E **37**
Hill Crest Gro. *Nott* —4F **33**
Hill Crest Pk. Ind. Est. *C'tn* —2H **11**
Hillcrest Rd. *Keyw* —3G **79**
Hillcrest Vw. *Cltn* —6D **34**
Hill Dri. *Bing* —4D **50**
Hill Farm Ct. *Edw* —3C **68**
Hillfield Gdns. *Nott* —3C **20**
Hillfield Rd. *S'fd* —3H **53**
Hillgrove Gdns. *Nott* —5E **21**
Hilliers Ct. *Nott* —5D **20**
Hillingdon Av. *Nott* —4D **30**
Hillington Ri. *Nott* —6G **21**
Hill Ri. *Trow* —5G **41**
Hill Rd. *Bees* —2B **64**
Hill Rd. *B Vil* —1C **20**
Hill Rd. *Hean* —4B **14**
Hillsford Clo. *Nott* —4G **43**
Hillside. *Lan M* —2E **15**
Hill Side. *Nott* —6B **44**
Hillside Av. *Nott* —3C **34**
Hillside Cres. *Bees* —3E **55**
Hillside Dri. *Bur J* —2F **37**
Hillside Dri. *Long E* —5D **62**
Hillside Gro. *Sand* —5C **52**
Hillside Rd. *Bees* —2A **64**
  (Highfield Rd.)
Hillside Rd. *Bees* —2C **54**
  (Ullswater Cres.)
Hillside Rd. *Rad T* —6G **49**
Hills Rd. *Wd'p* —3A **34**
Hill Syke. *Low* —3G **25**
Hillview Av. *Nott* —5H **33**
Hillview Rd. *Bees* —3A **64**
Hill Vw. Rd. *Cltn* —6C **34**
Hilton Clo. *Long E* —3B **72**
Hilton Ct. *W Bri* —6D **58**
Hilton Cres. *W Bri* —6D **58**
Hilton Rd. *Nott* —5B **34**
Hinchin Brook. *Lent* —5C **44**
Hinshelwood Ct. *Nott* —5A **66**
Hinsley Clo. *Arn* —5D **22**
Hinsley Ct. *Nott* —4C **42**
Hirst Ct. *Nott* —4E **45** (2A **4**)
Hirst Cres. *Nott* —5F **43**
Hoare Rd. *Bees* —3B **64**
Hobart Clo. *Nott* —2G **57**
Hobart Dri. *S'fd* —2H **53**
Hobson Dri. *Ilk* —3A **40**
Hockerwood. *Nott* —1C **66**
Hockley. *Nott* —5H **45** (4G **5**)

Hodgkin Clo. *Nott* —4A **66**
Hodgkinson St. *N'fld* —3A **48**
Hodson Ho. *Nott* —5G **33**
Hoefield Cres. *Nott* —1G **31**
Hoe Hill Vw. *Toll* —4F **69**
Hoewood Rd. *Nott* —6G **19**
Hogan Gdns. *Nott* —4E **21**
Hogarth Clo. *S'fd* —5G **53**
Hogarth St. *Nott* —3B **46**
Hoggbarn La. *Los* —1B **14**
Hoggetts Clo. *Bees* —5B **54**
Hogg La. *Rad T* —6E **49**
  (in two parts)
Hoggs Fld. *Eastw* —3B **16**
Holbeck Rd. *Huck* —2H **7**
Holbeck Rd. *Nott* —3B **44**
Holborn Av. *Nott* —4B **46**
Holborn Clo. *Nut* —4D **30**
Holborn Pl. *Bulw* —6A **20**
Holbrook Ct. *Nott* —5C **66**
Holbrook St. *Hean* —3E **15**
Holby Clo. *Nott* —5D **20**
Holcombe Clo. *Nott* —5H **31**
Holdale Rd. *Nott* —3D **46**
Holden Ct. *Nott* —4E **45** (2A **4**)
Holden Cres. *Nut* —1C **30**
Holden Gdns. *S'fd* —5G **53**
Holden Rd. *Bees* —4E **55**
Holden St. *Nott* —4E **45** (2A **4**)
Holgate. *Nott* —3A **66**
Holgate Rd. *Nott* —2G **57**
Holgate Wlk. *Huck* —5E **7**
Holkham Av. *Bees* —6C **54**
Holkham Clo. *Arn* —1C **34**
Holkham Clo. *Ilk* —4G **27**
Holland Clo. *Got* —6H **75**
Holland Mdw. *Long E* —2F **73**
Holland St. *Nott* —2D **44**
Holles Cres. *Nott* —6E **45** (6A **4**)
Hollies Dri. *Edw* —1C **68**
Hollies, The. *Eastw* —3B **16**
Hollies, The. *Sand* —6C **52**
Hollington Rd. *Nott* —3G **43**
Hollingworth Av. *Sand* —2D **62**
Hollins, The. *C'tn* —3A **12**
Hollinwell Av. *Nott* —4H **43**
Hollinwell Ct. *Edw* —2D **68**
Hollinwood La. *C'tn* —4D **10**
  (in two parts)
Hollis St. *Nott* —6E **33**
Hollows, The. *Long E* —5A **64**
Hollows, The. *Nott* —1E **67**
Hollowstone. *Nott* —5H **45** (5G **5**)
  (in two parts)
Holly Av. *Breas* —4B **62**
Holly Av. *Cltn* —2F **47**
Holly Av. *Nott* —3F **57**
Holly Av. *T'wd* —2C **46**
Hollybrook Gro. *Watn* —6B **18**
Holly Clo. *Bing* —5G **51**
Holly Clo. *Huck* —6H **7**
Holly Copse Nature Reserve.
  —5H **29**
Holly Ct. *Bees* —3C **54**
Holly Ct. *Nott* —2B **46**
Hollycroft. *W Bri* —1C **68**
Hollydale Rd. *Nott* —3D **46**
Hollydene Clo. *Huck* —6C **6**
Hollydene Cres. *Nott* —3H **31**
Hollyfarm Ct. *Newt* —4E **17**
Holly Gdns. *Nott* —2B **46**
Hollygate Ind. Pk. *Cotg* —1G **71**
Hollygate La. *Cotg* —2F **71**
Holly La. *Bees* —6E **55**
Holly Rd. *Watn* —6H **17**
Hollythorpe Pl. *Huck* —6D **6**
Holme Clo. *Ilk* —5H **27**
Holme Clo. *Wdbgh* —1D **24**
Holme Cft. *W Hal* —2C **38**
Holmefield Cres. *Ilk* —1C **40**
Holme Gro. *W Bri* —1D **58**
Holme La. *Hol P & Rad T* —6B **48**
Holme Lea. *Sand* —5D **52**
Holme Lodge. *Cltn* —3G **47**
Holme Pierrepont Country Pk.
  —6A **48**
Holme Pierrepont Hall. —6B **48**
Holme Pierrepont National
  Watersports Cen. —1G̈ **59**

Holme Rd. *Bing* —5F **51**
Holme Rd. *W Bri* —2B **58**
Holmes Clo. *Lan M* —2E **15**
Holmesfield Dri. *Hean* —5D **14**
Holmes Rd. *Breas* —5A **62**
Holmes St. *Hean* —3B **14**
Holme St. *Nott* —1A **58**
Holmewood Cres. *Nott* —1E **33**
Holmewood Dri. *Gilt* —5D **16**
Holmfield Rd. *Bees* —2C **64**
Holmsfield. *Keyw* —5G **79**
Holroyd Av. *Nott* —5B **46**
Holt Gro. *C'tn* —3H **11**
Holwood Ct. *Nott* —1G **31**
Holyoake Dri. *Long E* —6H **63**
Holyoake Rd. *Nott* —4E **35**
Holyrood Ct. *Bees* —2C **54**
Holywell Rd. *Ilk* —4G **27**
Home Clo. *Arn* —5H **21**
Home Cft., The. *Bees* —4B **54**
Home Farm Clo. *Got* —6G **75**
Homefield Av. *Arn* —3C **22**
Homefield Rd. *Nott* —2B **44**
Homestead. *Lan M* —1E **15**
Homewell Wlk. *Nott* —2D **66**
Honeysuckle Clo. *Nott* —6E **31**
Honeysuckle Gro. *Bing* —6D **50**
Honeysuckle Gro. *Nott* —3H **31**
Honeywood Ct. *Nott* —2C **46**
Honeywood Dri. *Nott* —2C **46**
Honingham Clo. *Arn* —2B **34**
Honingham Rd. *Ilk* —4G **27**
Honister Clo. *Gam* —4E **59**
Honister Clo. *Nott* —6B **66**
Honiton Clo. *Bees* —3A **64**
Honiton Rd. *Nott* —6E **31**
Hood Cotts. *Nott* —5H **33**
Hood St. *Nott* —5H **33**
Hooley Clo. *Long E* —1D **72**
Hooley Pl. *Nott* —4H **33**
Hoopers Wlk. *Nott* —1G **57**
Hooton Rd. *Cltn* —2E **47**
Hooton St. *Nott* —4B **46**
Hope Clo. *Nott* —1F **57**
Hopedale Clo. *Nott* —4C **44**
Hope Dri. *Nott* —6F **45** (6B **4**)
Hope St. *Bees* —4E **55**
Hope St. *Ilk* —2B **40**
Hopewell Clo. *Rad T* —4G **49**
Hopewell Wlk. *Ilk* —2B **28**
Hopkins Ct. *Eastw* —2B **16**
Horace Av. *S'fd* —4E **53**
Hornbeam Clo. *Ilk* —2D **40**
Hornbeam Gdns. *Nott* —6F **19**
Hornbuckle Ct. *Nott* —4D **44**
Hornchurch Rd. *Nott* —1D **42**
Hornsby Wlk. *Nott* —5C **20**
Horridge St. *Ilk* —3B **28**
Horsecroft Clo. *Ilk* —5G **27**
Horsendale Av. *Nut* —3E **31**
Horsham Dri. *Nott* —5D **20**
Horsley Cres. *Lan M* —2E **15**
Hoselett Fld. Rd. *Long E* —2G **73**
Hoten Rd. *Nott* —6B **46**
Hotspur Clo. *Nott* —2C **32**
Hotspur Rd. *Colw* —3G **47**
Houghton Clo. *Nut* —3E **31**
Houldsworth Ri. *Arn* —3A **22**
Hound Rd. *W Bri* —3A **58**
Hounds Ga. *Nott* —5G **45** (5C **4**)
  (in two parts)
Houseman Gdns. *Nott* —1G **57**
Houston Clo. *Nott* —4C **20**
Hovenden Gdns. *Nott* —2C **44**
Hove Rd. *Nott* —2C **32**
Howard Clo. *Long E* —4G **63**
Howard St. *Nott* —4G **45** (2E **5**)
Howarth Clo. *Long E* —6C **62**
Howbeck Rd. *Arn* —5D **22**
Howden Rd. *Nott* —3A **20**
Howell Jones Rd. *Bees* —2B **64**
Howells Clo. *Nott* —5G **21**
Howick Dri. *Nott* —6F **19**
Howitt St. *Hean* —3D **14**
Howitt St. *Long E* —6G **63**
Hoylake Cres. *Nott* —2D **42**
Hoylake Wlk. *Nott* —5E **21**
Hoyland Av. *Nott* —1C **56**
Hoyle Rd. *C'tn* —2H **11**

Hubert Ct. *Nott* —3D **44**
Hubert St. *Nott* —3D **44**
Huckerby Rd. *Ilk* —5G **27**
Hucknall Aerodrome. —3E **19**
Hucknall By-Pass. *Huck* —4E **7**
Hucknall Clo. *Strel* —5D **30**
Hucknall Cres. *Ged* —5G **35**
Hucknall Ind. Pk. *Huck* —1F **19**
Hucknall La. *Nott* —1H **57**
Hucknall Leisure Cen. —3H **7**
Hucknall Rd. *Nott* —4B **20**
Hudson St. *Nott* —3B **46**
Hufton's Ct. *Hean* —6E **15**
Hufton's Dri. *Hean* —6D **14**
Hugessen Av. *Huck* —3A **8**
Huggett Gdns. *Nott* —4E **21**
Humber Clo. *Nott* —1G **57**
Humber Lodge. *Bees* —4G **55**
Humber Rd. *Bees* —4G **55**
Humber Rd. *Long E* —4E **63**
Humber Rd. S. *Bees* —5H **55**
Humberston Rd. *Nott* —6C **42**
Hungerhill La. *Wdbgh* —3H **23**
Hungerhill Rd. *Nott* —2H **45**
Hunger Hill Yd. *Ilk* —3C **40**
Hungerton St. *Nott* —6D **44**
Hunston Clo. *Nott* —2G **43**
Hunt Av. *Hean* —3C **14**
Hunter Rd. *Arn* —1E **35**
Hunters Clo. *Nott* —5E **57**
Huntingdon Dri. *Nott*
—5F **45** (5B **4**)
Huntingdon St. *Nott* —3G **45** (1D **4**)
Huntingdon Wlk. *Sand* —6D **52**
Huntingdon Way. *Bees* —3H **63**
Huntley Clo. *Nott* —4E **67**
Hurcomb St. *Nott* —2B **46**
Hurley Ct. *W Hal* —1C **38**
Hurst Dri. *Stan* —3A **38**
Hurts Cft. *Bees* —1D **64**
Hurt's Yd. *Nott* —4G **45** (3D **4**)
Huss's La. *Long E* —6H **63**
Hutchinson Grn. *Nott*
—3H **45** (1F **5**)
Hutton Clo. *Bees* —2D **54**
Hutton St. *Nott* —6B **46**
Huxley Clo. *Nott* —2D **42**
Hyde Clo. *Nott* —1D **66**
Hyde Pk. Clo. *W Bri* —6G **57**
Hyson Clo. *Nott* —1D **44**
Hyson Clo. *Nott* —2D **44**

Ian Gro. *Cltn* —1H **47**
Ikea Way. *Gilt* —6E **17**
Ilam Sq. *Ilk* —2A **28**
Ilford Clo. *Ilk* —4H **27**
Ilkeston Rd. *Hean* —4D **14**
Ilkeston Rd. *Ilk* —6B **40**
Ilkeston Rd. *Nott* —4B **44** (3A **4**)
(in two parts)
Ilkeston Rd. *Sand* —2E **53**
Ilkeston Rd. *S'fd & Bees* —1G **53**
Ilkeston Rd. *Trow* —4D **40**
Imperial Av. *Bees* —5E **55**
Imperial Av. *Ged* —6G **35**
Imperial Rd. *Bees* —5E **55**
Imperial Rd. *Nott* —1B **32**
Inchwood Clo. *Bees* —3H **63**
Incinerator Rd. *Nott* —1A **58**
Independent St. *Nott* —3D **44**
Indoor Athletics Arena. —2F **43**
Indoor Bowls Hall. —5A **64**
Info. Cen. —4E **5**
Ingham Gro. *Nott* —6C **44**
Ingham Rd. *Long E* —3E **63**
Ingleborough Gdns. *Long E*
—5C **62**
Ingleby Clo. *Cotg* —3F **71**
Ingleby Clo. *Nott* —5B **42**
Ingleby Rd. *Long E* —3B **72**
Inglefield Rd. *Ilk* —3B **40**
Inglewood Rd. *Nott* —4C **66**
Ingram Rd. *Nott* —1A **32**
Ingram Ter. *Nott* —1A **32**
Inham Cir. *Bees* —5C **54**
Inham Clo. *Bees* —6A **54**
Inham Rd. *Bees* —6A **54**
Innes Clo. *Cltn* —2E **47**

Instow Ri. *Nott* —3H **45** (1G **5**)
Intake Rd. *Keyw* —4F **79**
International Model Cen. —4E **9**
Iona Dri. *Trow* —4F **41**
Iona Gdns. *Nott* —4E **21**
Ipswich Cir. *Nott* —4C **46**
Ireland Av. *Bees* —6G **55**
Ireland Clo. *Bees* —6G **55**
Iremonger Rd. *Nott* —1H **57**
Irene Ter. *Nott* —5D **32**
Ireton Gro. *Bees* —3D **64**
Ireton St. *Bees* —5E **55**
Ireton St. *Nott* —4E **45** (2A **4**)
Irwin Dri. *Nott* —2F **31**
Isaac Newton Cen. *Nott* —2B **56**
Isaacs La. *S'fd* —4F **53**
Isabella St. *Nott* —6G **45** (6D **4**)
Isandula Rd. *Nott* —5D **32**
Island, The. *Eastw* —4B **16**
Islay Clo. *Arn* —4B **22**
Islay Clo. *Trow* —4F **41**
Ivatt Dri. *Nott* —6B **46**
Ives Clo. *W Bri* —1G **67**
Ivy Clo. *Watn* —4H **17**
Ivy Gro. *Cltn* —2F **47**
Ivy Gro. *Nott* —1E **45**
Ivy La. *Eastw* —3A **16**

Jacklin Gdns. *Nott* —4E **21**
Jackson Av. *Ilk* —6A **28**
Jackson Av. *Sand* —5C **52**
James St. *Arn* —5A **22**
James St. *Kimb* —1H **29**
Japonica Dri. *Nott* —3H **31**
Jardines, The. *Bramc* —2C **54**
Jarrow Gdns. *Nott* —3D **20**
Jarvis Av. *Nott* —3D **46**
Jasmine Clo. *Bees* —2D **54**
Jasmine Clo. *Clif* —4A **66**
Jasmine Clo. *Strel* —6E **31**
Jasmine Ct. *Hean* —4G **15**
Jasmine Rd. *Nott* —4C **32**
Jasper Clo. *Rad T* —1E **61**
Jayne Clo. *Ged* —5A **36**
Jayne Clo. *Nott* —3E **43**
J.B's Bingo & Entertainment Cen.
—4C **66**
Jebb's La. *Bing* —5F **51**
Jedburgh Clo. *Kimb* —6G **17**
Jedburgh Clo. *Nott* —3H **45** (1G **5**)
Jedburgh Wlk. *Nott* —3H **45** (1G **5**)
Jenned Rd. *Arn* —3C **22**
Jenner St. *Nott* —6F **33**
Jenness Av. *Nott* —4C **20**
Jennison St. *Nott* —6A **20**
Jenny Burton Way. *Huck* —6A **8**
Jermyn Dri. *Arn* —4E **21**
Jersey Gdns. *Nott* —3A **46** (1H **5**)
Jervis Ct. *Ilk* —4B **28**
Jesmond Rd. *Nott* —1B **32**
Jessamine Ct. *Bees* —5G **55**
Jessops La. *Ged* —4H **35**
Joan Av. *Hean* —3C **14**
John Carroll Ct. *Nott* —3B **46**
John Carrol Leisure Cen. —4D **44**
John Quinn Ct. *Nott* —6D **32**
Johnson Av. *Huck* —6H **7**
Johnson Dri. *Hean* —3D **14**
Johnson Rd. *Nott* —5C **44**
John's Pl. *Hean* —4B **14**
Johns Rd. *Rad T* —6G **49**
John St. *Hean* —3B **14**
John St. *Ilk* —6B **28**
John St. *New B* —6D **32**
Joseph Ct. *Ilk* —4A **28**
Joyce Av. *Bees* —2H **63**
Joyce Av. *Nott* —3H **33**
Joyce Clo. *Nott* —3H **33**
Jubilee Ct. *Nott* —6D **30**
Jubilee Rd. *Day* —1A **34**
Jubilee St. *Kimb* —6G **17**
Jubilee St. *Nott* —5B **46**
Judson Av. *S'fd* —5H **53**
Julian Clo. *Ilk* —3D **40**
Julian Rd. *W Bri* —3D **58**
Julie Av. *Hean* —4E **15**
Jumelles Dri. *C'tn* —4F **11**
Junction Rd. *Long E* —1A **74**

Juniper Clo. *Nott* —4A **66**
Juniper Ct. *Gilt* —5E **17**
Juniper Ct. Nott —3E **45**
(off Waterloo Promenade)
Juniper Gdns. *Bing* —5G **51**

Kappler Clo. *N'fld* —2A **48**
Karen Ri. *Arn* —4C **22**
Katherine Dri. *Bees* —2H **63**
Kayes Ct. *S'fd* —4F **53**
Kayes Wlk. *Nott* —5H **45** (5F **5**)
Keats Clo. *Day* —6H **21**
Keats Clo. *Long E* —2D **72**
Keats Clo. *Nut* —1B **30**
Keats Dri. *Huck* —5D **6**
Kedleston Clo. *Bees* —6C **54**
Kedleston Clo. *Long E* —2C **72**
Kedleston Dri. *Ilk* —4H **27**
Kedleston Dri. S. *Ilk* —4A **28**
Keeling Clo. *Newt* —4D **16**
Keepers Clo. *B Vil* —1C **20**
Kegworth Rd. *Got* —6F **75**
Keighton Rd. *Nott* —2A **56**
Keilder Dri. *Bing* —5C **50**
Kelfield Clo. *Nott* —2C **32**
Kelham Grn. *Nott* —3B **46**
Kelham M. *Nott* —1D **46**
Kelham Way. *Eastw* —2A **16**
Kelling Clo. *Nott* —1E **33**
Kelly Wlk. *Nott* —4F **57**
Kelsey Clo. *Bees* —2E **65**
Kelso Gdns. *Nott* —1F **57**
Kelstern Clo. *Nott* —4H **31**
Kelvedon Gdns. *Nott*
—3A **46** (1H **5**)
Kelvin Clo. *S'fd* —6E **53**
Kelvin Rd. *Nott* —2C **46**
Kemmel Rd. *Nott* —2B **32**
Kempsey Clo. *Nott* —5C **20**
Kempson St. *Rud* —6G **67**
Kempton Clo. *Kimb* —6G **17**
Kempton Dri. *Arn* —4C **22**
Kendal Clo. *Huck* —3F **7**
Kendal Ct. *W Bri* —3D **58**
Kendal Dri. *Bees* —3D **54**
Kendale Ct. *Nott* —6B **34**
Kendleston Wlk. *Nott* —5E **21**
Kendrew Ct. *Nott* —4A **66**
Kenia Clo. *Cltn* —1F **47**
Kenilworth Ct. *Bees* —3G **55**
Kenilworth Ct. *Nott* —6F **45** (6B **4**)
Kenilworth Dri. *Ilk* —4G **39**
Kenilworth Rd. *Bees* —4G **55**
Kenilworth Rd. *Nott* —6F **45** (6B **4**)
Ken Martin Pool & Lido. —4A **20**
Kenmore Gdns. *Nott*
—3H **45** (1G **5**)
Kennedy Av. *Long E* —2E **73**
Kennedy Clo. *Day* —6H **21**
Kennedy Dri. *S'fd* —2G **53**
Kennel La. *Ann* —2A **6**
Kenneth Rd. *Arn* —3B **22**
Kennington Rd. *Nott* —4B **44**
Kenrick Rd. *Nott* —6C **34**
Kenrick St. *N'fld* —2A **48**
(in two parts)
Kensal St. *W Bri* —3A **58**
Kensington Av. *Hean* —4A **14**
Kensington Clo. *Bees* —4A **64**
Kensington Ct. Nott —4G **33**
(off St Albans St.)
Kensington Gdns. *Cltn* —2G **47**
Kensington Gdns. *Ilk* —2C **40**
Kensington Pk. Clo. *W Bri* —6G **57**
Kensington Rd. *Sand* —1C **62**
Kensington St. *Ilk* —3B **40**
Kenslow Av. *Nott* —2C **44**
Kent Av. *Bees* —1F **65**
Kentmere Clo. *Gam* —4E **59**
Kenton Av. *Nut* —4D **30**
Kenton Ct. *Nott* —2H **57**
Kent Rd. *Gilt* —4E **17**
Kent Rd. *Nott* —5B **34**
Kent Rd. *S'fd* —5F **53**
Kent St. *Nott* —4H **45** (3F **5**)
Kentwood Rd. *Nott* —5B **46**
Kenyon Rd. *Nott* —6B **44**
Keppel Ct. *Ilk* —4B **28**

Kersall Ct. *Nott* —2B **32**
Kersall Dri. *Nott* —2B **32**
Kersall Gdns. *Huck* —4H **7**
Kersall Gdns. Cres. *Huck* —4H **7**
Kestrel Clo. *Cltn* —6D **34**
Kestrel Clo. *Quar H* —5B **40**
Kestrel Dri. *Bing* —6F **51**
Keswick Clo. *Bees* —3D **54**
Keswick Clo. *Gam* —4E **59**
Keswick Clo. *Ilk* —4H **39**
Keswick Ct. *Long E* —3D **62**
Keswick Clo. *Nott* —5A **46** (4H **5**)
Keswick St. *Nott* —5A **46** (4H **5**)
Kett St. *Nott* —6H **19**
Keverne Clo. *Nott* —5A **32**
Kevin Rd. *Nott* —1D **54**
Kew Clo. *W Bri* —2G **67**
Kew Cres. *Hean* —4F **15**
Kew Gdns. *Nut* —4E **31**
Keys Clo. *Nott* —6G **19**
Key St. *Nott* —4B **46**
Keyworth La. *Bun* —6B **78**
Keyworth Rd. *Ged* —4F **35**
Kibworth Clo. *Nott* —3D **32**
(in two parts)
Kiddier Av. *Arn* —6D **22**
Kilbourne Rd. *Arn* —4D **22**
Kilbourn St. *Nott* —3G **45**
Kilburn Clo. *Bees* —1B **54**
Kilburn Dri. *Ilk* —4H **27**
Kilby Av. *Nott* —2B **46**
Kilby Ho. *Long E* —6F **63**
Kildare Rd. *Nott* —1B **46**
Kildonan Clo. *Nott* —5D **30**
Killerton Grn. *Nott* —6D **66**
Killerton Pk. Dri. *W Bri* —1F **67**
Killisick Ct. *Arn* —5D **22**
Killisick La. *Arn* —3D **22**
Killisick Rd. *Arn* —5C **22**
Kilnbrook Av. *Arn* —4D **22**
Kiln Clo. *W Hal* —6C **26**
Kilnwood Clo. *Nott* —2C **46**
Kilsby Rd. *Nott* —3D **66**
Kilverston Rd. *Sand* —5C **52**
Kilverton Clo. *Nott* —5A **44**
Kilvington Rd. *Arn* —6D **22**
Kimber Clo. *Nott* —3D **42**
Kimberley Clo. *Kimb* —2H **29**
Kimberley Eastwood By-Pass.
Eastw —3H **15**
Kimberley Recreation Cen.
—1A **30**
Kimberley Rd. *Nut* —2B **30**
Kimberley St. *Nott* —5C **46**
Kimbolton Av. *Nott* —4D **44**
Kindlewood Dri. *Bees* —4B **64**
King Charles St. *Nott*
—5F **45** (5C **4**)
King Edward Ct. *Nott*
—4H **45** (3F **5**)
King Edward Gdns. *Sand* —5D **52**
King Edward St. *Huck* —5G **7**
King Edward St. *Nott*
—4H **45** (3F **5**)
King Edward St. *Sand* —5D **52**
Kingfisher Clo. *Bees* —6H **55**
Kingfisher Clo. *Nott* —1E **57**
Kingfishers Ct. *W Bri* —1E **69**
Kingfisher Wharf. *Nott* —1E **57**
King George Av. *Ilk* —1A **40**
King John's Arc. *Nott* —4E **5**
King John's Chambers. *Nott* —4E **5**
Kinglake Pl. *Nott* —1G **57**
Kingrove Av. *Bees* —5D **54**
Kings Av. *Ged* —5G **35**
Kingsbridge Av. *Nott* —1E **35**
Kingsbridge Way. *Bees* —5C **54**
Kingsbury Dri. *Nott* —1G **43**
Kings Clo. *Hean* —4D **14**
Kingsdale Clo. *Long E* —2C **72**
Kingsdown Mt. *Nott* —1E **55**
Kingsford Av. *Nott* —3C **44**
Kingsley Cres. *Long E* —3D **72**
Kingsley Dri. *N'fld* —3A **48**
Kingsley Rd. *Nott* —5C **46**
Kingsmead Av. *Trow* —1F **53**
King's Mdw. Rd. *Nott* —1E **57**
Kingsmoor Clo. *Nott* —6C **20**
King's Pl. *Nott* —5H **45** (4F **5**)

Kings Rd. *Sand* —5D **52**
Kingsthorpe Clo. *Nott* —6B **34**
Kingston Av. *Ilk* —5C **40**
Kingston Ct. *Nott* —5A **46** (4H **5**)
Kingston Ct. *W Hal* —1B **38**
Kingston Dri. *Cotg* —4F **71**
Kingston Rd. *W Bri* —5A **58**
King St. *Bees* —5G **55**
King St. *Eastw* —3B **16**
King St. *Ilk* —6B **28**
King St. *Long E* —5E **63**
King St. *Nott* —5G **45** (4D **4**)
Kingsway. *Hean* —3B **14**
Kingsway. *Ilk* —4B **40**
Kingsway. *Rad T* —1E **61**
Kingsway Av. *Huck* —1E **19**
Kingsway Rd. *Huck* —1E **19**
Kingswell Rd. *Arn* —6B **22**
Kingswood Clo. *W Bri* —6H **57**
Kingswood Rd. *Nott* —4H **43**
Kingswood Rd. *W Bri* —6H **57**
Kinlet Rd. *Nott* —1E **33**
Kinoulton La. *Nott* —6H **81**
Kinross Cres. *Nott* —3G **43**
Kinsale Wlk. *Nott* —3C **66**
Kippis St. *Nott* —4H **45** (3F **5**)
Kirby Clo. *Newt* —2C **16**
Kirby Rd. *Newt* —2C **16**
Kirkbride Ct. *Bees* —1B **64**
Kirk Bldgs. *Cltn* —2F **47**
Kirkby Av. *Ilk* —3B **40**
Kirkby Gdns. *Nott* —1H **57**
Kirk Clo. *Bees* —1D **64**
Kirk Cotts. *Nott* —3C **32**
Kirkdale Clo. *Nott* —5B **42**
Kirkdale Gdns. *Long E* —1D **72**
Kirkdale Rd. *Long E* —2D **72**
Kirkdale Rd. *Nott* —3D **46**
Kirkewhite Ct. *Nott* —1H **57**
Kirkewhite St. W. *Nott* —1G **57**
Kirkewhite Wlk. *Nott* —1G **57**
Kirkfell Clo. *W Bri* —6E **59**
Kirkfield Dri. *Breas* —5A **62**
Kirkham Clo. *Hean* —4B **14**
Kirkham Dri. *Bees* —3H **63**
Kirkhill. *Bing* —4G **51**
Kirkland Dri. *Bees* —3C **64**
Kirk La. *Rud* —6G **67**
Kirkley Gdns. *Arn* —5C **22**
Kirkman Rd. *Los* —1A **14**
Kirk Rd. *Nott* —5C **34**
Kirkstead Gdns. *Nott* —2D **44**
Kirkstead St. *Nott* —2D **44**
Kirkstone Ct. *Long E* —3D **62**
Kirkstone Dri. *Gam* —4E **59**
Kirkwhite Av. *Long E* —6F **63**
Kirtle Clo. *Nott* —1H **43**
Kirtley Dri. *Nott* —1E **57**
Kirton Av. *Long E* —6F **63**
Kittiwake M. *Lent* —5C **44**
Kiwi Clo. *Huck* —6D **6**
Knapp Av. *Eastw* —4B **16**
Kneesall Gro. *Huck* —4H **7**
Kneeton Clo. *Ged* —3F **35**
Kneeton Clo. *Nott* —3G **33**
Kneeton Va. *Nott* —3G **33**
Knighton Av. *Nott* —3C **44**
Knighton Rd. *Wd'p* —2H **33**
Knightsbridge Ct. *Nott* —*4G* **33**
(off Newstead St.)
Knightsbridge Dri. *Nut* —4E **31**
Knightsbridge Dri. *W Bri* —1G **67**
Knightsbridge Gdns. *Huck* —1F **7**
Knightsbridge Way. *Huck* —2E **7**
Knights Clo. *Bees* —3H **63**
Knights Clo. *Nott* —5D **20**
Knight's Clo. *W Bri* —2G **67**
Knight St. *N'fld* —3H **47**
Knightwood Dri. *B Vil* —6F **9**
Kniveton Pk. *Ilk* —2H **39**
Knole Rd. *Nott* —4E **43**
Knole Street Baths. —1D **44**
Knoll Av. *Huck* —6D **6**
Knowle Hill. *Kimb* —2A **30**
(in two parts)
Knowle La. *Kimb* —3A **30**
Knowle Pk. *Kimb* —2A **30**

Knowles Wlk. *Arn* —5G **21**
Kozi Kots. *N'fld* —2H **47**
Krebs Clo. *Nott* —4A **66**
Kyle Vw. *Nott* —4E **21**
Kyme St. *Nott* —4D **44**
Kynance Gdns. *Nott* —6F **57**

Labray Rd. *C'tn* —3G **11**
Laburnum Av. *Keyw* —5A **80**
Laburnum Clo. *Sand* —4D **52**
Laburnum Gdns. *Nott* —2C **32**
Laburnum Gro. *Bees* —6H **55**
Laburnum Gro. *Huck* —6H **7**
Laburnum St. *Nott* —2H **45**
Lace Cen. & Costume Mus.—5D **4**
Lace Hall Mus. —5F **5**
Lace Market. —4F **5**
Lace Market Theatre. —5F **5**
Lace Rd. *Bees* —4F **55**
Lace St. *Nott* —2B **56**
Lacey Av. *Huck* —6G **7**
Lacey Clo. *Ilk* —4G **27**
Lacey Fields Rd. *Hean* —4E **15**
Ladbrooke Cres. *Nott* —4A **32**
Ladybank Ri. *Arn* —5E **23**
Lady Bay Av. *W Bri* —2B **58**
Lady Bay Bri. *Nott & W Bri* —1A **58**
Lady Bay Ct. *W Bri* —2C **58**
Lady Bay Rd. *W Bri* —2C **58**
Ladybridge Clo. *Bees* —2E **65**
Ladycroft Av. *Huck* —4G **7**
Ladylea Rd. *Long E* —3C **72**
Ladysmith St. *Nott* —5C **46**
Ladysmock Gdns. *Nott* —1H **57**
Ladywood Rd. *Ilk* —5E **39**
Lake Av. *Los* —1A **14**
Lakehead Ho. *Nott* —4C **66**
Lakeland Av. *Huck* —6A **8**
Lakeside Av. *Long E* —3E **73**
Lakeside Bus. Cen. *Ship* —1E **27**
Lakeside Cres. *Long E* —2E **73**
Lake St. *Nott* —3D **44**
Lamartine St. *Nott* —4H **45** (2G **5**)
Lamb Clo. Dri. *Newt* —1C **16**
Lambert Cotts. *Nott* —4F **45** (3B **4**)
Lambert Gdns. *Nott* —1A **44**
Lambert St. *Nott* —2C **44**
Lambeth Ct. *Bees* —4H **55**
Lambeth Rd. *Arn* —3E **21**
Lambie Clo. *Nott* —4A **44**
Lambley Almshouses. *Nott* —1H **45**
Lambley Av. *Nott* —4D **34**
Lambley Bridle Rd. *Bur J* —1D **36**
Lambley Ct. *Nott* —4D **34**
Lambley La. *Bur J* —2D **36**
Lambley La. *Ged* —4G **35**
Lambley Rd. *Low* —5G **25**
Lambley St. *Nott* —6H **19**
Lambourne Dri. *Nott* —4F **43**
Lambourne Gdns. *Wd'p* —2C **34**
Lambton Clo. *Ilk* —4A **28**
Lamcote Gdns. *Rad T* —6E **49**
Lamcote Gro. *Nott* —2H **57**
Lamcote M. *Rad T* —6E **49**
Lamcote St. *Nott* —2H **57**
Laming Gap La. *Cotg* —5C **80**
Lamins La. *B Vil* —6F **9**
Lammas Gdns. *Nott* —1H **57**
Lamorna Gro. *Nott* —6H **57**
Lamplands. *Cotg* —2E **71**
Lamp Wood Clo. *C'tn* —4G **11**
Lanark Clo. *Nott* —6A **44**
Lancaster Av. *Sand* —1C **62**
Lancaster Av. *S'fd* —5G **53**
Lancaster Ct. *Nott* —2D **46**
Lancaster Rd. *B Vil* —1C **20**
Lancaster Rd. *Huck* —1D **18**
Lancaster Rd. *Nott* —2D **46**
Lancaster Way. *Nott* —5D **30**
Lancelot Dri. *Watn* —4H **17**
Lancelyn Gdns. *W Bri* —1A **68**
Landcroft Cres. *Nott* —1E **33**
Landmere Clo. *Ilk* —4G **27**
Landmere Gdns. *Nott* —6B **34**
Landmere La. *Rud & Edw* —3H **67**
(in two parts)
Landmere La. *W Bri* —2F **67**
Landsdown Gro. *Long E* —4H **63**

Landseer Clo. *Nott* —3C **44**
Laneham Av. *Arn* —6C **22**
Laneside Av. *Bees* —3G **63**
Lane, The. *Aws* —3E **29**
Laneward Clo. *Ilk* —3H **27**
Langar Clo. *Nott* —3G **33**
Langar Rd. *Bing* —6E **51**
Langbank Av. *Nott* —4C **20**
Langdale Dri. *Long E* —1C **72**
Langdale Gro. *Bing* —5B **50**
Langdale Rd. *Nott* —4A **46**
Langden Ct. *Long E* —1G **73**
Langdon Clo. *Long E* —4C **62**
Langdown Clo. *Nott* —5G **19**
Langford Rd. *Arn* —6D **22**
Langham Av. *Nott* —3C **46**
Langham Dri. *Bur J* —2F **37**
Langley Av. *Arn* —1B **34**
Langley Av. *Ilk* —2H **27**
Langley Mill By-Pass. *Brins* —1E **15**
Langstrath Dri. *W Bri* —1E **69**
Langstrath Rd. *Nott* —4C **66**
Langton Clo. *Colw* —3G **47**
Langtree Gdns. *Bing* —4F **51**
Langtry Gro. *Nott* —6E **33**
Lansdown Clo. *Bees* —1B **64**
Lansdowne Dri. *W Bri* —1H **67**
Lansdowne Rd. *Nott* —3C **32**
Lansing Clo. *Nott* —5D **66**
Lanthwaite Clo. *Nott* —4D **66**
Lanthwaite Rd. *Nott* —4D **66**
Lapford Clo. *Nott* —1F **35**
Larch Clo. *Arn* —5G **21**
Larch Clo. *Bing* —5G **51**
Larch Clo. *Huck* —6H **7**
Larch Cres. *Bees* —4E **55**
Larch Cres. *Eastw* —3A **16**
Larchdene Av. *Nott* —6D **42**
Larch Gdns. *Nott* —6G **19**
Larch Way. *Keyw* —5A **80**
Largs Clo. *Nott* —3C **20**
Lark Clo. *Bees* —6A **54**
Larkdale St. *Nott* —3E **45** (1A **4**)
Larkfield Rd. *Nut* —2B **30**
Larkland's Av. *Ilk* —2C **40**
Larkspur Av. *Red* —3A **22**
Larwood Gro. *Nott* —3G **33**
Lascelles Av. *Ged* —5F **35**
Latham St. *Nott* —6H **19**
Lathkill Av. *Ilk* —2A **28**
Lathkill Clo. *Nott* —6H **19**
Lathkill Clo. *W Hal* —1C **38**
Lathkilldale Cres. *Long E* —2C **72**
Latimer Clo. *Nott* —1A **32**
Latimer Dri. *Bees* —6B **42**
Laughton Av. *W Bri* —1G **67**
Laughton Cres. *Huck* —1E **19**
Launceston Cres. *Nott* —1E **67**
Launder St. *Nott* —1G **57**
Laurel Av. *Keyw* —5H **79**
Laurel Cres. *Long E* —1E **73**
Laurel Cres. *Nut* —6B **18**
Laurel Rd. *Cltn* —1F **47**
Laurie Av. *Nott* —1E **45**
Laurie Clo. *Nott* —1E **45**
Lauriston Dri. *Nott* —3B **32**
Lavender Clo. *Nott* —6E **31**
Lavender Cres. *Cltn* —6F **35**
Lavender Gdns. *Hean* —4F **15**
Lavender Gro. *Bees* —6H **55**
Lavender Wlk. *Nott* —2H **45**
Laver Clo. *Arn* —6D **22**
Lawdon Rd. *Arn* —4C **22**
Lawley Av. *Bees* —2G **55**
Lawrence Av. *Aws* —2E **29**
Lawrence Av. *Breas* —5A **62**
Lawrence Av. *Colw* —4G **47**
Lawrence Av. *Eastw* —3B **16**
Lawrence Clo. *Cotg* —2F **71**
Lawrence St. *Long E* —5F **63**
Lawrence St. *Sand* —4D **52**
Lawrence St. *S'fd* —5F **53**
Lawrence Way. *Nott* —1E **57**
Lawson Av. *Long E* —6G **63**
Lawson St. *Nott* —3E **45** (1A **4**)

Lawton Dri. *Nott* —4A **20**
Laxton Av. *Nott* —2B **32**
Laxton Dri. *Huck* —5E **7**
Leabrook Clo. *Nott* —2A **66**
Leabrook Gdns. *Huck* —3A **8**
Leacroft Rd. *Nott* —2B **44**
Leadale Av. *Huck* —3A **8**
Leaf Clo. *Huck* —2H **7**
Leafe Clo. *Bees* —3C **64**
Leafield Grn. *Nott* —3C **66**
Leafy La. *Hean* —4D **14**
Leahurst Gdns. *W Bri* —6D **58**
Leahurst Rd. *W Bri* —6C **58**
Leahy Gdns. *Nott* —1D **32**
Leake Rd. *Got* —6H **75**
Leamington Dri. *Bees* —1C **64**
Leander Clo. *Nott* —5F **57**
Leas, The. *Bul* —2H **37**
Lechlade Clo. *W Hal* —1B **38**
Lechlade Rd. *Nott* —1E **33**
Ledbury Va. *Nott* —1H **43**
Leech Ct. *Gilt* —6D **16**
Lee Cres. *Ilk* —1D **40**
Lee La. *Hean* —4F **15**
Leen Clo. *B Vil* —1D **20**
Leen Clo. *Huck* —3A **8**
Leen Ct. *Nott* —1C **56**
Leen Dri. *Bulw* —4A **20**
Leen Dri. *Huck* —2H **7**
Leen Ga. *Nott* —1B **56**
Leen Mills La. *Huck* —2H **7**
Leen Pl. *Nott* —4C **44**
Leen Valley Golf Course. —4B **8**
Leen Valley Way. *Huck* —6A **8**
Leen Vw. Ct. *Nott* —1G **31**
Lee Rd. *Bur J* —2G **37**
Lee Rd. *C'tn* —3F **11**
Lees Barn Rd. *Rad T* —1D **60**
Lees Hill Footpath. *Nott* —6A **46**
Lees Hill St. *Nott* —5A **46**
Lees Rd. *Nott* —6C **34**
Leicester Ho. *S'fd* —3H **53**
Leicester St. *Long E* —1G **73**
Leigh Clo. *W Bri* —5G **57**
Leigh Rd. *Bees* —2H **63**
Leighton St. *Nott* —3B **46**
Leiston Gdns. *Nott* —5E **21**
Leisure Cen. —4C **66**
(Nottingham)
Leisure Cen. —5B **22**
(Rushcliffe Comp. Sch.)
Leivers Av. *Arn* —5B **22**
Lema Clo. *Nott* —5B **20**
Lendal Ct. *Nott* —4E **45** (2A **4**)
Lendrum Ct. *Bur J* —3F **37**
Leniscar Av. *Los* —1A **14**
Len Maynard Ct. *Nott* —2C **46**
Lennox St. *Nott* —4H **45** (3G **5**)
Lenton Av. *Nott* —5E **45**
Lenton Av. *Toll* —4E **69**
Lenton Baths. —6D **44**
Lenton Boulevd. *Nott* —4D **44**
Lenton Cir. *Toll* —4E **69**
Lenton Ct. *Nott* —6E **45** (6A **4**)
(Lenton Av.)
Lenton Ct. *Nott* —5D **44**
(Lombard Clo.)
Lenton Hall Dri. *Nott* —1A **56**
Lenton La. *Nott* —1D **56**
(in two parts)
Lenton Mnr. *Nott* —6C **44**
Lenton Rd. *Nott* —6E **45** (6A **4**)
Lenton St. *Sand* —5E **53**
Leonard Av. *Nott* —5F **33**
Leonard Cheshire Clo. *Hean*
—4F **15**
Leonard St. *Bulw* —2H **31**
Leopold St. *Long E* —5F **63**
Le Page Ct. *Nott* —2G **43**
Leroy Wallace Av. *Nott* —3D **44**
Lerwick Clo. *Nott* —4E **67**
Leslie Av. *Bees* —6F **55**
Leslie Av. *Kimb* —2H **29**
Leslie Av. *Nott* —1E **45**
Leslie Gro. *C'tn* —4H **11**
Leslie Rd. *Nott* —1E **45**
Letchworth Cres. *Bees* —1C **64**
Letcombe Rd. *Nott* —2C **66**
Levens Clo. *W Bri* —6E **59**

Leverton Ct. W Bri —6B 58
Leverton Grn. Nott —3C 66
Leverton Wlk. Arn —5C 22
Levick Ct. Nott —1G 57
Lewcote La. W Hal —6E 27
Lewindon Dri. Wd'p —3A 34
Lewis Clo. Nott —3H 45 (1F 5)
Lexington Gdns. Nott —3H 33
Leybourne Dri. Nott —1C 32
Leyland Clo. Bees —3H 63
Leys Ct. Rud —1G 77
Leys Rd. Rud —1G 77
Leys, The. Keyw —6H 69
Leys, The. Nott —4A 66
Ley St. N'fld —2A 48
Leyton Cres. Bees —6H 55
Library Rd. Nott —2A 56
Lichfield Clo. Bees —2G 63
Lichfield Clo. Long E —6H 63
Lichfield Rd. Nott —5C 46
Liddell Gro. Nott —4F 43
Liddington St. Nott —6D 32
Lido. —6G 33
Lilac Av. Cltn —1E 47
Lilac Clo. Keyw —5A 80
Lilac Clo. Nott —6E 31
Lilac Ct. Nott —4A 66
Lilac Cres. Bees —6H 55
Lilac Gro. Bees —6H 55
Lilac M. Ilk —4H 27
Lilac Rd. Huck —6H 7
Lilacs, The. Bees —5G 55
Lilian Hind Ct. Nott —5F 19
Lilleker Ri. Arn —4A 22
Lillie Ter. Nott —5B 46
Lillington Rd. Nott —6H 19
Lily Av. N'fld —2A 48
Lily Gro. Bees —6H 55
Lime Av. Lan M —3G 15
Lime Clo. Nut —1A 30
Lime Clo. Rad T —6F 49
Limefield Ct. W Bri —2C 58
Lime Gro. Long E —5F 63
Lime Gro. Sand —5D 52
Lime Gro. S'fd —6F 53
Lime Gro. Av. Bees —6E 55
Limekiln Ct. Nott —5G 19
Lime La. Arn —6A 10
Limes, The. Bar F —1E 75
Limes, The. M'ley —4C 26
Lime St. Ilk —2B 40
Lime St. Nott —6H 19
Lime Ter. Long E —5F 63
Lime Tree Av. Nott —4H 31
(Broxtowe La.)
Lime Tree Av. Nott —6H 43
(Digby Av.)
Limetree Clo. Keyw —5H 79
Lime Tree Cres. Bees —2G 55
Limetree Ct. Ilk —3G 39
Limetree Ri. Ilk —3G 39
Lime Tree Rd. Huck —1H 19
Limmen Gdns. Nott —3A 46 (1H 5)
Limpenny St. Nott —3E 45
Linby Av. Huck —4H 7
Linby Clo. Ged —5G 35
Linby Clo. Nott —2H 33
Linby Dri. Strel —5D 30
Linby Gro. Huck —3H 7
Linby La. L'by & Pap —1A 8
Linby Rd. Huck —3H 7
Linby St. Nott —5A 20
Linby Wlk. Huck —3G 7
Lincoln Av. Sand —1C 62
Lincoln Cir. Nott —5E 45 (5A 4)
Lincoln Clo. S'fd —2G 53
Lincoln Clo. Nott —2E 43
Lincoln Gro. Rad T —6F 49
Lincoln St. Nott —4G 45 (3E 5)
Lincoln St. Old B —4C 32
Lindale Clo. Gam —5E 59
Lindbridge Rd. Nott —5F 31
Linden Av. Nott —4A 66
Linden Ct. Bees —6G 55
Linden Gro. Bees —6G 55
Linden Gro. Ged —6B 36
Linden Gro. Sand —4C 52
Linden Gro. S'fd —5G 53
Linden St. Nott —2H 45

Lindfield Clo. Nott —5G 31
Lindfield Rd. Nott —5F 31
Lindisfarne Gdns. Nott —4E 21
Lindley St. Newt —1D 16
Lindley Ter. Nott —2C 44
Lindrick Clo. Edw —1E 69
Lindsay St. Nott —2D 44
Lindum Gro. Nott —6B 46
Lindum Rd. Nott —4B 32
Linette Clo. Nott —5E 33
Linford St. Bees —5B 42
Ling Cres. Rud —5G 67
Lingfield Ct. Nott —6D 42
Lingford. Cotg —2G 71
Lingford St. Huck —5H 7
Lingmell Clo. W Bri —5E 59
Lingwood La. Wdbgh —3B 24
Linkin Rd. Bees —5C 54
Linkmel Clo. Nott —2E 57
Linkmel Rd. Eastw —2G 15
Linksfield Ct. W Bri —3G 67
Linnell St. Nott —3B 46
Linsdale Clo. Nott —4B 42
Linsdale Gdns. Ged —3F 35
Linton Ri. Nott —3C 46
Linwood Cres. Eastw —4B 16
Lion Clo. Nott —5A 32
Lismore Clo. Nott —4C 44
Lissett Av. Ilk —2A 40
Lister Ct. Nott —1C 56
Listergate. Nott —5G 45 (5E 5)
Listergate Sq. Nott —5G 45 (5E 5)
Listowel Cres. Nott —5C 66
Litchen Clo. Ilk —5B 28
Litchfield Ri. Arn —3A 22
Littlebounds. W Bri —4H 57
Littlegreen Rd. Wd'p —2B 34
Lit. Hallam Hill. Ilk —4A 40
Lit. Hallam La. Ilk —3B 40
Lit. Hayes. W Bri —1G 67
Lit. John Wlk. Nott —2H 45
Little La. C'tn —4F 11
Little La. Kimb —2H 29
Little La. Toll —6G 69
Lit. Lime La. Arn —6A 10
(in two parts)
Lit. Lunnon. Bar F —1E 75
Lit. Meadow. Cotg —3G 71
Littlemore La. Bradm —4A 78
Lit. Oakwood Dri. Nott —3B 20
Lit. Ox. Colw —5H 47
Lit. Tennis St. Nott —6C 46
Lit. Tennis St. S. Nott —1C 58
Littlewell La. Stan D —1B 52
Lit. Wood Ct. Huck —6E 7
Littlewoods Gdns. Nott —4C 42
Litton Clo. Ilk —3A 28
Litton Clo. Wd'p —3A 34
Liverpool St. Nott —4A 46 (3H 5)
Llanberis Gro. Nott —5A 32
Lloyd St. Nott —5G 33
Loach Ct. Nott —4A 44
Lobelia Clo. Nott —2H 45
Lock Clo. Bees —2G 65
Lock Clo. Ilk —3G 39
Lockerbie St. Cltn —3H 47
Lock La. Long E —3D 72
Lock La. Sand —6D 52
Locksley La. Nott —1C 66
Lockton Av. Hean —5C 14
Lockwood Clo. Bees —1A 66
Lockwood Clo. Nott —4E 21
Lodge Clo. Nott —1B 44
Lodge Clo. Red —3A 22
Lodge Farm La. Arn —4A 22
Lodge Rd. Long E —2F 73
Lodge Rd. M'ley —4C 26
Lodge Rd. Newt —5C 16
Lodge Row. M'ley —4C 26
Lodgewood Clo. Nott —1G 31
Lodore Clo. W Bri —5E 59
Logan Sq. Nott —3C 32
Logan St. Nott —1A 32
Lois Av. Nott —6D 44
Lombard Clo. Nott —6D 44
Lombardy Lodge. Bees —4A 64
London Rd. Nott —5H 45 (6G 5)
(in two parts)
Long Acre. Bing —5E 51

Long Acre. Huck —4D 6
Longacre. Wd'p —3B 34
Long Acre E. Bing —5F 51
Longbeck Av. Nott —6C 34
Longbridge La. Hean —2B 14
Longclose Ct. Nott —1G 31
Longdale Rd. Nott —1H 33
Longden Clo. Bees —1H 53
Longden St. Nott —4A 46 (3H 5)
Long Eaton Stadium. —5H 63
Longfellows Clo. Nott —5F 21
Longfield Cres. Ilk —4B 40
Longfield La. Ilk —4B 40
Longford Cres. Nott —3A 20
Long Hill Ri. Huck —5H 7
Longlands Clo. Bees —1H 65
Longlands Dri. W Bri —6F 59
Longlands Rd. Bees —1H 65
Longleat Cres. Bees —6C 54
Longmead Clo. Nott —1G 33
Longmead Dri. Nott —1G 33
Long Mdw. Hill. Low —3F 25
Longmoor Gdns. Long E —3C 62
Longmoor La. Breas —4A 62
Longmoor La. Sand —3C 62
Longmoor Rd. Long E —3C 62
Longore Sq. Nott —5B 44
Longridge Rd. Wd'p —3B 34
Long Row. Nott —5G 45 (4D 4)
Long Row E. Nott —5G 45 (4E 5)
Long Row W. Nott —5G 45 (4D 4)
Long Stairs. Nott —5H 45 (5G 5)
Longthorpe Ct. Arn —6B 22
Longue Dri. C'tn —4F 11
(in two parts)
Longwall Av. Q Dri & Nott —2E 57
Long W. Cft. C'tn —3E 11
Longwood Ct. Nott —5D 20
Lonscale Clo. W Bri —6E 59
Lonsdale Dri. Bees —3G 63
Lonsdale Rd. Nott —3C 44
Lord Haddon Rd. Ilk —6A 28
Lord Nelson St. Nott —5B 46
Lord St. Nott —5B 46
Lorimer Av. Ged —4H 35
Lorna Ct. Nott —6H 33
Lorne Clo. Nott —2G 45
Lorne Gro. Rad T —6F 49
Lorne Wlk. Nott —2G 45
Lortas Rd. Nott —5D 32
Loscoe-Denby La. Den V & Los —1A 14
Loscoe Gdns. Nott —6F 33
Loscoe Grange. Los —2A 14
Loscoe Mt. Rd. Nott —5G 33
Loscoe Rd. Hean —2B 14
Loscoe Rd. Nott —6G 33
Lothian Rd. Toll —4E 69
Lothmore Ct. Nott —1F 57
Lotus Clo. Nott —2A 46
Loughborough Av. Nott —5B 46
Loughborough Rd. Bradm —2H 77
Loughborough Rd. W Bri & Rud —5A 58
Loughrigg Clo. Nott —2F 57
Louis Av. Bees —4E 55
Louise Av. N'fld —1A 48
Lovell Clo. Nott —2F 31
Lowater St. Cltn —2D 46
Lowcroft. Wd'p —3B 34
Lowdham La. Wdbgh —1D 24
Lowdham Rd. Epp —1G 25
Lowdham Rd. Ged —4E 35
Lowdham St. Nott —4A 46 (3H 5)
Lwr. Beauvale. Newt —2C 16
Lwr. Bloomsgrove Rd. Ilk —5B 28
Lwr. Brook St. Long E —6G 63
Lwr. Canaan. Rud —5H 67
Lwr. Chapel St. Ilk —6B 28
Lwr. Clara Mt. Rd. Hean —4E 15
Lower Ct. Bees —4G 55
Lwr. Dunstead Rd. Lan M —2E 15
Lwr. Eldon St. Nott —5A 46 (5H 5)
Lwr. Gladstone St. Hean —3C 14
Lwr. Granby St. Ilk —5B 28
Lwr. Maples. Ship —5E 15

Lwr. Middleton St. Ilk —6C 28
Lwr. Nelson St. Hean —3B 14
Lwr. Orchard St. S'fd —4F 53
Lwr. Park St. S'fd —5E 53
Lwr. Parliament St. Nott —4H 45 (3E 5)
Lwr. Regent St. Bees —5G 55
Lower Rd. Bees —4H 55
Lwr. Stanton Rd. Ilk —3B 40
Lwr. Whitworth Rd. Ilk —3B 40
Loweswater Ct. Gam —4E 59
Lowlands Dri. Keyw —3H 79
Lowlands Lea. Hean —3D 14
Low Pavement. Nott —5G 45 (5E 5)
Lows La. Stan D —1B 52
(in two parts)
Low Wood Rd. Nott —2E 31
Loxley Clo. Nott —1H 43
Lucerne Clo. Nott —5F 57
Lucknow Av. Nott —1H 45
Lucknow Ct. Nott —1H 45
Lucknow Dri. Nott —1H 45
Lucknow Rd. Nott —1H 45
Ludford Rd. Nott —5A 20
Ludgate Clo. Arn —3E 21
Ludham Av. Nott —5H 19
Ludlam Av. Gilt —6C 16
Ludlow Av. Nott —4B 58
Ludlow Clo. Bees —2D 54
Ludlow Hill Rd. W Bri —6B 58
Lulworth Clo. W Bri —6G 57
Lulworth Ct. Kimb —6H 17
Lune Clo. Bees —2E 65
Lupin Clo. Nott —2H 45
Luther Clo. Nott —2A 46
Luton Clo. Nott —6B 32
Lutterell Ct. W Bri —6H 57
Lutterell Way. W Bri —6D 58
Lybster M. Nott —1F 57
Lychgate Ct. Wat —5H 17
Lydia Gdns. Eastw —4A 16
Lydney Pk. W Bri —5F 57
Lyle Clo. Kimb —6G 17
Lyme Pk. W Bri —6F 57
Lymington Gdns. Nott —3B 46
Lymn Av. Ged —5H 35
Lynam Ct. Nott —6H 19
Lyncombe Gdns. Keyw —3H 79
Lyndale Rd. Bees —3A 54
Lynden Av. Long E —1F 73
Lyndhurst Gdns. W Bri —1H 67
Lyndhurst Gro. Long E —4F 63
Lyndhurst Rd. Nott —5B 46
Lynmouth Cres. Nott —2C 44
Lynmouth Dri. Ilk —4H 27
Lynncroft. Eastw —2C 16
Lynstead Dri. Huck —6C 6
Lynton Ct. Nott —2B 46
Lynton Gdns. Arn —5C 22
Lynton Rd. Bees —5C 54
Lyons Clo. Rud —5F 67
Lytham Dri. Edw —2E 69
Lytham Gdns. Nott —4E 21
Lythe Clo. Nott —6E 57
Lytton Clo. Nott —4A 46 (2H 5)

Mabel Gro. W Bri —3C 58
Mabel St. Nott —1H 57
Macauley Gro. Nut —1B 30
Macdonald Sq. Ilk —4G 39
Machins La. Edw —2C 68
Mackinley Av. S'fd —2G 53
Maclaren Gdns. Rud —1H 77
Maclean Rd. Cltn —2E 47
Macmillan Clo. Nott —5B 34
Madford Bus. Pk. Day —1H 33
Madryn Wlk. Nott —5E 21
Mafeking St. Nott —5C 46
Magdala Rd. Nott —1G 45
Magdalene Way. Huck —3G 7
Magnolia Clo. Nott —6E 31
Magnolia Ct. Bees —2D 54
Magnolia Gro. Huck —1H 19
Magnus Ct. Bees —5G 55
Magnus Rd. Nott —4G 33
Magson Clo. Nott —4A 46
Maiden La. Nott —5H 45 (4G 5)
Maidens Dale. Arn —7H 21

Maid Marian Way. *Nott*
—5F **45** (4C **4**)
Maidstone Dri. *Nott* —1D **54**
Main Rd. *Cotg* —4D **60**
Main Rd. *Ged* —6H **35**
Main Rd. *Lent* —5A **56**
Main Rd. *Plum* —5G **69**
Main Rd. *Rad T* —6E **49**
Main Rd. *Shelf* —1H **49**
Main Rd. *Watn* —4H **17**
Main Rd. *Wilf* —5F **57**
Main St. *Aws* —2E **29**
Main St. *Bradm* —4A **78**
Main St. *Breas* —5A **62**
Main St. *Bulw* —1H **31**
(in two parts)
Main St. *Bur J* —3F **37**
Main St. *C'tn* —3D **10**
Main St. *Eastw* —4B **16**
Main St. *Epp* —5E **13**
Main St. *Gam* —4E **59**
Main St. *Keyw* —6G **79**
Main St. *Kimb* —1H **29**
Main St. *Lamb* —6B **24**
Main St. *L'by* —1G **7**
Main St. *Long E* —6G **63**
Main St. *M'ley* —2E **29**
Main St. *Newt* —3E **17**
Main St. *Oxt* —1B **12**
Main St. *Pap* —1B **8**
Main St. *Stan D* —3B **52**
Main St. *Strel* —5B **30**
Main St. *Wdbgh* —1B **24**
Main St. Bulwell. *Bulw* —6H **19**
Maitland Av. *Wd'p* —3B **34**
Maitland Rd. *Wd'p* —3B **34**
Major St. *Nott* —4G **45** (2D **4**)
Malbon Clo. *Nott* —1B **46**
Malcolm Clo. *Nott* —2G **45**
Maldon Clo. *Bees* —1C **64**
Maldon Clo. *Long E* —2G **73**
Malin Hill. *Nott* —5H **45** (5F **5**)
Malkin Av. *Rad T* —5G **49**
Mallard Clo. *Bing* —6G **51**
Mallard Clo. *Nott* —3D **32**
Mallard Ct. *Bees* —6G **55**
Mallard Rd. *Cltn* —3B **48**
Malling Wlk. *Nott* —6A **34**
Mallow Way. *Bing* —5C **50**
(in two parts)
Malmesbury Rd. *Nott* —3C **34**
Maltby Clo. *Nott* —5H **31**
Maltby Rd. *Nott* —3C **34**
Malt Cotts. *Nott* —6D **32**
Malt Cross Music Hall, The.
—4D **4**
Malthouse Clo. *Eastw* —4B **16**
Malthouse Rd. *Ilk* —4B **40**
Malting Clo. *Rud* —1G **79**
Maltings, The. *Nott* —2B **46**
Maltmill La. *Nott* —5H **45** (5E **5**)
Malton Rd. *Nott* —5D **32**
Malt St. *Got* —6H **75**
Malvern Clo. *Nott* —6A **34**
Malvern Ct. *Bees* —5H **55**
Malvern Cres. *W Bri* —6B **58**
Malvern Gdns. *Long E* —5C **62**
Malvern Rd. *Nott* —6A **34**
Malvern Rd. *W Bri* —6A **58**
Manchester St. *Long E* —1F **73**
Mandalay St. *Nott* —3B **32**
Manesty Cres. *Nott* —6C **66**
Manifold Gdns. *Nott* —1G **57**
Manly Clo. *Nott* —5C **20**
Manners Av. *Ilk* —6H **27**
Manners Ind. Est. *Ilk* —6H **27**
Manners Rd. *Ilk* —6A **28**
Manners St. *Ilk* —3C **40**
Manning St. *Nott* —2H **45**
Manning Vw. *Ilk* —5B **28**
Mannion Cres. *Long E* —2D **72**
Manns Leys. *Cotg* —3E **71**
Mann St. *Nott* —1D **44**
Manor Av. *Bees* —5F **55**
(Dovecote La.)
Manor Av. *Bees* —2E **65**
(Kelsey Clo.)
Manor Av. *Nott* —5A **46**
Manor Av. *S'fd* —3F **53**

Manor Clo. *Edw* —2D **68**
Manor Ct. *Bees* —4B **54**
Manor Ct. *Breas* —5A **62**
Manor Ct. *Cltn* —2H **47**
Manor Cres. *Cltn* —1H **47**
Manor Cft. *Nott* —4C **32**
Mnr. Farm La. *Nott* —3C **66**
Mnr. Fields Dri. *Ilk* —2H **39**
Manor Grn. Wlk. *Cltn* —1H **47**
Manor Ho. Rd. *Long E* —6H **63**
Manor Leigh. *Breas* —5A **62**
Manor Pk. *Rud* —6F **67**
Manor Rd. *Bar F* —1E **75**
Manor Rd. *Bing* —5F **51**
Manor Rd. *C'tn* —4G **11**
Manor Rd. *Cltn* —1H **47**
Manor Rd. *Eastw* —4B **16**
Manor Rd. *Ilk* —6A **28**
Manor Rd. *Keyw* —4G **79**
Manor St. *Nott* —5A **46**
Manorwood Rd. *Cotg* —3F **71**
Mansell Clo. *Eastw* —4D **16**
Mansfield Ct. *Nott* —1F **45**
Mansfield Gro. *Nott* —3F **45** (1C **4**)
Mansfield La. *C'tn* —2H **11**
Mansfield Rd. *Eastw* —1A **16**
Mansfield Rd. *Hean* —3D **14**
Mansfield Rd. *Nott* —2F **45** (1D **4**)
Mansfield Rd. *R'hd* —1F **9**
Mansfield St. *Nott* —5G **33**
Manston M. *Nott* —3D **44**
Manthorpe Cres. *Nott* —4B **34**
Manton Cres. *Bees* —3F **55**
Manvers Ct. *Nott* —5A **46** (4H **5**)
Manvers Gro. *Rad T* —6F **49**
Manvers Rd. *W Bri* —5B **58**
Manvers St. *N'fld* —3A **48**
Manvers St. *Nott* —5A **46** (4H **5**)
Manville Clo. *Bees* —6B **42**
Manville Clo. *Nott* —3A **44**
Maori Av. *Huck* —6D **6**
Maple Av. *Bees* —6H **55**
Maple Av. *Sand* —4D **52**
Maplebeck Rd. *Arn* —6C **22**
Maple Clo. *Bing* —5G **51**
Maple Clo. *Keyw* —5A **80**
Maple Clo. *Rad T* —1F **61**
Maple Ct. *Kimb* —1H **29**
Mapledene Cres. *Nott* —6C **42**
Maple Dri. *Ged* —5B **36**
Maple Dri. *Huck* —6E **7**
Maple Dri. *Nut* —1B **30**
Maple Gdns. *Hean* —4B **14**
Maple Gro. *Breas* —5B **62**
Maples St. *Nott* —2D **44**
Maplestead Av. *Nott* —5F **57**
Mapletree Clo. *Nott* —6F **21**
Maple Way. *Nott* —1A **68**
Mapperley Golf Course. —3D **34**
Mapperley Cres. *Nott* —5A **34**
Mapperley Hall Dri. *Nott* —6G **33**
Mapperley Hall Gdns. *Nott* —6H **33**
Mapperley La. *M'ley & W Hal*
—5C **26**
Mapperley Orchard. *Arn* —6D **22**
Mapperley Pk. Dri. *Nott* —1G **45**
Mapperley Plains. *Nott* —2D **34**
Mapperley Reservoir Nature Trail.
—3C **26**
Mapperley Ri. *Nott* —5A **34**
Mapperley Rd. *Nott* —2G **45**
Mapperley St. *Nott* —5G **33**
March Clo. *Nott* —6C **20**
Marchesi Clo. *Huck* —1E **19**
Marchwood Clo. *Nott* —4B **44**
Mardale Clo. *W Bri* —6E **59**
Margaret Av. *Ilk* —1B **40**
Margaret Av. *Long E* —4H **63**
Margaret Av. *Sand* —1D **62**
Margaret Cres. *Ged* —5G **35**
Margaret Pl. *Bing* —4D **50**
Margarets Ct. *Bees* —5H **55**
Marham Clo. *Nott* —6A **46**
Marhill Rd. *Cltn* —2H **47**
Maria Ct. *Park T* —6E **45** (6A **4**)
Marie Gdns. *Huck* —6G **7**
Marina Av. *Bees* —6F **55**
Marina Rd. *Smal* —5A **14**

Mariner Ct. *Nott* —1G **31**
Marion Av. *Huck* —2A **8**
Marion Murdoch Ct. *Ged* —5G **35**
Maris Clo. *Nott* —3A **66**
Maris Dri. *Bur J* —3E **37**
Market Pl. *Bing* —5E **51**
Market Pl. Bulw —6H **19**
(off Main St., in two parts)
Market Pl. *Huck* —4G **7**
Market Pl. *Ilk* —1A **40**
Market Pl. *Long E* —5G **63**
Market Side. Nott —6H **19**
(off Bulwell High Rd.)
Market St. *Bing* —5E **51**
Market St. *Hean* —3C **14**
Market St. *Ilk* —1B **40**
Market St. *Nott* —4G **45** (3D **4**)
Markham Cres. *Nott* —3G **33**
Markham Rd. *Bees* —2D **54**
Mark St. *Sand* —4E **53**
Marlborough Ct. *Bees* —3F **55**
Marlborough St. *W Bri* —4B **58**
Marlborough Rd. *Bees* —3F **55**
Marlborough Rd. *Long E* —4H **63**
Marlborough Rd. *Wd'p* —2H **33**
Marlborough St. *Nott* —2C **56**
Marldon Clo. *Nott* —4B **42**
Marlow Av. *Nott* —5C **32**
Marlow Cres. *W Hal* —1B **38**
Marl Rd. *Rad T* —6H **49**
Marlwood. *Cotg* —4G **71**
Marmion Rd. *Nott* —2C **46**
Marnham Dri. *Nott* —6A **34**
Marple Sq. *Nott* —2G **45**
Marriott Av. *Bees* —6A **54**
Marriott Clo. *Bees* —6A **54**
Marsant Clo. *Nott* —4A **44**
Marshall Dri. *Bees* —3H **53**
Marshall Hill Dri. *Nott* —6D **34**
Marshall Rd. *Nott* —6C **34**
Marshall St. *Hean* —3D **14**
Marshall St. *Nott* —5G **33**
Marshall Way. *Ilk* —3H **39**
Marston Rd. *Nott* —2D **46**
Martell Ct. *Bees* —2C **64**
Martin Clo. *Blen I* —5F **19**
Martin Ct. *Blen I* —5G **19**
Martindale Clo. *Gam* —4E **59**
Martinmass Clo. *Nott* —6C **44**
Martin's Hill. *Cltn* —2G **47**
Martin's Pond Nature Reserve.
—4F **43**
Marton Rd. *Bees* —2C **64**
Marton Rd. *Nott* —4A **20**
Marvin Rd. *Bees* —6A **54**
Marwood Cres. *Cltn* —5E **35**
Marwood Rd. *Cltn* —6E **35**
Mary Ct. *Nott* —6A **34**
Maryland Ct. *S'fd* —2G **53**
Mary Rd. *Eastw* —4D **16**
Masonic Pl. *Nott* —4F **45** (3C **4**)
Mason Rd. *Ilk* —5H **27**
Massey Clo. *Bur J* —4E **37**
Massey Gdns. *Nott* —3A **46** (1H **5**)
Masson Ct. *Nott* —4E **21**
Matlock Ct. *Long E* —2B **72**
Matlock Ct. *Nott* —4G **45** (2D **4**)
Matlock St. *N'fld* —2H **47**
Matthews Ct. *S'fd* —1H **53**
(in two parts)
Mattingly Rd. *Nott* —1G **31**
Maud St. *Nott* —6E **33**
Maun Av. *Nott* —3B **44**
Maun Gdns. *Nott* —3B **44**
Maurice Dri. *Nott* —5A **34**
Maws La. *Kimb* —6G **17**
Maxtoke Rd. *Nott* —6E **45** (6A **4**)
Maxwell Clo. *Nott* —6D **44**
Maxwell St. *Breas* —5B **62**
Maxwell St. *Long E* —6G **63**
May Av. *Nott* —5E **43**
May Cotts. *Nott* —3C **32**
May Ct. *Nott* —6F **33**
Maycroft Gdns. *Nott* —2C **46**
Maydene Clo. *Nott* —4B **66**
Mayes Ri. *B Vil* —1C **20**
Mayfair Gdns. *Nott* —2D **32**
Mayfield Av. *Bur J* —2F **37**

Mayfield Av. *Hean* —4C **14**
Mayfield Ct. *Nott* —1G **57**
Mayfield Dri. *S'fd* —1H **53**
Mayfield Gro. *Long E* —4G **63**
Mayfield Rd. *Cltn* —2D **46**
Mayflower Clo. *W Bri* —4C **58**
Mayflower Rd. *Newt* —5D **16**
Mayland Clo. *Nott* —3C **42**
Maylands Av. *Breas* —5A **62**
Mayo Rd. *Nott* —6F **33**
Maypole. *Nott* —2C **66**
Maypole Yd. *Nott* —4G **45** (3E **5**)
May's Av. *Cltn* —3E **47**
Mays Clo. *Cltn* —3E **47**
May St. *Ilk* —3A **28**
Maythorn Clo. *W Bri* —2G **67**
Maythorne Wlk. *Nott* —6C **22**
Maywood Golf Course. —5A **52**
McIntosh Rd. *Ged* —4F **35**
Meadowbank Ct. *Eastw* —2H **15**
Meadowbank Way. *Eastw* —2H **15**
Meadow Clo. *Breas* —6A **62**
Meadow Clo. *Eastw* —1B **16**
Meadow Clo. *Ged* —1A **36**
Meadow Clo. *Huck* —6D **6**
Meadow Clo. *Nott* —1A **58**
Meadow Cotts. *N'fld* —2H **47**
Meadow Ct. *Nott* —1B **58**
(Brand St.)
Meadow Ct. *Nott* —1A **58**
(Meadow Clo.)
Meadow Dri. *Keyw* —4A **80**
Meadow End. *Got* —6H **75**
Meadow End. *Rad T* —6H **49**
Meadow Gdns. *Bees* —1E **65**
Meadow Gdns. *Hean* —4F **15**
Meadow Gro. *Nott* —1A **58**
Meadow La. *Bees* —6E **55**
Meadow La. *Bur J* —3F **37**
Meadow La. *Long E* —6H **63**
(in two parts)
Meadow La. *Nott* —2A **58**
Meadow Ri. *Nott* —1F **31**
Meadow Rd. *Aws* —2E **29**
Meadow Rd. *Bees* —6G **55**
Meadow Rd. *N'fld* —3H **47**
Meadows, The. *Aws* —2E **29**
Meadows, The. *Hean* —4C **14**
Meadows, The. *Wdbgh* —1B **24**
Meadow St. *Ilk* —6B **28**
Meadows Way. *Nott* —2F **57**
Meadowsweet Hill. *Bing* —5C **50**
Meadow Trad. Est. *Nott* —6A **46**
Meadowvale Cres. *Nott* —4C **66**
Medawar Clo. *Nott* —4A **66**
Medbank Ct. *Nott* —6E **57**
Meden Clo. *Nott* —2C **66**
Meden Gdns. *Nott* —2B **44**
Medina Dri. *Toll* —4F **69**
Medway Clo. *Bees* —6C **54**
Medway St. *Nott* —4B **44**
Meeks Rd. *Arn* —5D **22**
Meerbrook Pl. *Ilk* —4G **39**
Meer Rd. *Bees* —6A **54**
Melbourne Ct. *Long E* —3B **72**
Melbourne Ct. *Nott* —6A **32**
Melbourne Rd. *Nott* —1H **43**
Melbourne Rd. *S'fd* —1G **53**
Melbourne Rd. *W Bri* —2B **58**
Melbury Rd. *Nott* —1D **42**
Melbury Rd. *Wd'p* —3B **34**
Meldreth Rd. *Nott* —3E **43**
Melford Hall Dri. *W Bri* —1G **67**
Melford Rd. *Nott* —1D **42**
Melksham Rd. *Nott* —5G **21**
Mellbreak Clo. *W Bri* —5E **59**
Mellers Ct. *Nott* —2C **46**
Mellon Ter. *Nott* —4E **45** (2A **4**)
Mellors Rd. *Arn* —4B **22**
Mellors Rd. *W Bri* —6B **58**
Melrose Av. *Bees* —6G **55**
Melrose Av. *Nott* —4G **33**
Melrose Gdns. *W Bri* —1H **67**
Melrose St. *Nott* —4G **33**
Melton Ct. *Sand* —6C **52**
Melton Gdns. *Edw* —1C **68**
Melton Gro. *W Bri* —4A **58**
Melton Rd. *Edw & Toll* —4C **68**
Melton Rd. *Plum* —6H **69**

Melton Rd. *W Bri & Edw* —4A **58**
Melville Ct. *Nott* —1G **45**
Melville Gdns. *Nott* —3A **46** (1H **5**)
Melville St. *Nott* —6G **45** (6E **5**)
Melvyn Dri. *Bing* —5E **51**
Mendip Clo. *Long E* —4C **62**
Mendip Ct. *Nott* —5D **20**
Mensing Av. *Cotg* —2E **71**
Merchant St. *Nott* —5H **19**
(in two parts)
Mercia Clo. *Gilt* —5C **16**
Mercury Clo. *Nott* —2C **32**
Mere Av. *C'tn* —4H **11**
Mere Clo. *C'tn* —4H **11**
Meredith Clo. *Nott* —2F **57**
Meredith St. *S'fd* —1H **53**
Meregill Clo. *Nott* —4E **21**
Merevale Av. *Nott* —1D **66**
Mere Way. *Rud* —3H **77**
Meriac Clo. *Nott* —5D **20**
Meriden Av. *Bees* —3G **55**
Meridian Ct. *Nott* —4E **33**
Merlin Clo. *Nott* —3C **66**
Merlin Dri. *Huck* —1E **19**
Merlin Way. *Quar H* —5B **40**
Merrivale Ct. *Nott* —1G **45**
Mersey St. *Nott* —6H **19**
Merton Clo. *Arn* —4D **22**
Merton Ct. *S'fd* —2G **53**
Metcalf Rd. *Newt* —2D **16**
Mevell Ct. *Nott* —5E **45** (5A **4**)
Mews La. *C'tn* —4G **11**
Mews, The. *Nott* —1E **45**
Meynall Gro. *Nott* —6E **33**
Meynell Rd. *Long E* —2F **73**
MGM Cinema. —4C **4**
Miall Ct. *Nott* —4C **44**
Miall St. *Nott* —4C **44**
Michael Gdns. *Nott* —6F **33**
Michael Rayner Ct. *Nott* —4B **32**
Mickleborough Av. *Nott* —1B **46**
Mickleborough Way. *W Bri*
—2G **67**
Mickledon Clo. *Long E* —5C **62**
Mickledon Clo. *Nott* —1F **57**
Micklemoor La. *Bing* —1H **51**
Middle Av. *Cltn* —1E **47**
Middlebeck Av. *Arn* —5E **23**
Middlebeck Dri. *Arn* —5D **22**
Middledale Rd. *Cltn* —3E **47**
Middlefell Way. *Nott* —4B **66**
Middle Furlong Gdns. *Nott* —1F **57**
Middle Furlong M. *Nott* —1F **57**
Middle Hill. *Nott* —5G **45** (5E **5**)
Middle La. *Bees* —6E **55**
Middle Nook. *Nott* —4E **43**
Middle Orchard St. *S'fd* —4F **53**
Middle Pavement. *Nott*
—5G **45** (5E **5**)
Middle St. *Bees* —5F **55**
Middleton Boulevd. *Nott* —5A **44**
Middleton Clo. *Nut* —1C **30**
Middleton Cres. *Bees* —2E **55**
Middleton Rd. *Ilk* —4C **40**
Middleton St. *Aws* —3E **29**
Middleton St. *Bees* —4E **55**
Middleton St. *Ilk* —6C **28**
Middleton St. *Nott* —4C **44**
Midhurst Clo. *Bees* —1C **64**
Midhurst Way. *Nott* —3C **66**
Midlame Gdns. *Nott* —6F **19**
Midland Av. *N'fld* —2A **48**
Midland Av. *Nott* —6C **44**
Midland Av. *S'fd* —6E **53**
Midland Clo. *Nott* —3B **44**
Midland Cotts. *W Bri* —4B **58**
Midland Ct. *Nott* —6F **33**
(Edbury Rd.)
Midland Ct. *Nott* —4B **44**
(Midland Clo.)
Midland Cres. *Cltn* —2H **47**
Midland Gro. *N'fld* —1A **48**
Midland Rd. *Cltn* —2H **47**
Midland Rd. *Eastw* —3B **16**
Midland Rd. *Hean* —3C **14**
Midland St. *Long E* —5G **63**
Midland Ter. *Long E* —4G **63**
Midway, The. *Nott* —3C **56**

Mikado Rd. *Long E* —2E **73**
Mike Powers Pottery. —6G **67**
Milburn Gro. *Bing* —5C **50**
Mildenhall Cres. *Nott* —5G **21**
Mile End Rd. *Colw* —4G **47**
Milford Av. *Long E* —2D **62**
Milford Clo. *Nott* —5G **19**
Milford Ct. *Day* —1H **33**
Milford Dri. *Ilk* —4H **27**
Milford Dri. *Nott* —2E **47**
Mill Acre Clo. *Ilk* —5H **27**
Millbank. *Hean* —4E **15**
(in two parts)
Millbank Clo. *Ilk* —4H **27**
Millbank Ct. *Nott* —1G **31**
Millbeck Av. *Nott* —5C **42**
Millbeck Clo. *Gam* —5E **59**
Mill Clo., The. *Old B* —4C **32**
Mill Cres. *Arn* —5A **22**
Milldale Clo. *Nott* —3A **66**
Milldale Rd. *Long E* —1D **72**
Millennium Ct. *Nott* —2B **32**
Millennium Way. *Nott* —3G **31**
Millennium Way E. *Nott* —3G **31**
Millennium Way W. *Nott* —3G **31**
Miller Hives Clo. *Cotg* —2E **71**
Millers Bri. *Cotg* —3E **71**
Millers Clo. *Shelf* —6H **37**
Millers Ct. *Nott* —3C **44**
Millers Dale Av. *Ilk* —2A **28**
Mill Fld. Clo. *Bur J* —4E **37**
Millfield Clo. *Ilk* —4G **27**
Millfield Rd. *Ilk* —2C **40**
Millfield Rd. *Kimb* —6G **17**
Mill Hill La. *Breas* —4A **62**
Mill Hill Rd. *Bing* —6D **50**
Millicent Gro. *W Bri* —3B **58**
Millicent Rd. *W Bri* —3A **58**
Mill Lakes Country Pk. —1B **20**
Mill La. *Arn* —5A **22**
Mill La. *Bradm* —3B **78**
Mill La. *Clip* —4D **70**
Mill La. *Coss* —1D **40**
Mill La. *Cotg* —1E **71**
Mill La. *Lamb* —6B **24**
Mill La. *Sand* —5E **53**
Mill Rd. *Hean* —5E **15**
Mill Rd. *Newt* —2C **16**
Mill Rd. *S'fd* —3F **53**
Mill St. *Ilk* —6B **28**
Mill St. *Nott* —4B **32**
Millview Clo. *Nott* —5B **46**
Mill Vw. Ct. *Nott* —5A **46** (5H **5**)
Mill Yd. *Huck* —4G **7**
Milner Rd. *Long E* —5F **63**
Milner Rd. *Nott* —5G **33**
Milnhay Rd. *Lan M* —3G **15**
Milton Av. *Ilk* —3A **28**
Milton Ct. *Arn* —6D **22**
Milton Ct. *Nott* —4F **33**
Milton Cres. *Bees* —3D **64**
Milton Ri. *Huck* —6D **6**
Milton St. *Ilk* —3A **28**
Milton St. *Long E* —6F **63**
Milton St. *Nott* —4G **45** (2E **5**)
Milton Ter. *Long E* —6F **63**
Milverton Rd. *Nott* —5G **21**
Milward Rd. *Los* —3B **14**
Mimosa Clo. *Nott* —4A **66**
Minerva St. *Nott* —5H **19**
(in two parts)
Minster Clo. *Huck* —3H **7**
Minster Ct. *Nott* —2F **45**
Minster Gdns. *Newt* —4D **16**
Mint Gro. *Long E* —5C **62**
Minton Clo. *Bees* —6B **64**
Minver Cres. *Nott* —6G **31**
Mirberry M. *Nott* —6C **44**
Miriam Ct. *W Bri* —4A **58**
Misk Hollows. *Huck* —3F **7**
Misk Vw. *Eastw* —3D **16**
Mission St. *Nott* —5A **34**
Mitchell Av. *Lan M* —1E **15**
Mitchell Clo. *Nott* —1G **31**
Mitchell St. *Long E* —6G **63**
Mitchell Ter. *Ilk* —4C **40**
Moffat Clo. *Nott* —2B **46**
Moira Ho. *Arn* —6A **22**

Mollington Sq. *Nott* —3H **31**
Monarch Way. *Hean* —3A **14**
Mona Rd. *W Bri* —2C **58**
Mona St. *Bees* —5G **55**
Monks Clo. *Ilk* —1C **40**
Monk's La. *Got* —6H **75**
Monksway. *Nott* —1E **67**
Monkton Clo. *Ilk* —4H **27**
Monkton Dri. *Nott* —2E **43**
Monmouth Clo. *Nott* —5B **42**
Monroe Wlk. *Nott* —6E **21**
Monsaldale Clo. *Long E* —1D **72**
Monsall Av. *Ilk* —2A **28**
Monsall St. *Nott* —6D **32**
Monsell Dri. *Red* —4A **22**
Montague Rd. *Huck* —3G **7**
Montague St. *Bees* —4E **55**
Montague St. *Nott* —6A **20**
Montfort Cres. *Nott* —3H **33**
Montfort St. *Nott* —4E **45**
Montgomery Clo. *Bees* —3C **64**
Montgomery St. *Nott*
—3E **45** (1A **4**)
Montpelier Rd. *Nott* —2C **56**
Montrose Ct. *S'fd* —2G **53**
Monyash Clo. *Ilk* —4A **28**
Moorbridge Cotts. *Nott* —3B **20**
Moorbridge Ct. *Bing* —4E **51**
Moorbridge La. *S'fd* —2F **53**
Moorbridge Rd. *Bing* —4E **51**
Moorbridge Rd. E. *Bing* —4E **51**
Moore Clo. *W Bri* —2D **58**
Moore Ga. *Bees* —5F **55**
Moore Rd. *Map* —5C **34**
Moores Av. *Sand* —4E **53**
Moor Farm Cvn. Pk. *C'tn* —5C **12**
Moor Farm Inn La. *Bramc* —1A **54**
Moorfield Ct. *S'fd* —2G **53**
Moorfield Cres. *Sand* —6D **52**
Moorfields Av. *Eastw* —2B **16**
Moorgate St. *Nott* —4E **45** (2A **4**)
Moorgreen. *Newt* —1E **17**
Moorgreen Bus. Pk. *Newt* —1D **16**
Moorgreen Dri. *Strel* —5D **30**
Moorgreen Ind. Pk. *Newt* —1D **16**
Moorhouse Rd. *Nott* —3E **43**
Moorings, The. *Nott* —1D **56**
Moorland Av. *S'fd* —5F **53**
Moorlands Clo. *Long E* —3D **62**
Moor La. *Bees* —1B **54**
Moor La. *Bing* —4E **51**
Moor La. *Bradm* —5H **77**
Moor La. *Bun* —6G **77**
Moor La. *C'tn* —5C **12**
Moor La. *Dal A* —6D **38**
Moor La. *Got* —6H **75**
Moor La. *Rud* —1G **77**
Moor Rd. *B Vil* —2B **20**
Moor Rd. *C'tn* —4A **12**
Moor Rd. *Pap* —1B **8**
Moor Rd. *Strel* —6D **30**
Moorsholm Dri. *Nott* —5C **42**
Moor St. *N'fld* —2H **47**
Moor, The. *Trow* —4A **54**
Moray Ct. *Kimb* —6H **17**
Morden Clo. *Nott* —1D **42**
Morden Rd. *Gilt* —5E **17**
Moreland Ct. *Cltn* —2E **47**
Moreland Ct. *Nott* —6B **46**
Moreland Pl. *Nott* —6B **46**
Moreland St. *Nott* —6B **46**
Morello Av. *Cltn* —1H **47**
Moreton Rd. *Nott* —6C **66**
Morgan Ct. *Bees* —6H **55**
Morgan M. *Nott* —3B **66**
Morkinshire Cres. *Cotg* —1F **71**
Morkinshire La. *Cotg* —1E **71**
Morley Av. *Nott* —5A **34**
Morley Ct. *Nott* —5A **46** (3H **5**)
Morley Dri. *Ilk* —4H **27**
Morley Gdns. *Nott* —6F **33**
Morley Rd. *Nott* —6C **34**
Morley St. *Day* —1A **34**
Mornington Clo. *Sand* —5E **53**
Mornington Cres. *Nut* —4D **30**
Morrell Bank. *Nott* —1D **32**
Morris Av. *Bees* —4B **64**
Morris Rd. *Nott* —6D **30**
Morris St. *N'fld* —2A **48**

Mortimer's Hole Cave. —6F **45**
(off Castle)
Morton Clo. *Rad T* —6H **49**
Morton Gdns. *Rad T* —6H **49**
Morval Rd. *Nott* —2E **43**
Morven Av. *Huck* —5H **7**
Mosley St. *Huck* —5G **7**
Mosley St. *Nott* —1D **44**
Moss Clo. *Arn* —5G **21**
Mosscroft Av. *Nott* —4B **66**
Mossdale Rd. *Nott* —2G **33**
Moss Dri. *Bees* —4B **54**
Moss Ri. *Nott* —5D **34**
Moss Rd. *Huck* —4F **7**
Moss Rd. *Ilk* —2A **40**
Moss Side. *Nott* —2E **67**
Mosswood Cres. *Nott* —6F **21**
Mottram Rd. *Bees* —5C **54**
Mountbatten Ct. *Ilk* —4B **28**
Mountbatten Gro. *Ged* —5G **35**
Mountbatten Way. *Bees* —3C **64**
Mountfield Av. *Sand* —1C **62**
Mountfield Dri. *Nott* —6E **21**
Mt. Hooton. *Nott* —3E **45**
Mt. Hooton Rd. *Nott* —2E **45**
Mt. Pleasant. *Cltn* —2G **47**
Mt. Pleasant. *Ilk* —3A **28**
Mt. Pleasant. *Keyw* —4H **79**
Mt. Pleasant. *Nott* —5B **32**
Mt. Pleasant. *Rad T* —6E **49**
Mt. Sorrel Dri. *W Bri* —5D **58**
Mount St. *Breas* —6B **62**
Mount St. *Hean* —4C **14**
Mount St. *New B* —6D **32**
Mount St. *Nott* —5F **45** (5C **4**)
(in two parts)
Mount St. *S'fd* —4G **53**
Mount St. Arc. *Nott* —4C **4**
Mount, The. *B Vil* —1C **20**
Mount, The. *Nott* —5E **35**
(Elmhurst Av.)
Mount, The. *Nott* —6E **31**
(Wyrale Dri.)
Mount, The. *Red* —4H **21**
Mount, The. *S'fd* —5F **53**
Mowbray Ct. *Nott* —4H **45** (2G **5**)
Mowbray Gdns. *W Bri* —6B **58**
Mowbray Ri. *Arn* —5B **22**
Moyra Dri. *Arn* —6G **21**
Mozart Clo. *Nott* —4C **44**
Mudpie La. *W Bri* —2D **58**
Muir Av. *Toll* —5F **69**
Muirfield Rd. *Arn* —4D **20**
Mulberry Clo. *W Bri* —6F **57**
Mulberry Gdns. *Nott* —5G **19**
Mulberry Gro. *Huck* —1H **19**
Mundella Rd. *Nott* —2H **57**
Mundy's Dri. *Hean* —5D **14**
Mundy St. *Hean* —4C **14**
Mundy St. *Ilk* —5B **28**
Munford Cir. *Nott* —4G **31**
Munks Av. *Huck* —4F **7**
Murby Cres. *Nott* —5H **19**
Murden Way. *Bees* —5H **55**
Muriel Rd. *Bees* —4F **55**
Muriel St. *Nott* —1A **46**
Museum of Nottingham Lace.
—5F **5**
Muskham Av. *Ilk* —4B **28**
Muskham St. *Nott* —2H **57**
Musters Ct. *Huck* —5A **8**
Musters Ct. *W Bri* —5A **58**
Musters Cres. *W Bri* —6B **58**
Musters Cft. *Colw* —6H **47**
Musters Rd. *Bing* —5D **50**
Musters Rd. *Rud* —1F **77**
Musters Rd. *W Bri* —3A **58**
Musters Wlk. *Nott* —6G **19**
Muston Clo. *Nott* —6B **34**
Myrtle Av. *Long E* —1E **73**
Myrtle Av. *Nott* —1H **45**
Myrtle Av. *S'fd* —5G **53**
Myrtle Gro. *Bees* —4G **55**
Myrtle Rd. *Cltn* —1E **47**
Myrtus Clo. *Nott* —3A **66**

Nabarro Ct. *C'tn* —4G **11**
Nabbs La. *Huck* —5D **6**

Naburn Ct. *Nott* —6B **32**
Nairn Clo. *Arn* —4D **22**
Nairn M. *Cltn* —2G **47**
Nanranjan M. *Nott* —3E **45** (1A **4**)
Nansen Gdns. *Nott* —1D **32**
Nansen St. *Nott* —1A **32**
Naomi Ct. *Nott* —4A **20**
Naomi Cres. *Nott* —4A **20**
Narrow La. *Wat* —4H **17**
Naseby Clo. *Nott* —3D **32**
Naseby Dri. *Long E* —3G **73**
Nathaniel Rd. *Long E* —6H **63**
Nathans La. *Rad T* —4A **60**
Nature Reserve. —2F 67
(Rushcliffe)
Navenby Wlk. *Nott* —3C **66**
Naworth Clo. *Nott* —2C **32**
Naylor Av. *Got* —6H **75**
Neal Ct. *Lan M* —2E **15**
Neale St. *Long E* —6G **63**
Nearsby Dri. *W Bri* —5D **58**
Needham Rd. *Arn* —5C **22**
Needham St. *Bing* —5E **51**
Needwood Av. *Trow* —1F **53**
Negus Ct. *Lamb* —6B **24**
Neighwood Clo. *Bees* —3G **63**
Nell Gwyn Cres. *Nott* —4G **21**
Nelper Cres. *Ilk* —4C **40**
Nelson Rd. *Bees* —1G **65**
Nelson Rd. *Day* —6A **22**
Nelson Rd. *Nott* —6A **20**
Nelson St. *Ilk* —3B **28**
Nelson St. *Long E* —1F **73**
Nelson St. *Nott* —5H **45** (4G **5**)
Nene Clo. *Huck* —2E **19**
Nepps Cft. *Epp* —5G **13**
Nesfield Ct. *Ilk* —6A **28**
Nesfield Rd. *Ilk* —6A **28**
Neston Dri. *Nott* —3H **31**
Nether Clo. *Eastw* —1B **16**
Nether Clo. *Nott* —3C **46**
Netherfield La. *Locki* —6B **72**
Netherfield Rd. *Long E* —3D **72**
Netherfield Rd. *Sand* —6D **52**
Nethergate. *Nott* —3A **66**
(in two parts)
Nether Pasture. *N'fld* —3A **48**
Nether St. *Bees* —5G **55**
Nettlecliff Wlk. *Nott* —5C **20**
Neville Rd. *C'tn* —4H **11**
Neville Sadler Ct. *Bees* —4G **55**
Newall Dri. *Bees* —3C **64**
Newark Av. *Nott* —5A **46** (5H **5**)
Newark Ct. *Nott* —2D **32**
Newark Cres. *Nott* —5A **46** (5H **5**)
Newark St. *Nott* —5A **46** (5H **5**)
Newbery Av. *Long E* —1H **73**
Newbridge Clo. *W Hal* —1B **38**
Newbury Clo. *Nott* —3C **34**
Newbury Ct. *Nott* —1F **45**
Newbury Dri. *Nut* —4D **30**
Newcastle Av. *Bees* —5F **55**
Newcastle Av. *Ged* —6G **35**
Newcastle Chambers. *Nott*
—5G **45** (4D **4**)
Newcastle Cir. *Nott* —5E **45** (5A **4**)
Newcastle Ct. *Park T*
—5E **45** (5A **4**)
Newcastle Dri. *Nott* —5E **45** (4A **4**)
Newcastle Farm Dri. *Nott* —4A **32**
Newcastle St. *Nott* —5A **20**
(Carey Rd.)
Newcastle St. *Nott* —4G **45** (3E **5**)
(Up. Parliament St.)
Newcastle Ter. *Nott* —4E **45** (3A **4**)
(Newcastle Dri.)
Newcastle Ter. *Nott* —6B **32**
(Nuthall Rd.)
Newcombe Dri. *Arn* —6E **23**
New Derby Rd. *Eastw* —2H **15**
Newdigate Rd. *Watn* —6A **18**
Newdigate St. *Ilk* —3C **40**
Newdigate St. *Kimb* —1H **29**
Newdigate St. *Nott* —4E **45** (2A **4**)
Newdigate St. *W Hal* —1A **38**
Newdigate Vs. *Nott* —4E **45** (2A **4**)
New Eaton Rd. *S'fd* —6G **53**
New Farm La. *Nut* —1C **30**

Newfield Rd. *Nott* —4D **32**
Newgate Clo. *Cltn* —2G **47**
Newgate Ct. *Nott* —5D **44**
Newgate St. *Bing* —4E **51**
Newhall Gro. *W Bri* —2B **58**
Newham Clo. *Hean* —4E **15**
Newholm Dri. *Nott* —6E **57**
Newland Clo. *Bees* —3A **64**
Newland Clo. *Nott* —4A **44**
Newlands Clo. *Edw* —1B **68**
Newlands Dri. *Ged* —6H **35**
Newlands Dri. *Hean* —2C **14**
New Lawn Rd. *Ilk* —1A **40**
Newlyn Dri. *Nott* —1B **44**
Newlyn Gdns. *Nott* —1B **44**
Newmanleys Rd. *Eastw* —5A **16**
Newmanleys Rd. S. *Eastw* —4A **16**
Newman Rd. *C'tn* —3G **11**
Newmarket Rd. *Nott* —1H **31**
Newmarket Way. *Bees* —3H **63**
Newport Dri. *Nott* —6B **32**
Newquay Av. *Nott* —2C **44**
New Rd. *Bar F* —1E **75**
New Rd. *Newt* —1F **17** & 5A **6**
(in two parts)
New Rd. *Nott* —3B **44**
New Rd. *Rad T* —6F **49**
New Rd. *S'fd* —2F **53**
New Row. *Cltn* —2F **47**
Newstead Av. *Nott* —5D **34**
Newstead Av. *Rad T* —5G **49**
Newstead Clo. *Nott* —5E **43**
Newstead Ct. *Nott* —2C **34**
Newstead Dri. *W Bri* —4D **58**
Newstead Gro. *Bing* —5C **50**
Newstead Gro. *Nott* —3F **45** (1C **4**)
Newstead Ind. Est. *Arn* —6C **22**
Newstead Rd. *Long E* —2E **63**
Newstead Rd. N. *Ilk* —4H **27**
Newstead Rd. S. *Ilk* —4H **27**
Newstead St. *Sher* —4G **33**
Newstead Ter. *Huck* —3G **7**
Newstead Way. *Strel* —5D **30**
New St. *Long E* —5G **63**
New St. *Nott* —6F **33**
New St. *Red* —4A **22**
New St. *Stan* —3A **38**
New Ter. *Sand* —5D **52**
Newthorpe Comn. *Newt* —4C **16**
Newthorpe St. *Nott* —1H **57**
Newton Airfield. —1A 50
Newton Av. *Bing* —5D **50**
(in two parts)
Newton Av. *Rad T* —5G **49**
Newton Clo. *Arn* —1D **34**
Newtondale Clo. *Nott* —6B **32**
Newton Dri. *S'fd* —5G **53**
Newton Dri. *W Bri* —1G **67**
Newton Gdns. *Nwtn* —3C **50**
Newton's La. *Coss* —4D **28**
Newton St. *Bees* —5E **55**
Newton St. *Nott* —3C **56**
New Tythe St. *Long E* —6H **63**
New Va. Rd. *Colw* —4F **47**
New Windmill St. *Nott* —5B **46**
New Works Cotts. *Bur J* —1C **48**
Nicholas Rd. *Bees* —2D **54**
Nicker Hill. *Keyw* —3H **79**
Nicklaus Ct. *Nott* —5E **21**
(off Crossfield Dri.)
Nidderdale. *Nott* —5C **42**
Nidderdale Clo. *Nott* —6C **42**
Nightingale Clo. *Nott* —2G **55**
Nightingale Clo. *Nut* —1D **30**
Nightingale Way. *Bing* —6G **51**
Nile St. *Nott* —4H **45** (3G **5**)
Nine Acre Gdns. *Nott* —6F **19**
Nine Corners. *Kimb* —1H **29**
Nixon Ri. *Huck* —6D **6**
Nobel Rd. *Nott* —5A **66**
Noel St. *Kimb* —1A **29**
Noel St. *Nott* —1D **44**
No Man's La. *Ris & Sand* —4A **52**
Nook End Rd. *Hean* —4B **14**
Nook, The. *Bees* —4G **55**
(Kenilworth Rd.)
Nook, The. *Bees* —1E **65**
(Meadow La.)
Nook, The. *C'tn* —4H **11**

Nook, The. *Kimb* —2A **30**
Nook, The. *Los* —1A **14**
Nook, The. *Nott* —5E **43**
Norbett Clo. *Bees* —2C **64**
Norbett Ct. *Arn* —4C **22**
Norbett Rd. *Arn* —5C **22**
Norbreck Clo. *Nott* —4H **31**
Norburn Cres. *Nott* —4D **32**
Norbury Way. *Sand* —5C **52**
Nordean Rd. *Nott* —2C **34**
Norfolk Av. *Bees* —4A **64**
Norfolk Clo. *Huck* —6D **6**
Norfolk Pk. *Arn* —2D **34**
Norfolk Pl. *Nott* —4G **45** (3D **4**)
Norfolk Rd. *Long E* —4H **63**
Norfolk Wlk. *Sand* —6D **52**
Norland Clo. *Nott* —2A **46**
Normanby Rd. *Nott* —6C **42**
Norman Clo. *Bees* —6C **54**
Norman Clo. *Nott* —3G **45** (1E **5**)
Norman Cres. *Ilk* —4A **28**
Norman Dri. *Eastw* —3D **16**
Norman Dri. *Huck* —1E **19**
Norman Rd. *Nott* —1C **46**
Norman St. *Ilk* —4A **28**
Norman St. *Kimb* —6H **17**
Norman St. *N'fld* —3A **48**
Norman St. N. *Ilk* —3A **28**
Normanton La. *Keyw* —4H **79**
Northall Av. *Nott* —1H **31**
Northampton St. *Nott* —3A **46**
North Av. *Sand* —5C **52**
N. Church St. *Nott* —4G **45** (2D **4**)
N. Circus St. *Nott* —5F **45** (4C **4**)
Northcliffe Av. *Nott* —5D **34**
Northcote St. *Long E* —6G **63**
Northcote Way. *Nott* —2A **32**
Northdale Rd. *Nott* —2D **46**
Northdown Dri. *Bees* —1C **64**
Northdown Rd. *Nott* —3A **44**
North Dri. *Bees* —5E **55**
Northern Ct. *Nott* —3B **32**
Northern Dri. *B Vil* —1D **20**
Northern Dri. *Trow* —6F **41**
Northern Rd. *Hean* —3B **14**
Northfield Av. *Ilk* —5A **28**
Northfield Av. *Long E* —3D **72**
Northfield Av. *Rad T* —5H **49**
Northfield Cres. *Bees* —1H **63**
Northfield Rd. *Bees* —1A **64**
Northfields. *Long E* —3D **72**
North Ga. *Nott* —2B **66**
(College Dri.)
North Ga. *Nott* —6D **32**
(Radford Rd.)
North Ga. Pl. Nott —6D **32**
(off High Chu. St.)
Northgate St. *Ilk* —6A **28**
North Grn. *C'tn* —2F **11**
N. Hill Av. *Huck* —4F **7**
N. Hill Cres. *Huck* —4F **7**
Northolme Av. *Nott* —6A **20**
Northolt Dri. *Nut* —4D **30**
North Rd. *Long E* —1E **73**
North Rd. *Nott* —5E **45** (4A **4**)
North Rd. *Rud* —5F **67**
North Rd. *W Bri* —5A **58**
N. Sherwood St. *Nott*
—2F **45** (1D **4**)
Northside Wlk. *Arn* —3B **22**
North St. *Bees* —5E **55**
North St. *Ilk* —6B **28**
North St. *Kimb* —2A **30**
North St. *Lan M* —2F **15**
North St. *Newt* —3E **17**
North St. *Nott* —5A **46** (4H **5**)
Northumberland Clo. *Nott*
—3H **45** (1F **5**)
Northville Ct. *Nott* —2H **45**
Northwold Av. *W Bri* —5H **57**
Northwood Cres. *Nott* —1G **33**
Northwood Rd. *Nott* —1G **33**
Northwood St. *S'fd* —3F **53**
Norton St. *Nott* —3D **44**
(in two parts)
Norwich Gdns. *Nott* —4H **19**
Norwood Rd. *Nott* —4C **44**
Notintone Pl. *Nott* —5A **46**
Notintone St. *Nott* —5A **46**

Nottingham Airport. *Rad T* —6H **59**
Nottingham Archives. —6G 45
Nottingham Bowl. —4G 5
Nottingham Castle. —6C 4
Nottingham City Golf Course.
—4G 19
Nottingham Forest F.C. —2A 58
Nottingham Greyhound Stadium.
—6D 46
Nottingham Indoor Bowls Cen.
—2G 43
Nottingham Industrial Mus.
—6G 43
Nottingham International Clothing
Cen. *Huck* —2E **7**
Nottingham National Ice Cen.,The.
—4G 5
Nottingham Race Course. —6E 47
Nottingham Rd. *Bing* —5B **50**
Nottingham Rd. *Borr* —1A **62**
(in three parts)
Nottingham Rd. *Bul* —2B **30**
Nottingham Rd. *Bur J* —4D **36**
Nottingham Rd. *Day* —1A **34**
Nottingham Rd. *Eastw & Newt*
—3B **16**
Nottingham Rd. *Got* —6H **75**
Nottingham Rd. *Huck* —6A **8**
Nottingham Rd. *Ilk* —2B **40**
Nottingham Rd. *Keyw* —5G **79**
Nottingham Rd. *Kimb* —1A **30**
Nottingham Rd. *Long E & Bees*
—5G **63**
Nottingham Rd. *Nott* —4C **32**
(in two parts)
Nottingham Rd. *Nut* —2D **30**
Nottingham Rd. *Rad T* —1D **60**
Nottingham Rd. *S'fd* —4F **53**
Nottingham Rd. *Trow* —5E **41**
Nottingham Rd. *Wdbgh* —3F **23**
Nottingham Rd. E. *Eastw* —4D **16**
Nottingham S. & Wilford Ind. Est.
Nott —1F **67**
Nottingham Transport Heritage
Cen. —2G **77**
Nottingham University Sports Cen.
—2G **55**
Notts County F.C. —1A 58
(off County Rd.)
Nuart Rd. *Bees* —5F **55**
Nugent Gdns. *Nott* —3A **46** (1H **5**)
Nurseries, The. *Eastw* —3C **16**
Nursery Av. *Bees* —6C **54**
Nursery Av. *Sand* —6B **52**
Nursery Av. *W Hal* —2C **38**
Nursery Clo. *Huck* —1G **19**
Nursery Clo. *Rad T* —6H **49**
Nursery Dri. *Cltn* —1F **47**
Nursery Hollow. *Ilk* —3A **40**
Nursery La. *Nott* —3C **32**
Nursery Rd. *Arn* —6B **22**
Nursery Rd. *Bing* —5H **51**
Nursery Rd. *Rad T* —6H **49**
Nutbrook Cres. *Ilk* —5H **39**
Nuthall Circ. *Ilk* —5G **39**
Nuthall Gdns. *Nott* —1B **44**
Nuthall Rd. *Nott* —4H **31**

Oak Acres. *Bees* —6A **54**
Oak Apple Cres. *Ilk* —3A **40**
Oak Av. *Bing* —5G **51**
Oak Av. *Lan M* —1F **15**
Oak Av. *Rad T* —5E **49**
Oak Av. *Sand* —4C **52**
Oakdale Dri. *Bees* —1C **64**
Oakdale Rd. *Arn* —5D **22**
Oakdale Rd. *Cltn* —3F **47**
Oakdale Rd. *Nott* —3D **46**
Oak Dri. *Eastw* —3A **16**
Oak Dri. *Nut* —1B **30**
Oakenhall Av. *Huck* —4A **8**
Oakfield Clo. *Nott* —6C **42**
Oakfield Dri. *Sand* —2D **62**
Oakfield Rd. *Huck* —5H **7**
Oakfield Rd. *Nott* —6C **42**
Oakfield Rd. *S'fd* —4F **53**
Oakfields Rd. *W Bri* —2C **58**
Oak Flatt. *Bees* —6A **54**

Oakford Clo. *Nott* —5G **31**
Oak Gro. *Huck* —1H **19**
Oakham Clo. *Nott* —6D **20**
Oakham Rd. *Rud* —3H **67**
Oakham Way. *Ilk* —4H **27**
Oakington Clo. *Nott* —2F **33**
Oakland Av. *Long E* —2E **73**
Oakland Ct. *Bees* —2A **54**
Oakland Gro. *C'tn* —4H **11**
Oaklands Av. *Hean* —3E **15**
Oakland St. *Nott* —2C **44**
Oakland Ter. *Long E* —2E **73**
Oakleigh Av. *Nott* —5E **35**
Oakleigh St. *Nott* —3B **32**
Oakley M. *Nott* —1F **31**
Oakley's Rd. *Long E* —6G **63**
Oakley's Rd. W. *Long E* —1F **73**
Oak Lodge. *Bing* —5G **51**
Oak Lodge Dri. *Kimb* —6H **17**
Oakmead Av. *Nott* —1F **43**
Oakmere Clo. *Edw* —1E **69**
Oaks, The. *Nott* —4A **46** (2H **5**)
Oak St. *Nott* —6F **33**
Oak Tree Av. *Rad T* —5F **49**
Oak Tree Clo. *Huck* —1D **18**
Oak Tree Clo. *W Bri* —3C **58**
Oak Tree Dri. *Ged* —5A **36**
Oak Vw. *Nott* —3D **44**
Oakwell Cres. *Ilk* —1A **40**
Oakwell Dri. *Ilk* —1A **40**
Oakwood Dri. *Nott* —2A **44**
Oakwood Gdns. *Nut* —4D **30**
Oban Rd. *Bees* —5C **54**
Occupation Rd. *Huck* —6G **7**
Occupation Rd. *Nott* —2H **31**
Ockbrook Ct. *Ilk* —4B **28**
Ockerby St. *Nott* —1A **32**
Odeon Cinema. —4D **4**
Odesa Dri. *Bulw* —3H **31**
Ogdon Ct. *Nott* —3B **46**
Ogle Dri. *Nott* —6F **45** (6B **4**)
Ogle St. *Huck* —4G **7**
Okehampton Cres. *Nott* —1E **35**
Old Acres. *Wdbgh* —1D **24**
Old Bank Ct. *Nott* —5B **32**
Old Brickyard. *Nott* —2C **46**
Oldbury Clo. *Nott* —6B **66**
Old Chu. St. *Nott* —1C **56**
Old Coach Rd. *Nott* —3E **43**
(in three parts)
Old Coppice Side. *Hean* —5C **14**
(in two parts)
Old Derby Rd. *Eastw* —2H **15**
Old Dri. *Bees* —3D **54**
Old Epperstone Rd. *Low* —1G **25**
Old Farm Ct. *Bar F* —1E **75**
Old Farm Rd. *Nott* —5D **20**
Old Hall Clo. *C'tn* —4G **11**
Old Hall Dri. *Nott* —6H **33**
Oldham Ct. *Bees* —1C **64**
Oldknow St. *Nott* —3D **44**
Old Lenton St. *Nott* —4H **45** (3F **5**)
Old Lodge Dri. *Nott* —3H **33**
Old Main Rd. *Bul* —2G **37**
(in two parts)
Old Mnr. Clo. *Wdbgh* —1D **24**
Old Market Square. —4D **4**
Old Mkt. Sq. *Nott* —4D **4**
Old Melton Rd. *Keyw* —6G **69**
Old Mill Clo. *Bees* —3A **64**
Old Mill Clo. *B Vil* —2B **20**
Old Mill Clo. *Nott* —4D **44**
Old Mill Ct. *Bing* —4E **51**
Oldmoor Wood Nature Reserve.
—1H **41**
Old Oak Rd. *Nott* —3E **67**
Old Pk., The. *Cotg* —1F **71**
Old Pond, The. *Hean* —5E **15**
Old Rd. *Rud* —4H **67**
Old School Clo. *Nott* —5C **66**
Old St. *Nott* —4G **45** (2E **5**)
Old Tollerton Rd. *Gam* —6A **59**
Olga Rd. *Nott* —3B **46**
Olive Av. *Long E* —4F **63**
Olive Gro. *Bur J* —2F **37**
Oliver Clo. *Hean* —3F **15**
Oliver Clo. *Nott* —3E **45** (1A **4**)
Oliver Clo. *Ilk* —4G **39**
Oliver St. *Nott* —3E **45** (1A **4**)

Ollerton Rd. *Arn* —1A **22**
Olton Av. *Bees* —2F **55**
Olympus Ct. *Huck* —2D **18**
Onchan Av. *Cltn* —3G **47**
Onchan Dri. *Cltn* —3G **47**
Orange Gdns. *Nott* —1H **57**
Orby Clo. *Nott* —3B **46**
Orby Wlk. *Nott* —4B **46**
Orchard Av. *Bees* —5D **50**
Orchard Av. *Cltn* —2G **47**
Orchard Bus. Pk. *Ilk* —6H **27**
Orchard Clo. *Breas* —5B **62**
Orchard Clo. *Bur J* —2F **37**
Orchard Clo. *Nott* —3A **66**
Orchard Clo. *Rad T* —6E **49**
Orchard Clo. *Toll* —5F **69**
Orchard Clo. *W Hal* —2C **38**
Orchard Ct. *Cltn* —2G **47**
Orchard Ct. *Ged* —5F **35**
Orchard Ct. *Huck* —5G **7**
Orchard Ct. *Lan M* —2F **15**
Orchard Ct. *Nott* —1C **44**
Orchard Cres. *Bees* —6C **54**
Orchard Dri. *C'tn* —4A **12**
Orchard Gro. *Arn* —1G **33**
Orchard Pk. Ind. Est. *Sand* —5E **53**
Orchard Ri. *Hean* —3D **14**
Orchard Ri. *Lamb* —6C **24**
Orchards, The. *Ged* —6A **36**
Orchard St. *Got* —6H **75**
Orchard St. *Huck* —5G **7**
Orchard St. *Ilk* —2B **40**
Orchard St. *Kimb* —1H **29**
Orchard St. *Lan M* —2F **15**
Orchard St. *Long E* —6G **63**
Orchard St. *Newt* —4C **16**
Orchard, The. *Stan D* —3B **52**
Orchard Way. *Sand* —2C **62**
Orchid Clo. *W Bri* —1G **67**
Ordnance Clo. *Bees* —2C **64**
Orford Av. *Nott* —1D **66**
Orford Av. *Rad T* —1E **61**
Orion Clo. *Nott* —2E **43**
Orion Dri. *Nott* —2E **43**
Orlando Dri. *Cltn* —1H **47**
Orlock Wlk. *Nott* —2F **33**
Ormonde St. *Lan M* —1F **15**
Ormonde St. *Lan M* —1F **15**
Ormonde Ter. *Nott* —5G **33**
Ornsay Clo. *Nott* —4C **20**
Orpean Way. *Bees* —3G **63**
Orston Av. *Arn* —6C **22**
Orston Dri. *Nott* —5A **44**
Orston Grn. *Nott* —6B **44**
Orston Rd. E. *W Bri* —2B **58**
Orston Rd. W. *W Bri* —2A **58**
Orton Av. *Bees* —5C **54**
Ortzen Ct. *Nott* —3D **44**
Ortzen St. *Nott* —3D **44**
Orville Rd. *Nott* —2C **32**
Osborne Av. *Nott* —4G **33**
Osborne Clo. *Sand* —1D **62**
Osborne Gro. *Nott* —4G **33**
Osborne St. *Nott* —3C **44**
Osbourne Clo. *Watn* —6B **18**
Osgood Rd. *Arn* —2E **35**
Osier Rd. *Nott* —2G **57**
Osman Clo. *Nott* —2F **57**
Osmaston Clo. *Long E* —2B **72**
Osmaston St. *Nott* —6D **44**
Osmaston St. *Sand* —6E **53**
Osprey Clo. *Bing* —6F **51**
Osprey Clo. *Nott* —4A **66**
Ossington Clo. *Nott* —3G **45** (1D **4**)
Ossington St. *Nott* —3D **44**
Osterley Gro. *Nut* —5D **30**
Oulton Clo. *Arn* —1B **34**
Oulton Lodge. *Nott* —4B **20**
Oundle Dri. *Ilk* —2D **40**
Oundle Dri. *Nott* —6A **44**
Ousebridge Cres. *Cltn* —1A **48**
Ousebridge Dri. *Cltn* —1A **48**
Oval Gdns. *Nott* —1B **44**
Overdale Clo. *Long E* —1B **72**
Overdale Rd. *Nott* —5A **32**
Overstrand Clo. *Arn* —1B **34**
Owen Av. *Long E* —1A **74**
Owers Av. *Hean* —6D **14**
Owlston Clo. *Eastw* —2B **16**

Owsthorpe Clo. *Nott* —5E **21**
Owthorpe Gro. *Nott* —5F **33**
Owthorpe Rd. *Cotg* —3F **71**
Oxborough Rd. *Arn* —6G **21**
Oxbow Clo. *Nott* —2G **57**
Oxbury Rd. *Watn* —5H **17**
Oxclose La. *Arn* —1F **33**
Oxendale Clo. *W Bri* —5E **59**
Oxengate. *Arn* —1G **33**
Oxford Rd. *W Bri* —4C **58**
Oxford St. *Cltn* —6G **35**
Oxford St. *Eastw* —3B **16**
Oxford St. *Ilk* —2B **40**
Oxford St. *Long E* —5F **63**
Oxford St. *Nott* —5F **45** (4B **4**)
Oxton Av. *Nott* —3G **33**
Oxton By-Pass. *Oxt* —1B **12**
Oxton Rd. *Arn & C'tn* —4B **10**
Ozier Holt. *Colw* —6G **47**
Ozier Holt. *Long E* —1E **73**

P

Packman Dri. *Rud* —5H **67**
Paddington M. *Nott* —3C **46**
Paddock Clo. *C'tn* —4H **11**
Paddock Clo. *Nott* —2H **31**
Paddock Clo. *Rad T* —1E **61**
Paddock Farm Cotts. *Epp* —6G **13**
Paddocks, The. *Edw* —2D **68**
Paddocks, The. *Nut* —2B **30**
Paddocks, The. *Sand* —6C **52**
Paddocks Vw. *Long E* —5D **62**
Paddock, The. *Att* —3D **64**
Paddock, The. *Bing* —5E **51**
Padge Rd. *Bees* —5H **55**
Padgham Ct. *Nott* —5E **21**
Padley Ct. *Nott* —1G **31**
Padleys La. *Bur J* —2E **37**
Padstow Rd. *Nott* —1D **32**
Paget Cres. *Rud* —5G **67**
Paignton Clo. *Nott* —5H **31**
Paisley Gro. *Bees* —4C **64**
Palais, The. —3F **5**
Palatine St. *Nott* —6F **45** (6B **4**)
Palin Ct. *Nott* —2D **44**
Palin Gdns. *Rad T* —6G **49**
Palin St. *Nott* —3D **44**
Palm Cotts. *Nott* —4H **33**
Palm Ct. Ind. Cen. *Nott* —6D **32**
Palmer Av. *Huck* —3G **7**
Palmer Cres. *Cltn* —2F **47**
Palmer Dri. *S'fd* —6F **53**
Palmerston Gdns. *Nott*
(in two parts) —3G **45** (1E **5**)
Palm St. *Nott* —6D **32**
Palmwood Ct. *Nott* —3A **32**
Papplewick La. *Huck* —4H **7**
Park Av. *Aws* —2D **28**
Park Av. *Bur J* —3F **37**
Park Av. *Cltn* —1H **47**
Park Av. *Eastw* —2A **16**
Park Av. *Huck* —4F **7**
Park Av. *Ilk* —1B **40**
Park Av. *Keyw* —4F **79**
Park Av. *Kimb* —3A **30**
Park Av. *Nott* —1G **45**
Park Av. *Plum* —3H **79**
Park Av. *Stan* —3A **38**
Park Av. *W Bri* —3B **58**
Park Av. *Wdbgh* —1B **24**
Park Av. *Wd'p* —2A **34**
Park Av. E. *Keyw* —4F **79**
Park Av. W. *Keyw* —4F **79**
Park Chase. *Nott* —2H **31**
Park Clo. *Nott* —5A **34**
Park Clo. *Stan D* —3B **52**
Park Ct. *Hean* —4D **15**
Park Ct. *Nott* —2C **56**
Park Cres. *Eastw* —1B **16**
Park Cres. *Ilk* —1C **40**
Park Cres. *Nott* —5C **42**
Parkcroft Rd. *W Bri* —5B **58**
Parkdale Rd. *Nott & Cltn* —3D **46**
Park Dri. *Huck* —4F **7**
Park Dri. *Ilk* —2B **40**
Park Dri. *Nott* —5E **45** (5A **4**)
Park Dri. *Sand* —2C **62**
Parker Clo. *Arn* —5D **22**
Parker Gdns. *S'fd* —3H **53**

Parker St. *Huck* —4H **7**
Parkgate. *Huck* —2H **7**
Park Hall. *M'ley* —4B **26**
Pk. Hall La. *W Hal* —5B **26**
Parkham Rd. *Kimb* —6H **17**
Park Heights. *Nott* —6E **45** (6A **4**)
Park Hill. *Aws* —2D **28**
Park Hill. *Nott* —4E **45**
Park Ho. Gates. *Nott* —6H **33**
Parkland Clo. *Nott* —2A **66**
Parklands Clo. *Nott* —4F **21**
Park La. *Epp* —6G **13**
Park La. *Lamb* —6C **24**
Park La. *Nott* —3C **32**
Park M. *Nott* —1G **45**
Park Ravine. *Nott* —6E **45** (6A **4**)
Park Rd. *Bees* —5E **55**
(Bramcote Av.)
Park Rd. *Bees* —3H **53**
(Ewe Lamb La.)
Park Rd. *B Vil* —1C **20**
Park Rd. *C'tn* —3F **11**
Park Rd. *Cltn* —2H **47**
Park Rd. *Huck* —4F **7**
Park Rd. *Ilk* —2B **40**
Park Rd. *Nott* —6D **44**
Park Rd. *Plum* —3H **79**
Park Rd. *Rad T* —5F **49**
Park Rd. *Wd'p* —2A **34**
Park Rd. E. *C'tn* —3H **11**
Park Rd. N. *Bees* —5E **55**
Park Row. *Nott* —5F **45** (5C **4**)
Parkside. *Nott* —6E **43**
Parkside. *Plum* —3H **79**
Parkside Av. *Long E* —5D **62**
Parkside Dri. *Long E* —5D **62**
Parkside Gdns. N. *Nott* —6E **43**
Parkside Gdns. S. *Nott* —1E **55**
Parkside Ri. *Nott* —1E **55**
Parkstone Clo. *W Bri* —6G **57**
Park St. *Bees* —5E **55**
Park St. *Breas* —5B **62**
Park St. *Hean* —3B **14**
(in two parts)
Park St. *Long E* —4E **63**
Park St. *Nott* —5D **44**
Park St. *S'fd* —5E **53**
Park Ter. *Nott* —5F **45** (4B **4**)
Park Ter. *Plum* —2H **79**
Park, The. *Cotg* —1F **71**
Park Valley. *Nott* —5F **45** (5B **4**)
Park Vw. *Eastw* —4B **16**
Park Vw. *Nott* —5A **34**
Pk. View Ct. *Bees* —5D **54**
Pk. View Ct. *Nott* —4H **45** (3G **5**)
Parkview Dri. *Nott* —6E **21**
Parkway Ct. *Nott* —4D **42**
Parkwood Ct. *Nott* —2C **32**
Parkwood Cres. *Nott* —4A **34**
Parkyn Rd. *Day* —1H **33**
Parkyns St. *Rud* —6G **67**
Parliament Ter. *Nott* —4F **45** (3C **4**)
Parr Ga. *Bees* —6A **54**
Parrs, The. *Bees* —5H **55**
Parry Way. *Arn* —5D **22**
Parsons Mdw. *Colw* —5G **47**
Partridge Clo. *Bing* —6F **51**
Pasteur Ct. *Nott* —1C **56**
Pasture Clo. *Colw P* —5G **47**
Pasture La. *Long E* —1A **74**
Pasture La. *Rud* —1D **76**
Pasture Rd. *S'fd* —2F **53**
Pastures Av. *Nott* —5B **66**
Pastures, The. *C'tn* —4F **11**
Pastures, The. *Gilt* —5E **17**
Pateley Rd. *Nott* —3C **34**
Paton Rd. *Nott* —2C **32**
Patricia Dri. *Arn* —4C **22**
Patrick Rd. *W Bri* —3A **58**
Patterdale Clo. *Gam* —4E **59**
Patterdale Ct. *Bees* —6A **54**
Patterdale Rd. *Wd'p* —2B **34**
Patterson Rd. *Nott* —2D **44**
Pavilion Clo. *Nott* —2H **57**
Pavilion Rd. *Arn* —4F **21**
Pavilion Rd. *Ilk* —2A **28**
Pavilion Rd. *W Bri* —2A **58**
Paxton Gdns. *Nott* —4A **46** (2H **5**)

Payne Rd. *Bees* —2A **64**
Peache Way. *Bees* —4B **54**
Peachey St. *Nott* —4G **45** (2D **4**)
Peach St. *Hean* —4B **14**
Peacock Clo. *Rud* —1F **77**
Peacock Cres. *Nott* —3C **66**
Peacock Pl. *Ilk* —3H **27**
Peakdale Clo. *Long E* —1C **72**
Pearce Dri. *Nott* —2H **43**
Pearmain Dri. *Nott* —2B **46**
Pearson Av. *Bees* —6B **54**
Pearson Clo. *Bees* —6B **54**
Pearson Ct. *Bees* —5B **54**
Pearson Ct. *Day* —6A **22**
Pearson Ct. *N'fld* —3A **48**
Pearson St. *Nott* —5D **32**
Pear Tree Ct. *Nott* —3C **32**
Pear Tree Orchard. *Rad* —6G **67**
Peary Clo. *Nott* —1D **32**
Peas Hill Rd. *Nott* —3H **45** (1G **5**)
  (in two parts)
Peatburn Av. *Hean* —3A **14**
Peatfield Ct. *S'fd* —2F **53**
Peatfield Rd. *S'fd* —2F **53**
Peck La. *Nott* —5G **45** (4E **5**)
Pedestrian Way. *Nott* —5D **12**
Pedley St. *Ilk* —2B **40**
Pedmore Valley. *Nott* —6E **21**
Peel St. *Lan M* —2F **15**
Peel St. *Long E* —5G **63**
Peel St. *Nott* —3F **45** (1C **4**)
Peel Vs. *Nott* —5A **34**
Pelham Av. *Ilk* —6A **28**
Pelham Av. *Nott* —1F **45**
Pelham Cotts. Nott —5D **44**
  (off Pelham Cres.)
Pelham Cres. *Bees* —4H **55**
Pelham Cres. *Nott* —5D **44**
Pelham Rd. *Nott* —1F **45**
Pelham St. *Ilk* —6A **28**
Pelham St. *Nott* —5G **45** (4E **5**)
Pellham Ct. *Nott* —1F **45**
Pemberton St. *Nott* —5H **45** (5G **5**)
Pembrey Clo. *Trow* —1F **53**
Pembridge Clo. *Nott* —5B **32**
Pembroke Dri. *Nott* —6G **33**
Pembury Rd. *Nott* —4E **43**
Penarth Gdns. *Nott* —4A **34**
Penarth Ri. *Nott* —4A **34**
Pendennis Clo. *Ged* —6B **36**
Pendine Clo. *Red* —4H **21**
Pendle Cres. *Nott* —6B **34**
Pendock La. *Bradm* —5B **78**
Penhale Dri. *Huck* —6C **6**
Penhurst Clo. *Nott* —1E **67**
Penllech Clo. *Nott* —6E **21**
Penllech Wlk. *Nott* —6E **21**
Pen Moor Clo. *Long E* —1C **72**
Pennant Rd. *Nott* —5B **32**
Pennard Wlk. *Nott* —5B **66**
Penn Av. *Nott* —6C **44**
Pennhome Av. *Nott* —5G **33**
Pennie Clo. *Long E* —3F **73**
Pennine Clo. *Arn* —4F **21**
Pennine Clo. *Long E* —4C **62**
Pennyfields Boulevd. *Long E*
  —6C **62**
Pennyfoot St. *Nott* —5A **46** (5H **5**)
Penrhyn Clo. *Nott* —3H **45** (1F **5**)
Penrhyn Cres. *Bees* —1B **64**
Penrith Av. *Rad T* —5G **49**
Penrith Cres. *Nott* —5A **32**
Penshore Clo. *Nott* —4B **66**
Pentland Dri. *Arn* —3F **21**
Pentland Gdns. *Long E* —4C **62**
Pentridge Dri. *Ilk* —4G **27**
Pentwood Av. *Arn* —3B **22**
Peoples Hall Cotts. Nott
  —4H **45** (3F **5**)
  (off Heathcoat St.)
Peppercorn Gdns. *Nott* —3A **44**
Pepper La. *Stan D* —3A **52**
Pepper Rd. *C'tn* —3G **11**
Pepper St. *Nott* —5G **45** (5E **5**)
Percival Rd. *Nott* —5F **33**
Percy St. *Eastw* —3C **16**
Percy St. *Ilk* —2B **40**
Percy St. *Nott* —4B **32**
Peregrine Clo. *Lent* —5C **44**

Peri Va. Clo. *Nut* —4D **30**
Perlethorpe Av. *Ged* —5F **35**
Perlethorpe Av. *Nott* —5B **46**
Perlethorpe Clo. *Ged* —5G **35**
Perlethorpe Cres. *Ged* —5G **35**
Perlethorpe Dri. *Ged* —5F **35**
Perlethorpe Dri. *Huck* —4H **7**
Perry Gdns. *Nott* —4F **33**
Perry Gro. *Bing* —5F **51**
Perry Rd. *Nott* —5D **32**
Perth Dri. *S'fd* —2G **53**
Perth St. *Nott* —4G **45** (2E **5**)
Peters Clo. *Arn* —1E **35**
Peters Clo. *Newt* —3E **17**
Petersfield Clo. *Nott* —6D **20**
Petersgate. *Long E* —4C **62**
Petersgate Clo. *Long E* —3C **62**
Petersham M. *Nott* —6D **44**
Petersham Rd. *Long E* —3C **62**
Petworth Av. *Bees* —2H **63**
Petworth Dri. *Nott* —3D **32**
Peveril Ct. *W Bri* —4A **58**
Peveril Cres. *Long E* —2B **72**
Peveril Cres. *W Hal* —1C **38**
Peveril Dri. *Ilk* —5H **27**
Peveril Dri. *Nott* —6H **45** (6B **4**)
Peveril Dri. *W Bri* —2A **68**
Peveril M. *Nott* —5A **4**
Peveril Rd. *Bees* —3F **55**
Peveril St. *Huck* —3G **7**
Peveril St. *Nott* —3D **44**
Pewit Golf Course. —2H **39**
Philip Av. *Eastw* —4C **16**
Philip Av. *Nut* —1C **30**
Philip Gro. *Ged* —5G **35**
Phoenix Av. *Ged* —5G **35**
Phoenix Cen. *Nott* —3G **31**
Phoenix Clo. *Nott* —1F **57**
Phoenix Ct. *Eastw* —3C **16**
Phoenix Ct. *Nott* —3D **56**
Phoenix Rd. *Newt* —1D **16**
Phyllis Clo. *Huck* —2F **7**
Phyllis Gro. *Long E* —6H **63**
Piccadilly. *Nott* —1B **32**
Pickering Av. *Eastw* —3B **16**
Pieris Dri. *Nott* —4A **66**
Pierrepont Av. *Ged* —6G **35**
Pierrepont Rd. *W Bri* —3C **58**
Pilcher Ga. *Nott* —5H **45** (4E **5**)
Pilkington Rd. *Nott* —6C **34**
Pilkington St. *Nott* —6H **19**
Pimlico. *Ilk* —1A **40**
Pimlico Av. *Bees* —6B **42**
Pinder St. *Nott* —5H **45** (5G **5**)
Pine Av. *Lan M* —2E **15**
Pine Gro. *Huck* —1H **19**
Pine Hill Clo. *Nott* —4D **20**
Pinehurst Av. *Huck* —6C **6**
Pine Tree Wlk. *Eastw* —3A **16**
Pine Vw. *Nott* —3D **44**
Pinewood Av. *Arn* —4D **22**
Pinewood Gdns. *Nott* —5B **66**
Pinfold. *Bing* —5F **51**
Pinfold Clo. *Cotg* —1F **71**
Pinfold Clo. *Wdbgh* —1C **24**
Pinfold Cres. *Wdbgh* —1C **24**
Pinfold La. *Nott* —5F **57**
Pinfold La. *Shelf* —6H **37**
Pinfold La. *S'fd* —4F **53**
Pinfold Rd. *Gilt* —4E **17**
Pingle Cres. *Nott* —5D **20**
Pingle, The. *Long E* —4F **63**
Pintail Clo. *Cltn* —4B **48**
Pioneer Meadows Local Nature
  Reserve. —5H **39**
Piper Clo. *Huck* —2H **7**
Pippin Clo. *Nott* —2B **46**
Pitcairn Clo. *Nott* —2G **57**
Pit La. *Ship* —1F **27**
Plackett Clo. *S'fd* —3H **53**
Plains Farm Clo. *Nott* —4C **34**
Plains Gro. *Nott* —3C **34**
Plains Rd. *Nott* —4B **34**
Plane Clo. *Nott* —6F **19**
Plantagenet Ct. *Nott*
  —4H **45** (2G **5**)
Plantagenet St. *Nott*
  —4H **45** (2G **5**)
Plantation Clo. *Arn* —4F **21**

Plantation Rd. *Keyw* —4F **79**
Plantation Rd. *Nott* —5C **42**
Plantation Side. *Nott* —2C **44**
Plantations, The. *Long E* —5C **62**
Plant La. *Long E* —3C **72**
Platt La. *Keyw* —3H **79**
Platts Av. *Hean* —4A **14**
Player St. *Nott* —3C **44**
Playhouse. —4C **4**
Plaza Gdns. *Nott* —3D **32**
Pleasant Ct. *Nott* —2D **44**
Pleasant Row. *Nott* —2D **44**
Plough La. *Nott* —5A **46** (5H **5**)
Ploughman Av. *Wdbgh* —1D **24**
Plover Wharf. *Nott* —1E **57**
Plowman Ct. *S'fd* —5E **53**
Plowright Ct. *Nott* —2H **45**
Plowright St. *Nott* —2H **45**
Plumb Rd. *Huck* —4F **7**
Plumptre Almshouses. *Nott* —5G **5**
Plumptre Clo. *Eastw* —4B **16**
Plumptre Pl. *Nott* —5H **45** (5F **5**)
Plumptre Rd. *Lan M* —1F **15**
Plumptre Sq. *Nott* —5H **45** (5G **5**)
Plumptre St. *Nott* —5H **45** (5F **5**)
Plumptre Way. *Eastw* —4B **16**
Plumtree Gdns. *C'tn* —4H **11**
Plumtree Rd. *Cotg* —3D **70**
Plungar Clo. *Nott* —3H **43**
Podder La. *Nott* —1E **35**
Pointers Ct. *Nott* —2C **46**
Point, The. *Nott* —1H **45**
Polperro Way. *Huck* —6C **6**
Pond Hills La. *Arn* —5B **22**
Pool Mdw. *Colw* —5H **47**
Popham Ct. *Nott* —5H **45** (5F **5**)
Popham St. *Nott* —5H **45** (5F **5**)
Poplar Av. *Nott* —5E **33**
Poplar Av. *Sand* —4C **52**
Poplar Clo. *Bing* —5G **51**
Poplar Clo. *Cltn* —3F **47**
Poplar Cres. *Nut* —1A **30**
Poplar Rd. *Breas* —4B **62**
Poplars Av. *Bur J* —2G **37**
Poplars Clo. *Plum* —3H **79**
Poplars Rd. *Nott* —1D **56**
Poplars, The. *Bees* —4F **55**
Poplars, The. *Plum* —1G **79**
Poplars, The. *W Bri* —4B **58**
Poplar St. *Nott* —5H **45** (5G **5**)
Poplar Way. *Ilk* —4H **39**
Porchester Clo. *Huck* —4A **8**
Porchester Rd. *Bing* —5D **50**
Porchester Rd. *Nott* —4B **34**
Porlock Clo. *Long E* —4C **62**
Portage Clo. *Rad T* —1E **61**
Port Arthur Rd. *Nott* —5C **46**
Porter Clo. *Nott* —5A **66**
Porters Wlk. *Nott* —3C **46**
Portinscale Clo. *W Bri* —6E **59**
Portland Ct. *Nott* —2F **33**
Portland Cres. *S'fd* —5G **53**
Portland Gdns. *Huck* —4F **7**
Portland Grange. *Huck* —4E **7**
Portland Hill. *Nott* —2A **56**
Portland Leisure Cen. —1H **57**
Portland Pk. Clo. *Huck* —4F **7**
Portland Rd. *Bees* —4H **63**
Portland Rd. *Cltn* —5E **35**
Portland Rd. *Gilt* —5D **16**
Portland Rd. *Huck* —4H **7**
Portland Rd. *Ilk* —4B **28**
Portland Rd. *Long E* —3C **72**
Portland Rd. *Nott* —4E **45** (2A **4**)
Portland Rd. *W Bri* —5B **58**
Portland St. *Bees* —4G **55**
Portland St. *Day* —1H **33**
Portree Dri. *Nott* —4D **20**
Port Said Vs. *Nott* —6D **32**
Postern St. *Nott* —5F **45** (4C **4**)
Potomac M. *Nott* —5E **45** (5A **4**)
Potters Clo. *Nott* —6E **21**
Potters Ct. *Bees* —2D **54**
Potters Way. *Ilk* —1C **40**
Poulter Clo. *Nott* —2B **44**
Poulton Dri. *Nott* —6B **46**
Poultry. *Nott* —5G **45** (4E **5**)
Poultry Arc. *Nott* —4E **5**
Powers Rd. *Nott* —1B **46**

Powis St. *Nott* —6H **19**
Powtrell Clo. *Ilk* —3D **40**
Poynter Clo. *Hean* —4A **14**
Poynton St. *Nott* —4F **45** (3C **4**)
Poyser Clo. *New B* —6E **33**
Precinct, The. *Cotg* —2F **71**
Premier Rd. *Nott* —1E **45**
Prendwick Gdns. *Nott* —5F **21**
Prestwick Clo. *Nott* —5D **30**
Prestwood Dri. *Nott* —2H **43**
Pretoria Vs. *Nott* —5A **32**
Previn Gdns. *Nott* —3B **46**
Primrose Bank. *Bing* —5D **50**
Primrose Clo. *Nott* —2H **45**
Primrose Cres. *Cltn* —2H **47**
Primrose Hill. *Ilk* —4A **28**
Primrose Ri. *Newt* —5C **16**
Primrose St. *Cltn* —2H **47**
Primrose St. *Ilk* —4A **28**
Primula Clo. *Nott* —3A **66**
Prince Edward Cres. *Rad T* —1D **60**
Princess Av. *Bees* —5G **55**
Princess Clo. *Ged* —5G **35**
Princess Clo. *Hean* —3B **14**
Princess Dri. *Sand* —1D **62**
Princess St. *Long E* —5F **63**
Princes St. *Eastw* —2B **16**
Prince St. *Ilk* —3A **28**
Prince St. *Long E* —6D **63**
Prioridge. *Cotg* —3G **71**
Prior Rd. *Day* —1H **33**
Priors Clo. *Bing* —4G **51**
Priory Av. *Toll* —4E **69**
Priory Cir. *Toll* —4E **69**
Priory Clo. *Ilk* —3G **39**
Priory Ct. *Ged* —5H **35**
Priory Ct. *Nott* —6A **34**
Priory Cres. *Ged* —6H **35**
Priory M. *Nott* —1C **56**
Priory Rd. *Eastw* —4B **16**
Priory Rd. *Ged* —6H **35**
Priory Rd. *Huck* —4E **7**
Priory Rd. *W Bri* —3B **58**
Priory St. *Nott* —1C **56**
Pritchard Dri. *S'fd* —5G **53**
Private Rd. *Huck* —4E **7**
Private Rd. *Sher & Map* —5G **33**
Private Rd. *Wdbgh* —6B **12**
Private Rd. 8. *Colw I* —4H **47**
Private Rd. 5. *Colw I* —4B **48**
Private Rd. 4. *Colw I* —4B **48**
Private Rd. 1. *Colw I* —3H **47**
Private Rd. 3. *Colw I* —4A **48**
Private Rd. 2. *Colw I* —4H **47**
Prize Clo. *Nott* —4A **66**
Promenade. *Nott* —4H **45** (2G **5**)
Prospect Pl. *Nott* —6D **44**
Prospect Rd. *Cltn* —6C **34**
Prospect Rd. *Hean* —5E **15**
Prospect St. *Nott* —3C **44**
Prospect Ter. *Nott* —3C **44**
Providence Pl. *Ilk* —2A **28**
Prudhoe Ct. *Nott* —2H **57**
Pulborough Clo. *Nott* —3D **32**
Pullman Rd. *Nott* —5B **46**
Pumping Sta. Cotts. *Nott* —6C **46**
Purbeck Clo. *Long E* —5C **62**
Purbeck Dri. *W Bri* —6C **57**
Purchase Av. *Los* —3A **14**
Purdy Mdw. *Long E* —2B **72**
Pyatt St. *Nott* —2H **57**
Pygall Av. *Gor* —6G **75**
Pym Leys. *Long E* —2B **72**
Pym St. *Nott* —3B **46**
Pym Wlk. *Nott* —3A **46** (1H **5**)

Quantock Clo. *Arn* —3F **21**
Quantock Gro. *Bing* —5C **50**
Quantock Rd. *Long E* —4C **62**
Quarry Av. *Nott* —1H **31**
Quarrydale. *Huck* —2F **7**
Quarry Hill. *Stan D* —3B **52**
Quarry Hill Ind. Est. *Ilk* —4B **40**
Quarry Hill Rd. *Ilk* —4B **40**
Quayside Clo. *Nott* —2A **58**
Queen Elizabeth Rd. *Bees* —1A **64**
Queen Elizabeth Way. *Ilk* —4G **39**

Queens Av. *Ged* —5G **35**
Queens Av. *Hean* —3B **14**
Queens Av. *Ilk* —4C **40**
Queens Av. *Stan* —3A **38**
Queensberry St. *Nott* —3C **32**
Queen's Bower Rd. *Nott* —5G **21**
Queens Bri. Rd. *Nott* —6G **45**
Queensbury Av. *W Bri* —2G **67**
Queen's Ct. *Bing* —4D **50**
Queen's Dri. *Bees* —5G **55**
Queen's Dri. *Ilk* —1A **40**
Queen's Dri. *Nott* —4E **57**
Queens Dri. *Nut* —1C **30**
Queens Dri. *Sand* —1D **62**
Queen's Rd. *Bees* —6G **55**
Queens Rd. *Nott* —6G **45**
Queen's Rd. *Rad T* —5F **49**
Queen's Rd. E. *Bees* —4H **55**
Queens Rd. N. *Eastw* —3B **16**
Queens Rd. S. *Eastw* —4B **16**
Queen's Rd. W. *Bees* —1D **64**
Queen's Sq. *Eastw* —3B **16**
Queen St. *Arn* —4B **22**
Queen St. *Huck* —3F **7**
Queen St. *Ilk* —1A **40**
Queen St. *Lan M* —2G **15**
Queen St. *Long E* —6G **63**
Queen St. *Nott* —4G **45** (3D 4)
Queens Wlk. *Nott* —2F **57**
Queen Ter. *Ilk* —1A **40**
Querneby Av. *Nott* —5A **34**
Querneby Rd. *Nott* —5A **34**
Quinton Clo. *Nott* —6E **57**
Quorn Clo. *Bees* —2E **65**
Quorndon Cres. *Long E* —2F **73**
Quorn Gro. *Nott* —4E **33**
Quorn Rd. *Nott* —4E **33**

Racecourse Rd. *Nott* —5D **46**
Radbourne Rd. *Nott* —6B **46**
Radburn Ct. *S'fd* —2G **53**
Radcliffe Gdns. *Cltn* —1F **47**
Radcliffe Lodge. *Rad T* —6E **49**
Radcliffe Mt. *W Bri* —2B **58**
Radcliffe on Trent Golf Course.
—1H **61**
Radcliffe Rd. *Gam & Rad T* —3F **59**
Radcliffe Rd. *W Bri & Gam* —2A **58**
Radcliffe St. *Nott* —2H **57**
Radford Boulevd. *Nott* —3C **44**
Radford Bri. Rd. *Nott* —4A **44**
Radford Ct. *Nott* —4D **44**
Radford Ct. Ind. Est. *Nott* —4D **44**
Radford Cres. *Ged* —5G **35**
Radford Gro. La. *Nott* —3C **44**
Radford Rd. *Nott* —5C **32**
Radham Ct. *Nott* —5G **33**
Radley Sq. *Nott* —2B **32**
Radmarsh Rd. *Nott* —6C **44**
Rad Meadows. *Long E* —1E **73**
Radnor Gro. *Bing* —5C **50**
Radstock Rd. *Nott* —2C **46**
Radway Dri. *Nott* —6E **57**
Raeburn Dri. *Bees* —3G **63**
Ragdale Rd. *Nott* —5H **19**
(in two parts)
Raglan Clo. *Nott* —2H **45**
Raglan Ct. *Bees* —2G **55**
Raglan Dri. *Ged* —6H **35**
Raglan St. *Eastw* —4C **16**
Raibank Gdns. *Wd'p* —2A **34**
Railway Cotts. *Kimb* —1H **29**
Rainham Gdns. *Rud* —1G **77**
Raithby Clo. *Nott* —1E **33**
Raleigh Clo. *Ilk* —4B **28**
Raleigh Clo. *Nott* —4A **66**
Raleigh Ct. *Nott* —3E **45** (1A 4)
Raleigh M. *Nott* —4E **45** (2A 4)
Raleigh St. *Nott* —4E **45** (2A 4)
Ralf Clo. *W Bri* —1A **68**
Ramblers Clo. *Colw* —4G **47**
Ramsdale Av. *C'tn* —3F **11**
Ramsdale Cres. *Nott* —4H **33**
Ramsdale Pk. Golf Cen. —3D **10**
Ramsdale Rd. *Cltn* —6G **35**
Ramsey Clo. *S'fd* —1G **53**
Ramsey Dri. *Nott* —6F **33**
Ramsey Dri. *Arn* —1D **34**

Ranby Wlk. *Nott* —3B **46**
Rancliffe Av. *Keyw* —3F **79**
Randal Gdns. *Nott* —2D **44**
Randal St. *Nott* —2C **44**
(in two parts)
Ranelagh Gro. *Nott* —4G **43**
Ranmere Rd. *Nott* —2G **43**
Ranmoor Rd. *Ged* —6H **35**
Ranmore Clo. *Bees* —3B **54**
Rannerdale Clo. *W Bri* —5E **59**
Rannoch Ri. *Arn* —4B **22**
Rannock Gdns. *Keyw* —4H **79**
Ranskill Gdns. *Nott* —5E **21**
Ransom Dri. *Nott* —6A **34**
Ransom Rd. *Nott* —6A **34**
Ranson Rd. *Bees* —4C **64**
Ratcliffe St. *Eastw* —3B **16**
Rathgar Clo. *Nott* —5D **42**
Rathmines Clo. *Nott* —6C **44**
Rathvale Ct. *Bees* —1A **64**
Ravena Clo. *Colw* —3G **47**
Raven Av. *Nott* —3F **33**
Ravenhill Clo. *Bees* —1B **64**
Ravens Ct. *Nott* —2F **33**
Ravensdale Av. *Long E* —3D **62**
Ravensdale Dri. *Nott* —6C **42**
Ravensdene Ct. *Nott* —1G **45**
Ravensmore Rd. *Nott* —5F **33**
Ravenswood Rd. *Arn* —6B **22**
Ravensworth Rd. *Nott* —5H **19**
Rawson St. *Nott* —6D **32**
Raymede Clo. *Nott* —1D **32**
Raymede Dri. *Nott* —1C **32**
Raymond Dri. *Bing* —5G **51**
Rayneham Rd. *Ilk* —4G **27**
Rayner Ct. *Nott* —4D **44**
Raynford Av. *Bees* —1D **64**
Rays Av. *Hean* —4C **14**
Ray St. *Hean* —3B **14**
Read Av. *Bees* —5G **55**
Read Lodge. *Bees* —4G **55**
Readman Rd. *Bees* —2A **64**
Rearsby Clo. *Nott* —4D **42**
Recreation Rd. *Sand* —5D **52**
Recreation St. *Long E* —5H **63**
Recreation Ter. *S'fd* —5F **53**
Rectory Av. *Nott* —5E **43**
Rectory Ct. *Nott* —5F **43**
Rectory Ct. *W Bri* —4B **58**
Rectory Dri. *Ged* —5H **35**
Rectory Gdns. *Nott* —5F **43**
Rectory Pl. *Bar F* —1E **75**
Rectory Rd. *Breas* —5A **62**
Rectory Rd. *Colw* —4G **47**
Rectory Rd. *Cotg* —2E **71**
Rectory Rd. *W Bri* —4A **58**
Redbourne Dri. *Nott* —3A **44**
Redbridge Dri. *Nut* —4D **30**
Redcar Clo. *Ged* —5G **35**
Redcliffe Gdns. *Nott* —1G **45**
Redcliffe Rd. *Nott* —1G **45**
Redfield Rd. *Lent L* —3C **56**
Redfield Way. *Nott* —2C **56**
Redgates Ct. *C'tn* —3F **11**
Redhill Leisure Cen. —4A **22**
Redhill Lodge Dri. *Red* —4H **21**
Redhill Rd. *Arn* —4A **22**
Redland Av. *Cltn* —1H **47**
Redland Clo. *Bees* —1C **64**
Redland Clo. *Ilk* —4B **28**
Redland Dri. *Bees* —2C **64**
Redland Gro. *Cltn* —1G **47**
Red Lion Sq. *Hean* —3C **14**
Redmays Dri. *Bul* —1H **37**
Redmile Rd. *Nott* —5A **32**
Redoubt St. *Nott* —4C **44**
Redruth Clo. *Nott* —3C **42**
Redwood. *W Bri* —5F **57**
Redwood Av. *Nott* —6D **42**
Redwood Ct. *Huck* —3F **7**
Redwood Cres. *Bees* —6G **55**
Reedham Wlk. *Nott* —1C **32**
Reedman Rd. *Long E* —3D **72**
Rees Gdns. *Nott* —4E **21**
Regatta Way. *Nott* —3E **59**
Regency Ct. *Bees* —4G **55**
Regents Pk. Clo. *W Bri* —6G **57**
Regent St. *Bees* —4G **55**
Regent St. *Ilk* —2B **40**

Regent St. *Kimb* —1H **29**
Regent St. *Lan M* —2F **15**
Regent St. *Long E* —5F **63**
Regent St. *New B* —6E **33**
Regent St. *Nott* —5F **45** (4B 4)
Regent St. *Sand* —6E **53**
Regina Clo. *Rad T* —1E **61**
Reid Gdns. *Watn* —6B **18**
Reigate Clo. *Bees* —3B **54**
Reigate Dri. *Bees* —3E **65**
Reigate Rd. *Nott* —5D **32**
Rempstone Dri. *Nott* —2B **32**
Renals Way. *C'tn* —5H **11**
Renfrew Dri. *Nott* —5E **43**
Renne Hogg Rd. *Nott* —3E **57**
Repton Dri. *Ilk* —2D **40**
Repton Rd. *Long E* —3B **72**
Repton Rd. *Nott* —1B **32**
Repton Rd. *W Bri* —6A **58**
Retford Rd. *Nott* —4E **33**
Retlaw Ct. *Bees* —6D **54**
Revelstoke Av. *Nott* —4B **20**
Revelstoke Way. *Nott* —4B **20**
Revesby Gdns. *Nott* —2A **44**
Revesby Rd. *Wd'p* —2B **34**
Revill Clo. *Ilk* —5G **27**
Revill Cres. *S'fd* —3H **53**
Reydon Dri. *Nott* —6B **32**
Reynolds Dri. *Nott* —4F **43**
Rhyl Cres. *Ged* —5H **35**
Ribblesdale. *Ilk* —4G **39**
Ribblesdale Ct. *Bees* —1A **64**
Ribblesdale Rd. *Long E* —2C **72**
Ribblesdale Rd. *Nott* —2G **33**
Ribble St. *Nott* —4B **44**
Riber Clo. *Long E* —2F **73**
Riber Clo. *W Hal* —1C **38**
Riber Cres. *Nott* —2D **32**
Richard Herrod Bowls Cen., The.
—1E **47**
Richardson Clo. *Nott* —4A **66**
Richborough Pl. *Nott* —1D **54**
Richey Clo. *Arn* —6D **22**
Richmond Av. *Breas* —5C **62**
Richmond Av. *C'tn* —3A **12**
Richmond Av. *Ilk* —3B **28**
Richmond Av. *Newt* —3D **16**
Richmond Av. *Nott* —2B **46**
Richmond Av. *Sand* —1C **62**
Richmond Clo. *W Hal* —1B **38**
Richmond Ct. *Bees* —6E **55**
Richmond Dri. *Bees* —6E **55**
Richmond Dri. *Nott* —5H **33**
Richmond Dri. *Rad T* —5F **49**
Richmond Gdns. *Red* —4A **22**
Richmond Rd. *W Bri* —2B **58**
Richmond Ter. *Rad T* —6F **49**
Ricklow Ct. *Nott* —5E **21**
Rick St. *Nott* —4H **45** (3F 5)
Ridding Ter. *Nott* —3G **45** (1E 5)
Ridge La. *Rad T* —4G **49**
Ridgeway. *Hean* —5D **14**
Ridge Way. *Nott* —6C **20**
Ridgeway Dri. *Ilk* —4F **39**
Ridgewood Dri. *Bees* —1C **64**
Ridgmont Wlk. *Nott* —5B **66**
(in two parts)
Ridgway Clo. *Nott* —6E **59**
Ridgway St. *Nott* —3A **46**
Ridings, The. *Bul* —2G **37**
Ridings, The. *Keyw* —4A **80**
Ridsdale Rd. *Nott* —2G **33**
Rifle St. *Nott* —4C **44**
Rigg Hill Ct. *Nott* —2G **31**
Rigley Av. *Ilk* —6B **28**
Rigley Dri. *Nott* —6C **20**
Ring Leas. *Cotg* —3F **71**
Ringstead Clo. *W Bri* —6G **57**
Ringstead Wlk. *Nott* —5F **21**
Ringwood Cres. *Nott* —4A **44**
Ringwood Rd. *Bing* —5G **50**
Ripon Rd. *Nott* —4D **46**
Riseborough Wlk. *Nott* —4H **19**
Rise Ct. *Nott* —1F **45**
Risegate. *Cotg* —2F **71**
Risegate Gdns. *Cotg* —2F **71**
Riseholme Av. *Nott* —6C **42**
Rise Pk. Rd. *Nott* —4B **20**

Rise, The. *Nott* —4H **33**
Risley Ct. *Ilk* —4B **28**
Risley Dri. *Nott* —1F **57**
Risley La. *Breas* —2A **62**
Riste's Pl. *Nott* —5H **45** (4F 5)
Ritchie Clo. *Cotg* —3G **71**
Ritson Clo. *Nott* —3H **45** (1G 5)
Riverdale Rd. *Bees* —3D **64**
Rivergreen. *Nott* —2C **66**
Rivergreen Clo. *Bees* —1C **54**
Rivergreen Cres. *Bees* —1C **54**
Rivermead. *Cotg* —2F **71**
Rivermead. *W Bri* —4H **57**
River Rd. *Colw* —5G **47**
Riverside. *Bur J* —1F **49**
Riverside Clo. *Bees* —2H **65**
Riverside Ind. Pk. *Nott* —3E **57**
Riverside Rd. *Bees* —2G **65**
Riverside Way. *Nott* —2F **57**
Riverview. *Nott* —2H **57**
Riverway Gdns. *Nott* —1H **57**
Rivington Rd. *Bees* —3G **63**
Robbie Burns Rd. *Nott* —5F **21**
Robbinetts La. *Coss* —6F **29**
Roberts La. *Huck* —4F **7**
Roberts St. *Ilk* —3C **40**
Roberts St. *Nott* —5A **46**
Roberts Yd. *Bees* —4G **55**
Robey Clo. *L'by* —2H **7**
Robey Dri. *Eastw* —1B **16**
Robey Ter. *Nott* —2D **44**
Robina Dri. *Gilt* —5E **17**
Robinet Rd. *Bees* —6F **55**
Robin Hood Chase. *Nott* —2H **45**
Robin Hood Clo. *Eastw* —4B **16**
Robin Hood Dri. *Huck* —1E **19**
Robin Hood Ind. Est. *Nott*
—4A **46** (2H 5)
Robin Hood Rd. *Arn* —4G **21**
Robin Hood St. *Nott*
—4A **46** (3H 5)
Robin Hood Ter. *Nott*
—4H **45** (2G 5)
Robin Hood Way. *Nott* —2F **57**
Robinia Ct. *W Bri* —6C **58**
Robinson Gdns. *Nott* —4A **66**
Robinson Rd. *Nott* —4B **34**
Robinsons Hill. *Nott* —6H **19**
Robinswood Ho. *Nott* —2H **43**
Robins Wood Rd. *Nott* —3H **43**
Rob Roy Av. *Nott* —6D **44**
Roche Clo. *Arn* —6E **23**
Rochester Av. *N'fld* —2A **48**
Rochester Ct. *Nott* —1F **31**
Rochester Dri. *Long E* —6C **62**
Rochester Wlk. *Nott* —4D **66**
Rochford Ct. *Edw* —2E **69**
Rock Ct. *Nott* —4B **32**
Rock Dri. *Nott* —6E **45** (6A 4)
Rockford Ct. *S'fd* —2G **53**
Rockford Rd. *Nott* —4D **32**
Rockingham Gro. *Bing* —5C **50**
Rockley Av. *Newt* —4C **16**
Rockley Av. *Rad T* —5F **49**
Rockley Clo. *Huck* —5C **6**
Rockleys Vw. *Low* —3G **25**
Rock Side. *Kimb* —1H **29**
Rockside Gdns. *Huck* —4E **7**
Rock St. *Nott* —5G **19**
Rockwell Ct. *S'fd* —4G **53**
Rockwood Cres. *Huck* —5D **6**
Rockwood Wlk. *Huck* —5E **7**
Rodel Ct. *Nott* —3H **45** (1F 5)
Roden St. *Nott* —4A **46** (3H 5)
Roderick St. *Nott* —3B **32**
Rodney Rd. *W Bri* —5C **58**
Rodney Way. *Ilk* —4B **28**
Rodwell Clo. *Nott* —3A **44**
Roebuck Clo. *Nott* —5F **21**
Roecliffe. *W Bri* —1A **68**
Roehampton Dri. *Trow* —1F **53**
Roe Hill. *Wdbgh* —5C **12**
(in two parts)
Roe La. *Wdbgh* —1C **24**
Roes La. *C'tn* —4A **12**
Roker Clo. *Nott* —6G **31**
Roland Av. *Nut* —3E **31**
Roland Av. *Wilf* —4F **57**
Rolleston Clo. *Huck* —6D **6**

Rolleston Cres. *Watn* —4H **17**
Rolleston Dri. *Arn* —6C **22**
Rolleston Dri. *Newt* —5C **16**
Rolleston Dri. *Nott* —5D **44**
Roman Dri. *Nott* —3C **32**
Romans Ct. *Nott* —5C **32**
Romilay Clo. *Bees* —2G **55**
Romney Av. *Nott* —1D **54**
Romorantin Pl. *Long E* —6G **63**
Rona Ct. *Nott* —2C **32**
Ronald St. *Nott* —4D **44**
Rookery Gdns. *Arn* —5B **22**
Rookwood Clo. *Bees* —5E **55**
Roosa Clo. *Nott* —2F **31**
Roosevelt Av. *Long E* —2E **73**
Roper Av. *Hean* —5C **14**
Ropewalk Ind. Est. *Ilk* —6C **28**
Ropewalk, The. *Hean* —5D **14**
Ropewalk, The. *Ilk* —6C **28**
Ropewalk, The. *Nott* —4E **45** (3A **4**)
Ropewalk, The. *Stan C* —6A **26**
Ropsley Cres. *W Bri* —2C **58**
Roscoe Av. *Nott* —3H **79**
Roseacre. *Bees* —6G **55**
Rose Ash La. *Nott* —5F **21**
Rose Av. *Ilk* —5A **28**
Rosebank Dri. *Arn* —4D **22**
Roseberry Gdns. *Huck* —5A **8**
Roseberry St. *Nott* —3C **32**
Rosebery Av. *W Bri* —2A **58**
Rose Clo. *Nott* —2H **45**
Rose Cotts. *Bur J* —2E **37**
Rose Ct. *Long E* —4D **62**
Rosecroft Clo. *Nott* —1G **33**
Rosedale Clo. *Long E* —1D **72**
Rosedale Dri. *Nott* —5B **42**
Rosedale Rd. *Nott* —3E **47**
Rosegarth Wlk. *Nott* —3B **32**
Rose Gro. *Bees* —6H **55**
Rose Gro. *Keyw* —3H **79**
Rosegrove Av. *Arn* —4B **22**
Rose Hill. *Keyw* —4G **79**
Roseland Clo. *Keyw* —5G **79**
Roseleigh Av. *Nott* —5D **34**
Rosemary Clo. *Nott* —6E **31**
Roseneath Av. *Nott* —4C **20**
Rosetta Rd. *Nott* —6D **32**
(in two parts)
Rosewall Ct. *Arn* —6D **22**
Rosewood Cres. *Hean* —3F **15**
Rosewood Gdns. *Nott* —6F **19**
Rosewood Gdns. *W Bri* —2G **67**
Roslyn Av. *Ged* —5G **35**
Rossell Dri. *S'fd* —6F **53**
Rossendale. *Ilk* —3A **28**
Rossett Clo. *Gam* —5F **59**
Rossington Rd. *Nott* —4B **46**
Ross La. *Lamb* —6C **24**
Rosslyn Dri. *Huck* —3A **8**
Rosslyn Dri. *Nott* —1G **33**
Rosthwaite Clo. *W Bri* —6E **59**
Rothbury Av. *Trow* —1F **53**
Rothbury Gro. *Bing* —4C **50**
Rothesay Av. *Nott* —4D **44**
Rothley Av. *Nott* —4B **46**
Rothwell Clo. *Nott* —1E **67**
Roughs Woods. *Huck* —1D **18**
Roundwood Rd. *Arn* —6G **21**
Rowan Av. *S'fd* —1G **53**
Rowan Clo. *Bing* —5G **51**
Rowan Clo. *C'tn* —4F **11**
Rowan Clo. *Ilk* —4B **40**
Rowan Ct. *Nut* —1B **30**
Rowan Dri. *Keyw* —5A **80**
Rowan Dri. *Nott* —1E **67**
Rowan Gdns. *Nott* —6F **19**
Rowan Wlk. *Nott* —1C **46**
Rowe Gdns. *Nott* —1B **32**
Rowland Av. *Map* —5C **34**
Rowland M. *Nott* —2A **46**
Rowsley Av. *Long E* —2C **72**
Roxley Ct. *Bees* —4E **55**
Roxton Ct. *Kimb* —6H **17**
Royal Av. *Long E* —5C **62**
Royal Cen. *Nott* —4F **45** (3D **4**)
Royal Concert Hall. —3D **4**
Royal M. *Bees* —2C **64**
Royal Standard Ct. *Nott*
—5F **45** (5C **4**)

Roy Av. *Bees* —1H **65**
Royce Av. *Huck* —1E **19**
Royston Clo. *Nott* —2F **57**
Ruby Paddocks. *Kimb* —2H **29**
Ruddington Fields Bus. Pk. *Rud*
—2H **77**
Ruddington Framework Knitters
Mus. —1G **77**
Ruddington Grange Golf Course.
—4G **67**
Ruddington La. *Nott & Wilf* —5F **57**
Ruddington Village Mus. —6G **67**
Rudge Clo. *Nott* —4F **43**
Ruffles Av. *Arn* —2D **34**
Rufford Av. *Bees* —3A **54**
Rufford Av. *Ged* —5F **35**
Rufford Clo. *Huck* —5A **8**
Rufford Gro. *Bing* —5D **50**
Rufford Rd. *Long E* —3D **72**
Rufford Rd. *Nott* —4G **33**
Rufford Rd. *Rud* —6H **67**
Rufford Wlk. *Nott* —6H **19**
Rufford Way. *W Bri* —5D **58**
Ruffs Dri. *Huck* —6D **6**
Rugby Clo. *Nott* —6C **20**
Rugby Rd. *W Bri* —6G **57**
Rugby Ter. *Nott* —2D **44**
Rugeley Av. *Long E* —6H **63**
Ruislip Clo. *Kimb* —6G **17**
Runcie Clo. *Cotg* —3F **71**
Runnymede Ct. *Bees* —6G **55**
Runnymede Ct. *Nott* —4E **45** (2A **4**)
Runswick Dri. *Arn* —5B **22**
Runswick Dri. *Nott* —4G **43**
Runton Dri. *Nott* —3D **32**
Rupert Rd. *Bing* —5D **50**
Rupert St. *Ilk* —6C **28**
Ruscombe Pl. *Nott* —3H **45**
Rushcliffe Arena. —5H **57**
Rushcliffe Av. *Cltn* —1F **47**
Rushcliffe Av. *Rad T* —6F **49**
Rushcliffe Country Pk. —2G **77**
Rushcliffe Ct. *Nott* —1B **32**
Rushcliffe Ri. *Nott* —2H **33**
Rushcliffe Rd. *Huck* —6E **7**
Rushes, The. *Got* —6H **75**
Rushford Dri. *Nott* —5C **42**
Rush Leys. *Long E* —2F **73**
Rushmere Wlk. *Arn* —2B **34**
Rushton Gdns. *Nott* —2B **46**
Rushworth Av. *W Bri* —3A **58**
Rushworth Clo. *Nott* —2A **46**
(in two parts)
Rushworth Ct. *W Bri* —3A **58**
Rushy Clo. *Nott* —4D **42**
Rushy La. *Sand & Ris* —5A **52**
Ruskin Av. *Bees* —1D **64**
Ruskin Av. *Long E* —1C **72**
Ruskin Clo. *Day* —6H **21**
Ruskin St. *Nott* —4C **44**
Russell Av. *Nott* —4F **43**
Russell Ct. *Long E* —4F **63**
Russell Cres. *Nott* —4F **43**
Russell Dri. *Nott* —4E **43**
Russell Gdns. *Bees* —3C **64**
Russell Pl. *Nott* —4F **45** (3C **4**)
Russell Rd. *Nott* —1D **44**
Russell St. *Long E* —4F **63**
Russell St. *Nott* —3E **45** (1A **4**)
Russet Av. *Cltn* —2G **47**
Russley Rd. *Bees* —3A **54**
Ruth Dri. *Arn* —4C **22**
Rutherford Ho. *Nott* —2B **56**
Ruthwell Gdns. *Nott* —3E **21**
Rutland Av. *Bees* —3A **64**
Rutland Ct. *Man I* —6H **27**
Rutland Gro. *Sand* —6E **53**
Rutland Rd. *Bing* —5F **51**
Rutland Rd. *Ged* —4F **35**
Rutland Rd. *W Bri* —2B **58**
Rutland St. *Ilk* —6B **28**
Rutland Ter. *Ilk* —5B **28**
Rutland Ter. *Kimb* —2A **30**
Rutland Vs. *Nott* —5B **46**
Rydal Av. *Long E* —3D **62**
Rydal Dri. *Bees* —3D **54**
Rydal Dri. *Huck* —3F **7**
Rydale Rd. *Nott* —2G **33**

Rydal Gdns. *W Bri* —6C **58**
Rydal Gro. *Nott* —4C **32**
Ryder St. *Nott* —3B **32**
Ryecroft St. *S'fd* —2G **53**
Ryehill Clo. *Nott* —1H **57**
Ryehill St. *Nott* —1H **57**
Ryeland Gdns. *Nott* —1G **57**
Ryemere Clo. *Eastw* —3A **16**
Rye St. *Nott* —6D **32**
Rylands Clo. *Bees* —1H **65**
Rylands Ct. *Bees* —6G **55**
Ryton Ct. *Nott* —2H **57**
Ryton Sq. *Nott* —6H **31**

Sabina St. *Nott* —4H **45** (1G **5**)
Saddlers Yd. *Plum* —6G **69**
Saddleworth Ct. *Nott* —3G **45**
Saffron Gdns. *Nott* —1F **57**
St Agnes Clo. *Nott* —1D **42**
St Aidans Ct. *Nott* —3C **32**
St Albans Clo. *Long E* —2G **73**
St Albans Ct. *Arn* —3F **21**
St Albans M. *Nott* —1B **32**
St Albans Rd. *Arn* —6H **21**
St Albans Rd. *B Vil* —1C **20**
St Albans Rd. *Nott* —5A **20**
St Albans St. *Sher* —4G **33**
St Andrew Clo. *Got* —6H **75**
St Andrews Clo. *Huck* —3G **7**
St Andrews Clo. *Nott* —6A **20**
St Andrews Ct. *Nott* —6B **20**
St Andrew's Dri. *Ilk* —1A **40**
St Andrew's Rd. *Nott* —2F **45**
St Ann's Gdns. *Nott* —2A **46**
St Ann's Hill. *Nott* —2G **45**
St Ann's Hill Rd. *Nott* —2G **45**
St Ann's St. *Nott* —4G **45** (2E **5**)
St Ann's Valley. *Nott* —3A **46**
St Ann's Way. *Nott* —3G **45** (1E **5**)
St Ann's Well Rd. *Nott*
—4H **45** (2F **5**)
St Anthony Ct. *Nott* —1C **56**
St Augustines Clo. *Nott* —6E **33**
St Austell Dri. *Nott* —6F **57**
St Austins Ct. *Cltn* —1H **47**
St Austins Dri. *Cltn* —1H **47**
St Barnabas R.C. Cathedral.
—3B **4**
St Bartholomew's Rd. *Nott* —2B **46**
St Catherines St. *Rad T* —1E **61**
St Cecilia Gdns. *Nott* —3H **45**
St Chads. *Cltn* —2H **47**
St Chad's Rd. *Nott* —4A **46**
St Christopher St. *Nott* —5B **46**
St Cuthbert's Rd. *Nott* —4A **46**
St Ervan Rd. *Nott & Wilf* —5F **57**
St Georges Ct. *Huck* —3G **7**
St Georges Dri. *Bees* —3H **63**
St Georges Dri. *Nott* —1G **57**
St Helen's Cres. *Bur J* —3F **37**
St Helens Cres. *Trow* —5E **41**
St Helen's Gro. *Bur J* —4E **37**
St Helens Rd. *W Bri* —5B **58**
St Helen's St. *Nott* —4E **45** (3A **4**)
St Helier. *Nott* —5E **45** (5A **4**)
St James Av. *Ilk* —2C **40**
St James Ct. *Huck* —3G **7**
St James Ct. *Nott* —5D **34**
St James Ct. *Sand* —2D **62**
St James's St. *Nott* —5F **45** (5C **4**)
(in two parts)
St James's Ter. *Nott* —5F **45** (5C **4**)
St James St. *S'fd* —5E **53**
St James Ter. *S'fd* —5E **53**
St John's Ct. *Cltn* —2F **47**
St John's Cres. *Huck* —6A **8**
St John's Rd. *Rud* —6D **67**
St Johns St. *Long E* —6F **63**
St Judes Av. *Nott* —5H **33**
St Laurence Ct. *Long E* —1G **73**
St Lawrence Boulevd. *Rad T*
—1D **60**
St Lawrence Clo. *Hean* —3D **14**
St Leonards Dri. *Nott* —5F **43**
St Leven Clo. *Nott* —1D **42**
St Lukes Clo. *W Bri* —6D **58**
St Luke's St. *Nott* —4A **46** (3H **5**)

St Lukes Way. *Bur J* —1F **49**
St Margaret's Av. *Nott* —1A **44**
St Mark's St. *Nott* —4H **45** (2F **5**)
St Martins Clo. *Nott* —1E **43**
St Martin's Gdns. *Nott* —1D **42**
St Martin's Rd. *Nott* —1E **43**
St Mary's Av. *Ged* —5G **35**
St Mary's Clo. *Arn* —4B **22**
St Mary's Clo. *Bees* —4D **64**
St Mary's Cres. *Rud* —6G **67**
St Marys Ga. *Nott* —5H **45** (4F **5**)
St Mary's Pl. *Nott* —5H **45** (4F **5**)
St Marys Rd. *Bing* —4F **51**
St Mary St. *Ilk* —1A **40**
St Marys Way. *Huck* —3F **7**
St Matthias Rd. *Nott* —3A **46**
St Mawes Av. *Nott* —5F **57**
St Michael's Av. *Ged* —5G **35**
St Michael's Av. *Nott* —1D **42**
St Michaels Sq. *Bees* —3B **54**
St Michaels Vw. *Huck* —2H **7**
St Nicholas Clo. *Arn* —6A **22**
St Nicholas St. *Nott* —5H **45** (5D **4**)
St Norbert Dri. *Ilk* —4G **39**
St Patrick's Rd. *Huck* —4F **7**
St Patrick's Rd. *Nut* —1B **30**
St Pauls Av. *Nott* —2D **44**
St Paul's St. *Nott* —4B **44**
St Pauls Ter. *Nott* —2D **44**
St Peters Chambers. *Nott* —4E **5**
St Peter's Chu. Wlk. *Nott*
—5G **45** (4E **5**)
St Peters Cres. *Rud* —6G **67**
St Peter's Ga. *Nott* —5G **45** (4E **5**)
St Peter's Sq. *Nott* —4E **5**
St Peters St. *Nott* —4C **44**
St Saviours Gdns. *Nott* —1H **57**
St Stephens Av. *Nott* —5B **46**
St Stephen's Rd. *Nott* —5A **46**
St Vincent Clo. *Long E* —1G **73**
St Wilfrid's Rd. *W Hal* —2C **38**
St Wilfrid's Sq. *C'tn* —4H **11**
Salamander Clo. *Cltn* —5F **35**
Salcey Dri. *Trow* —1F **53**
Salcombe Cir. *Red* —4H **21**
Salcombe Clo. *Newt* —4E **17**
Salcombe Cres. *Rud* —5H **67**
Salcombe Dri. *Red* —4H **21**
Salcombe Rd. *Nott* —4D **32**
Salford Gdns. *Nott* —4H **45** (2G **5**)
Salisbury Clo. *Nott* —5A **34**
Salisbury Sq. *Nott* —5C **44**
Salisbury St. *Bees* —4G **55**
Salisbury St. *Long E* —6G **63**
Salisbury St. *Nott* —5C **44**
(in two parts)
Salmon Clo. *Nott* —6F **19**
Salop St. *Day* —6H **21**
Saltburn Rd. *Nott* —3G **43**
Saltby Grn. *W Bri* —2F **67**
Salterford Av. *C'tn* —3H **11**
Salterford Rd. *Huck* —6E **7**
Saltford Clo. *Ged* —5H **35**
Salthouse Clo. *Bees* —3G **55**
Salthouse Ct. *Bees* —4G **55**
Salthouse La. *Bees* —3G **55**
Saltney Way. *Nott* —2E **67**
Samson Ct. *Rud* —5F **67**
Sandale Clo. *Gam* —5E **59**
Sandays Clo. *Nott* —2G **57**
Sandby Ct. *Bees* —6C **54**
(in two parts)
Sanders Clo. *Ilk* —5G **27**
Sandfield Ct. *Nott* —1G **31**
Sandfield Rd. *Arn* —1B **34**
Sandfield Rd. *Bees* —3G **63**
Sandfield Rd. *Nott* —5D **44**
Sandford Av. *Long E* —6G **63**
Sandford Rd. *Nott* —5B **34**
Sandgate. *Bees* —2D **54**
Sandham Wlk. *Nott* —2C **66**
Sandhurst Dri. *Bees* —3C **64**
Sandhurst Dri. *Rud* —1F **77**
Sandiacre Friesland Sports Cen.
—6B **52**
Sandiacre Rd. *S'fd* —5E **53**
Sandon St. *Nott* —6E **33**
Sandown Rd. *Bees* —2H **63**

Sandpiper Way. *Lent* —5C **44**
Sandringham Av. *W Bri* —3A **58**
Sandringham Cres. *Nott* —4C **42**
Sandringham Dri. *Bees* —2C **54**
Sandringham Dri. *Hean* —1C **14**
Sandringham Pl. *Huck* —3H **7**
Sandringham Pl. *Ilk* —4H **39**
Sandringham Rd. *Nott* —5B **46**
Sandringham Rd. *Sand* —2D **62**
Sands Clo. *Colw* —4G **47**
Sandside. *Cotg* —3F **71**
Sandwell Clo. *Long E* —1C **72**
Sandyford Clo. *Nott* —4A **32**
Sandy La. *Bees* —1D **54**
Sandy La. *Hol P* —1B **60**
Sandy La. *Huck* —4G **7**
Sanger Clo. *Nott* —5A **66**
Sanger Gdns. *Nott* —5A **66**
Sankey Dri. *Nott* —6G **19**
Sapele Clo. *Ged* —5A **36**
Sargent Gdns. *Nott* —3B **46**
Saskatoon Clo. *Rad T* —1E **61**
Saunby Clo. *Arn* —6D **22**
Saunten Clo. *Edw* —1E **69**
Savages Rd. *Rud* —5G **67**
Savages Row. *Rud* —5G **67**
Saville Clo. *S'fd* —3G **53**
Saville Rd. *Wd'p* —2B **34**
Savoy Workshops. *Lent* —6D **44**
Sawley Bridge Marina. —5C **72**
Sawley Rd. *Breas* —6A **62**
Sawley Rd. *Dray* —2A **72**
Sawmand Clo. *Long E* —1E **73**
Sawmills Ind. Pk. *Los* —2B **14**
Saxelby Gdns. *Nott* —5H **19**
Saxondale Dri. *Nott* —2B **32**
Saxon Grn. *Nott* —6C **44**
Saxon Way. *Cotg* —4F **71**
Saxton Av. *Hean* —3D **14**
Saxton Clo. *Bees* —4H **55**
Scafell Clo. *W Bri* —6E **59**
Scafell Way. *Nott* —6B **66**
Scalby Clo. *Eastw* —3H **15**
Scalford Dri. *Nott* —5A **44**
Scarborough Av. *Ilk* —1H **39**
Scarborough St. *Nott*
　　　　—4H **45** (2G **5**)
Scarf Wlk. *Nott* —4F **57**
Scargill Av. *Newt* —4D **16**
Scargill Clo. *Newt* —4D **16**
Scargill Rd. *W Hal* —1C **38**
Scargill Wlk. *Eastw* —2D **16**
Sceptre St. *Nott* —5G **33**
School Av. *Huck* —1D **18**
School Clo. *Nott* —2H **57**
School La. *Bees* —1C **64**
School La. *Bing* —4E **51**
School La. *Stan D* —4B **52**
School Sq. *W Hal* —2C **38**
School Wlk. *B Vil* —1C **20**
School Way. *Nott* —2H **57**
Science Rd. *Nott* —2B **56**
Scotholme Av. *Nott* —1D **44**
Scotland Bank. *Cotg* —2F **71**
Scotland Rd. *Nott* —4D **32**
Scott Av. *Bees* —5F **55**
Scott Clo. *Nott* —2F **31**
Scottsdale Wlk. *Nott* —6A **34**
Scrimshire La. *Cotg* —2E **71**
Script Dri. *Nott* —3C **32**
Scrivelsby Gdns. *Bees* —1D **64**
Scrooby Row. *Nott* —5E **21**
Seaburn Rd. *Bees* —2G **63**
Seaford Av. *Nott* —4H **43**
Seaford Way. *Ilk* —2B **28**
Seagrave Ct. *Nott* —6A **22**
Seagrave Rd. *Nott* —6D **30**
Seamer Rd. *Kimb* —6H **17**
Seatallan Clo. *W Bri* —5E **59**
Seathwaite Clo. *Nott* —1E **69**
Seatoller Clo. *W Bri* —6E **59**
Seaton Cres. *Nott* —6G **31**
Second Av. *Bees* —3E **55**
Second Av. *Cltn* —2E **47**
Second Av. *Ged* —6H **35**
Second Av. *Ilk* —2B **40**
Second Av. *Lent* —5A **56**
Second Av. *Nott* —1F **45**

Second Av. *Ris* —1B **62**
Sedgebrook Clo. *Nott* —4A **32**
Sedgeley Rd. *Toll* —5F **69**
Sedgemoor Rd. *Long E* —2G **73**
Sedgewood Gro. *Nott* —2C **66**
Sedgley Av. *Nott* —4B **46**
Sedgwick St. *Lan M* —2F **15**
Sedley Av. *Nut* —1C **30**
Seely Av. *C'tn* —3F **11**
Seely Rd. *Nott* —4D **44**
Sefton Av. *S'fd* —3G **53**
Sefton Dri. *Nott* —6H **33**
Selby Clo. *Bees* —2G **63**
Selby La. *Keyw* —5G **79**
Selby Rd. *W Bri* —5B **58**
Selhurst Ct. *Nott* —2D **44**
Selhurst St. *Nott* —2D **44**
Selkirk Way. *Nott* —6F **33**
Sellars Av. *Rud* —1G **77**
Sellers Wood Dri. *Blen I* —5F **19**
Sellers Wood Dri. W. *Bulw* —6E **19**
Seller's Wood Nature Reserve.
　　　　—6E **19**
Selside Ct. *Bees* —1A **64**
Selston Dri. *Nott* —6A **44**
Selwyn Clo. *Nott* —2C **32**
Senna Ct. *Bees* —4H **55**
Serina Ct. *W Bri* —4A **58**
Serlby Ri. *Nott* —3B **46**
Serlby Rd. *Newt* —2C **16**
Service Rd. *Arn* —6G **21**
Seven Oaks Cres. *Bees* —2B **54**
Seven Oaks Rd. *Ilk* —2C **52**
Seventh Av. *Lent* —6A **56**
Severals. *S'fd* —4H **53**
Severn St. *Nott* —6H **19**
Seymour Rd. *Eastw* —4B **16**
Seymour Rd. *Huck* —6E **7**
Seymour Rd. *W Bri* —3D **58**
Seymour St. *Nott* —4A **46**
Shackleton Clo. *Nott* —5D **30**
Shacklock Clo. *Arn* —3E **21**
Shadwell Gro. *Rad T* —6E **49**
Shady La. *Bees* —3D **64**
Shaftesbury Av. *Bur J* —2G **37**
Shaftesbury Av. *Long E* —3D **72**
Shaftesbury Av. *Sand* —6C **52**
Shaftesbury St. *New B* —6E **33**
Shakespeare Clo. *Colw* —4G **47**
Shakespeare Av. *Long E* —4E **63**
Shakespeare St. *Nott*
　　　　—4F **45** (2C **4**)
Shakespeare Vs. *Nott*
　　　　—4G **45** (2D **4**)
Shaldon Clo. *Nott* —4D **20**
Shandwick Clo. *Arn* —3D **22**
Shanklin Dri. *S'fd* —4F **53**
Shanwell Clo. *Nott* —5D **30**
Shardale Gdns. *Nott* —3B **32**
Sharnford Way. *Bees* —5B **42**
Sharp Clo. *Ilk* —3G **39**
Sharp Clo. *Long E* —1E **73**
Sharphill Rd. *Edw* —1D **68**
Shaw Cres. *Huck* —1E **19**
Shaw Gdns. *Nott* —5A **66**
Shaw St. *Rud* —6G **67**
Shaw St. E. *Ilk* —3C **40**
Shaw St. W. *Ilk* —3C **40**
Shearing Clo. *Ged* —6A **36**
Shearing Hill. *Ged* —6A **36**
Sheepfold La. *Rud* —1G **77**
Sheet Stores Ind. Est. *Long E*
　　　　—2F **73**
Shelby Clo. *Lent* —5C **44**
Sheldon Clo. *Long E* —2D **62**
Sheldon Rd. *Los* —1A **14**
Shelford Clo. *Bees* —1D **64**
Shelford Clo. *Rad T* —5G **49**
Shelford Cres. *Bur J* —2G **37**
Shelford Dri. *Bing* —5D **50**
Shelford Ri. *Nott* —3C **46**
Shelford Rd. *Ged* —4E **35**
Shelford Rd. *Nwtn* —1A **50**
Shelford Rd. *Rad T & Shelf* —6F **49**
Shellburne Clo. *Nott* —5C **20**
Shelley Av. *Nott* —2C **66**
Shelley Clo. *Huck* —5D **6**
Shelley Clo. *Nut* —1B **30**
Shelley Rd. *Day* —6H **21**

Shelt Hill. *Wdbgh* —1D **24**
Shelton Av. *Huck* —1A **20**
Shelton Gdns. *Nott* —6F **67**
Shelton St. *Nott* —3G **45** (1E **5**)
Shenfield Gdns. *Nott* —4B **20**
Shepard Clo. *Nott* —1F **31**
Shepherd Ct. *Huck* —1D **18**
Shepherds Clo. *Nott* —2G **43**
Shepherds Wood Dri. *Nott* —2A **44**
Shepton Clo. *Ilk* —4H **27**
Shepton Cres. *Nott* —5H **31**
Sheraton Dri. *Nott* —6E **43**
Sherborne Rd. *Nott* —6G **31**
Sherborne Rd. *W Bri* —6B **58**
Sherbrook Av. *Day* —1H **33**
Sherbrooke Clo. *C'tn* —3G **11**
Sherbrooke Rd. *Nott* —6F **33**
Sherbrooke Ter. *Nott* —6F **33**
Sherbrook Rd. *Day* —1G **33**
Sherbrook Ter. *Day* —1H **33**
Sheridan Ct. *Nott* —1D **4**
Sheridan Ct. *S'fd* —1G **53**
Sheriffs La. *Bees* —3G **63**
Sheriffs Way. *Nott* —1G **57**
Sheringham Clo. *Arn* —1B **34**
Sherman Dri. *Bees* —3C **64**
Sherrington Clo. *Nott* —5A **66**
Sherwin Clo. *Nott* —3G **45** (1D **4**)
Sherwin Gro. *Nott* —6C **44**
Sherwin Rd. *Nott* —6C **44**
Sherwin Rd. *S'fd* —2H **53**
Sherwin Wlk. *Nott* —3G **45** (1D **4**)
Sherwood Av. *C'tn* —3F **11**
Sherwood Av. *Nott* —4H **33**
Sherwood Ct. *Bees* —2C **64**
Sherwood Gro. *C'tn* —3H **11**
Sherwood Gro. *Bing* —5D **50**
Sherwood Lodge Dri. *Arn* —1G **9**
Sherwood Ri. *Eastw* —4B **16**
Sherwood Ri. *Nott* —6E **33**
Sherwood Ri. *Huck* —5A **8**
Sherwood Va. *Nott* —5H **33**
Sherwood Wlk. *L'by* —1G **7**
Shilling Way. *Long E* —6C **62**
Shipley Comn. La. *Ilk* —3G **27**
Shipley Country Pk. & Vis. Cen.
　　　　—6C **14**
Shipley Ct. *Ilk* —6H **27**
Shipley Ga. *Eastw* —6A **16**
Shipley Hall. —2D **26**
(remains of)
Shipley La. *Hean* —2D **26**
Shipley Ri. *Cltn* —2G **47**
Shipley Rd. *Nott* —5F **31**
Shipstone St. *Ilk* —3D **40**
Shipstone St. *Nott* —1D **44**
Shipstones Yd. *Nott* —5A **20**
Shirebrook Clo. *Nott* —4A **32**
Shire Hall & Galleries. —5F **5**
Shirley Ct. *Bees* —3A **64**
Shirley Cres. *Breas* —5A **62**
Shirley Dri. *Arn* —6D **22**
Shirley Rd. *Nott* —1G **45**
Shirley St. *Long E* —3C **72**
Shores Wood Clo. *Nott* —5F **21**
Shortcross Av. *Nott* —3B **34**
Short Hill. *Nott* —5H **45** (5F **5**)
Short Stairs. *Nott* —5H **45** (5G **5**)
Shortwood Av. *Huck* —6F **7**
Shortwood Clo. *Nott* —5H **45** (5F **5**)
Shorwell Rd. *Nott* —2E **47**
Shotton Dri. *Arn* —3C **22**
Showcase Cinemas. —3C **56**
Shrewsbury Rd. *Nott* —5C **46**
Shrimpton Ct. *Rud* —1H **77**
Sibson Wlk. *Arn* —3B **22**
Sidlaw Ri. *Arn* —3F **21**
Sidmouth Clo. *Keyw* —3G **79**
Sidney Rd. *Bees* —4E **55**
Sidney St. *Kimb* —1H **29**
Sidney St. *Long E* —1F **73**
Silbury Clo. *Nott* —6B **66**
Silver Birch Clo. *Nott* —3H **31**
Silverdale. *S'fd* —6G **53**
Silverdale Rd. *Nott* —5D **32**
Silverhill Clo. *Strel* —5D **30**
Silverhow Clo. *W Bri* —6E **59**
Silverwood Rd. *Bees* —5E **55**
Simkin Av. *Nott* —6C **34**

Simone Gdns. *Nott* —3D **66**
Simons Ct. *Bees* —2D **54**
Sinclair Clo. *Hean* —5B **14**
Sir John Robinson Way. *Arn*
　　　　—6H **21**
Sisley Av. *S'fd* —5G **53**
Sixth Av. *Lent* —6A **56**
Skeavingtons La. *Ilk* —2A **28**
Skelwith Clo. *W Bri* —6E **59**
Sketchley Ct. *Nott* —6G **19**
Sketchley St. *Nott* —3B **46**
Skiddaw Clo. *W Bri* —6E **59**
Skipton Cir. *Nott* —3C **46**
Skipton Clo. *Ilk* —4H **27**
Skylark Clo. *Bing* —6F **51**
Skylark Dri. *Nott* —3B **32**
Slack La. *Hean* —5C **14**
Slack Rd. *Ilk* —4D **26**
Slade Clo. *Ilk* —4B **40**
Slade Rd. *Bees* —6A **54**
Slaidburn Av. *Nott* —6E **57**
Sloan Dri. *Bees* —6B **42**
Sloane Ct. *W Bri* —2G **67**
Sloethorne Gdns. *Arn* —5H **21**
Small's Cft. *Wdbgh* —1C **24**
Smedley Av. *Ilk* —2C **40**
Smedley Clo. *Nott* —5H **31**
Smedley's Av. *Sand* —6D **52**
Smeeton St. *Hean* —4F **15**
Smite Ct. *Nott* —3B **44**
Smith Dri. *Lan M* —2E **15**
Smithfield Av. *Trow* —5F **41**
Smithurst Rd. *Gilt* —5C **16**
Smithy Clo. *Nott* —3B **66**
Smithy Cres. *Arn* —5B **22**
Smithy Row. *Nott* —5G **45** (4E **5**)
Smithy Vw. *C'tn* —4G **11**
Smythson Dri. *Nott* —5E **43**
Snape Nook Ct. *Nott* —6F **19**
Snape Wood Rd. *Nott* —6F **19**
Snead Ct. *Nott* —4E **21**
Sneinton Boulevd. *Nott* —5B **46**
Sneinton Dale. *Nott* —5B **46**
Sneinton Hermitage. *Nott*
　　　　—6A **46** (6H **5**)
Sneinton Hollows. *Nott* —5B **46**
Sneinton Rd. *Nott* —5A **46** (4H **5**)
Snowdon Clo. *Nott* —4F **21**
Soarbank Clo. *Kimb* —6G **17**
Sobers Gdns. *Arn* —1D **34**
Softwood Clo. *Nott* —6F **19**
Soloman Rd. *Coss* —5D **28**
Solway Clo. *Bees* —6E **55**
Somerby Ct. *Bees* —5B **42**
Somersby Rd. *Wd'p & Map* —2B **34**
Somerset Clo. *Long E* —5A **64**
Somerton Av. *Nott* —1E **67**
Songthrush Av. *Nott* —3B **32**
Sophie Rd. *Nott* —4D **44**
Sorrel Dri. *Bing* —5C **50**
Soudan Dri. *Nott* —2F **57**
Southampton St. *Nott* —3A **46**
South Av. *Rad T* —5H **49**
South Charnwood Swimming Pool.
　　　　—6A **34**
Southchurch Ct. *Nott* —2D **66**
Southchurch Dri. *Nott* —4C **66**
Southcliffe Rd. *Cltn* —2F **47**
South Ct. *Bees* —1H **65**
Southdale Dri. *Cltn* —2F **47**
Southdale Rd. *Cltn* —2F **47**
(in two parts)
S. Devon Av. *Nott* —5D **34**
Southey St. *Nott* —3D **44**
Southfield Rd. *Nott* —3B **44**
Southfields. *Long E* —6G **63**
Southfields Ct. *Bees* —6B **54**
Southglade Rd. *Nott* —1C **32**
Southglade Sports Cen. —1D **32**
Southlea Rd. *Cltn* —2F **47**
South Pde. *Nott* —5G **45** (4D **4**)
Southport Ter. *Nott* —2C **44**
South Rd. *Bees* —1G **65**
South Rd. *Nott* —6E **45** (5A **4**)
South Rd. *W Bri* —4B **58**
S. Sherwood St. *Nott*
　　　　—4G **45** (2D **4**)
Southside. *Arn* —5E **23**
S. Snape Clo. *Nott* —6F **19**

Sycamore Gro. *Nott* —6B **34**
Sycamore Pl. *Nott* —1G **45**
Sycamore Ri. *Nott* —3H **31**
Sycamore Rd. *Aws* —2D **28**
Sycamore Rd. *Long E* —2E **73**
Sycamores, The. *Eastw* —5A **16**
Sydenham Ct. *Nott* —1C **56**
Syderstone Wlk. *Arn* —2B **34**
Sydney Gro. *Rad T* —6E **49**
Sydney Rd. *Nott* —4H **43**
Syke Rd. *Nott* —5D **20**
Synge Clo. *Nott* —5A **66**
Syon Pk. Clo. *W Bri* —6G **57**

Taft Av. *Sand* —5D **52**
Talbot Ct. *Rad T* —6E **49**
Talbot Dri. *S'fd* —1F **53**
Talbot St. *Nott* —4F **45** (3B **4**)
Tales of Robin Hood. —5C **4**
Tamarix Clo. *Ged* —5A **36**
Tambling Clo. *Arn* —1D **34**
Tame Clo. *Nott* —1C **66**
Tamworth Gro. *Nott* —3D **66**
Tamworth Rd. *Long E* —3D **72**
  (in two parts)
Tamworth Rd. *Shard* —6A **72**
Tangmere Cres. *Nott* —6E **31**
Tanners Wlk. *Nott* —5G **45** (5E **5**)
Tansy Way. *Bing* —6C **50**
Tantum Av. *Los* —1A **14**
Tanwood Rd. *Bees* —4B **64**
Tarbert Clo. *Nott* —1F **57**
Target St. *Nott* —4C **44**
Tatham's La. *Ilk* —5A **28**
  (in two parts)
Tattershall Dri. *Bees* —4H **55**
Tattershall Dri. *Nott* —5E **45** (4A **4**)
Taunton Rd. *W Bri* —5B **58**
Taupo Dri. *Huck* —6C **6**
Tavern Av. *Nott* —5A **32**
Tavistock Av. *Nott* —6G **33**
Tavistock Clo. *Huck* —6D **6**
Tavistock Ct. *Nott* —6G **33**
Tavistock Dri. *Nott* —6G **33**
Tavistock Rd. *W Bri* —5B **58**
Taylor Clo. *Nott* —5C **46**
Taylor Cres. *S'fd* —3H **53**
Taylor La. *Los* —2B **14**
Taylors Cft. *Wdbgh* —1B **24**
Taylor St. *Ilk* —6B **28**
TDG Pinnacle. *W Hal* —3C **38**
Teak Clo. *Nott* —2H **45**
Tealby Clo. *Nott* —6F **19**
Teal Clo. *Cltn* —3B **48**
Teal Wharf. *Nott* —1E **57**
Teasels, The. *Bing* —6D **50**
Technology Dri. *Bees* —6G **55**
Teesbrook Dri. *Nott* —5B **42**
Teesdale Ct. *Bees* —1A **64**
Teesdale Rd. *Long E* —1C **72**
Teesdale Rd. *Nott* —5E **33**
Telford Dri. *Newt* —2D **16**
Templar Lodge. *Bees* —5H **55**
Templar Rd. *Bees* —5H **55**
Temple Cres. *Nut* —3D **30**
Temple Dri. *Nut* —3E **31**
Templeman Clo. *Rud* —5F **67**
Templeoak Dri. *Nott* —6C **42**
Tenbury Cres. *Nott* —6H **31**
Tene Clo. *Arn* —3B **22**
Tennis Ct. Ind. Est. *Nott* —6C **46**
Tennis Dri. *Nott* —5E **45** (4A **4**)
Tennis M. *Nott* —5E **45** (4A **4**)
Tennis Vw. *Nott* —5E **45** (4A **4**)
Tennyson Av. *Ged* —6H **35**
Tennyson Ct. *Huck* —5D **6**
Tennyson Ct. *Nott* —4F **33**
Tennyson Dri. *Bees* —3D **64**
Tennyson Rd. *Wd'p* —3A **34**
Tennyson St. *Ilk* —4A **28**
Tennyson St. *Nott* —3E **45** (1A **4**)
  (in two parts)
Tenter Clo. *Long E* —2F **73**
Tenter Clo. *Nott* —5D **20**
Terrace Rd. *Nott* —2D **44**
Terrian Cres. *W Bri* —4B **58**
Terton Rd. *Nott* —5D **20**
Tetney Wlk. *Nott* —2G **43**

Tettenbury Rd. *Nott* —4D **32**
Teversal Av. *Nott* —5D **44**
Tevery Clo. *S'fd* —3G **53**
Teviot Rd. *Nott* —2D **32**
Tewkesbury Clo. *W Bri* —5C **58**
Tewkesbury Dri. *Kimb* —6G **17**
Tewkesbury Dri. *Nott* —3C **32**
Tewkesbury Rd. *Long E* —3G **73**
Thackeray's La. *Wd'p* —2H **33**
Thackeray St. *Nott* —4D **44**
Thames St. *Nott* —6H **19**
Thane Rd. *Nott* —5B **56**
Thaxted Clo. *Nott* —3D **42**
Theatre Royal. —3D **4**
Theatre Sq. *Nott* —4G **45** (3D **4**)
Thelda Rd. *Keyw* —4G **79**
Thetford Clo. *Arn* —1C **34**
Third Av. *Cltn* —1D **46**
  (in two parts)
Third Av. *Ged* —6H **35**
Third Av. *Ilk* —2B **40**
Third Av. *Lent* —5A **56**
Third Av. *Nott* —1F **45**
Thirlbeck. *Cotg* —3G **71**
Thirlmere. *W Bri* —6E **59**
Thirlmere Clo. *Long E* —3D **62**
Thirlmere Clo. *Nott* —2B **46**
Thirlmere Rd. *Long E* —3D **62**
Thirston Clo. *Nott* —6F **19**
Thistle Clo. *Newt* —5D **16**
Thistledown Rd. *Nott* —6C **66**
Thistle Grn. Clo. *Hean* —4F **15**
Thistle Rd. *Ilk* —5C **40**
Thomas Av. *Rad T* —5H **49**
Thomas Clo. *Nott* —3H **45** (1G **5**)
Thompson Clo. *Bees* —2C **64**
Thompson Gdns. *Nott* —4E **21**
Thompson St. *Lan M* —2F **15**
Thoresby Av. *Ged* —5F **35**
Thoresby Av. *Nott* —6B **46**
Thoresby Clo. *Rad T* —5G **49**
Thoresby Ct. *Nott* —1H **45**
Thoresby Dale. *Huck* —4H **7**
Thoresby Rd. *Bees* —2C **54**
Thoresby Rd. *Bing* —5C **50**
Thoresby Rd. *Long E* —1D **72**
Thoresby St. *Nott* —5A **46** (5H **5**)
Thor Gdns. *Nott* —4D **20**
Thornbury Way. *Nott* —6D **20**
Thorncliffe Ri. *Nott* —1G **45**
Thorncliffe Rd. *Nott* —1G **45**
Thorndale Rd. *C'tn* —4H **11**
Thorndale Rd. *Nott* —5A **32**
Thorn Dri. *Newt* —5D **16**
Thorndyke Clo. *Bees* —1H **65**
Thorner Clo. *Nott* —2C **32**
Thorney Hill. *Nott* —2B **46**
Thorneywood Mt. *Nott* —2B **46**
Thorneywood Ri. *Nott* —2B **46**
Thorneywood Rd. *Long E* —5H **63**
Thornfield Ind. Est. *Nott* —4B **46**
Thorn Gro. *Huck* —1H **19**
Thornhill Clo. *Bees* —1B **54**
Thornley St. *Nott* —2C **44**
Thornthwaite Clo. *W Bri* —5E **59**
Thornton Av. *Red* —4H **21**
Thornton Clo. *Nott* —5E **43**
Thorntons Clo. *Cotg* —2G **71**
Thornton Ter. *Nott* —2D **44**
Thorntree Clo. *Breas* —4B **62**
Thorn Tree Gdns. *Eastw* —1B **16**
Thorpe St. *Ilk* —4A **28**
Thrapston Av. *Arn* —3B **22**
Thraves Yd. *Rad T* —6E **49**
Three Tuns Rd. *Eastw* —3C **16**
Threlkeld Clo. *W Bri* —5E **59**
Thrumpton Av. *Long E* —6H **63**
Thrumpton Dri. *Nott* —2F **57**

Thrumpton Pk. —5A **74**
Thurgarton Av. *Nott* —5B **46**
Thurgarton St. *Nott* —5B **46**
Thurland St. *Nott* —5G **45** (3E **5**)
Thurlby La. *Keyw* —6B **80**
Thurlestone Dri. *Nott* —1E **35**
Thurloe Ct. *W Bri* —2G **67**
Thurman Dri. *Cotg* —2F **71**
Thurman St. *Ilk* —3C **40**
Thurman St. *Nott* —3D **44**
Thursby Rd. *Nott* —2C **66**
Thymus Wlk. *Nott* —4A **66**
Thyra Ct. *Nott* —6A **34**
Thyra Gdns. *Bees* —5G **55**
Thyra Gro. *Nott* —6H **33**
Tidworth Clo. *Nott* —3G **43**
Tilberthwaite Clo. *Gam* —5E **59**
Tilbury Ri. *Nott* —4G **31**
Tilford Gdns. *S'fd* —5G **53**
Tilstock Ct. *Watn* —5A **18**
Tilton Gro. *Ilk* —4G **39**
Tim La. *Bur J* —3F **37**
Tinker Cft. *Ilk* —2A **40**
Tinsley Rd. *Eastw* —4H **15**
Tintagel Grn. *Nott* —4C **66**
Tippett Ct. *Nott* —3B **46**
Tip Tree Clo. *Kimb* —6H **17**
Tiree Clo. *Trow* —6F **41**
Tishbite St. *Nott* —6H **19**
Tissington Clo. *Nott* —1E **45**
Tissington Rd. *Nott* —1E **45**
Titchfield Ct. *Huck* —5G **7**
Titchfield St. *Huck* —4H **7**
Titchfield Ter. *Huck* —4H **7**
Tithby Dri. *Nott* —3H **33**
Tithby Rd. *Bing* —6E **51**
Tithe Gdns. *Nott* —4E **21**
Tithe La. *C'tn* —4H **11**
Tiverton Clo. *Huck* —6D **6**
Tiverton Clo. *Nott* —5H **31**
Toad La. *Epp* —6G **13**
Tobias Clo. *Nott* —5D **20**
Todd Clo. *Nott* —5A **66**
Todd Ct. *Nott* —5A **66**
Toft Clo. *Cotg* —3E **71**
Toft Rd. *Bees* —2A **64**
Token Ho. Yd. *Nott* —4E **5**
Tollerton Grn. *Nott* —2B **32**
Tollerton La. *Toll* —5F **69**
Tollerton Rd. *Rad T* —5F **59**
Tollhouse Hill. *Nott* —4F **45** (3C **4**)
Tomlinson Av. *Got* —6G **75**
Tonbridge Mt. *Nott* —1D **54**
Tonnelier Rd. *Nott* —2C **56**
Top Rd. *Rud* —1G **77**
Top Row. *Bur J* —2D **48**
Top Valley Dri. *Nott* —5C **20**
Top Valley Way. *Nott* —6C **20**
Torbay Cres. *Nott* —1F **33**
Torkard Dri. *Nott* —5D **20**
Torrington Ct. *Nott* —5H **33**
Torvill Dri. *Nott* —4D **42**
Toston Dri. *Nott* —5A **44**
Totland Dri. *Nott* —5B **32**
Totland Rd. *Bees* —1C **54**
Totley Clo. *Nott* —3A **20**
Totnes Clo. *Huck* —5D **6**
Totnes Rd. *Nott* —4D **46**
Toton Clo. *Nott* —2B **32**
Toton La. *S'fd* —4F **53**
Tottle Gdns. *Nott* —3B **44**
Tottle Rd. *Nott* —3E **57**
Tourist Info. Cen. —4E **5**
Tower Cres. *Nott* —3A **30**
Towe's Mt. *Cltn* —2G **47**
Towle St. *Long E* —3C **72**
Towlson Ct. *Bees* —2D **64**
Towlsons Cft. *Nott* —4B **32**
Townsend Ct. *Nott* —4E **21**
Townside Clo. *Long E* —3D **72**
Town St. *Bees* —4A **54**
Town St. *Sand* —6D **52**
Town Vw. *Kimb* —6H **17**
Towson Av. *Lan M* —3G **15**
Towyn Ct. *Nott* —6E **21**
Tracy Clo. *Bees* —2E **55**
Trafalgar Clo. *Nott* —3D **44**

Trafalgar Rd. *Bees* —1G **65**
Trafalgar Rd. *Long E* —1F **73**
Trafalgar Rd. *Long E* —6H **63**
Trafalgar Ter. *Long E* —6G **63**
Traffic St. *Nott* —6G **45**
Trafford Gdns. *Nott* —2B **44**
Tranby Gdns. *Nott* —5F **43**
Travers Rd. *Sand* —5C **52**
Treegarth Sq. *Nott* —4F **21**
Tree Vw. Clo. *Arn* —4G **21**
Trefan Gdns. *Nott* —6E **21**
Trefoil Clo. *Bing* —6D **50**
Trelawn Clo. *Nott* —5H **33**
Tremadoc Ct. *Nott* —1F **45**
Tremayne Rd. *Nott* —3C **42**
Trenchard Clo. *Nwtn* —2B **50**
Trent Av. *Rud* —6F **67**
Trent Boulevd. *W Bri* —2B **58**
Trent Bri. *Nott* —2A **58**
Trent Bri. Bldgs. *W Bri* —2A **58**
Trent Cotts. *Long E* —3E **73**
Trent Ct. *W Bri* —2C **58**
Trent Cres. *Bees* —2E **65**
Trentdale Rd. *Cltn* —3F **47**
Trent Dri. *Huck* —2D **18**
Trent Gdns. *Bur J* —3G **37**
Trentham Dri. *Nott* —2A **44**
Trentham Gdns. *Bur J* —4D **36**
Trentham Gdns. *Nott* —2A **44**
Trent Ho. *Long E* —3C **72**
Trent La. *Bur J* —3F **37**
Trent La. *Long E* —4G **73**
Trent La. *Nott* —6B **46**
Trent Lock Golf Course. —3E **73**
Trenton Clo. *Bees* —2A **54**
Trenton Dri. *Long E* —5A **64**
Trent Rd. *Bees* —1G **65**
Trent Rd. *Ilk* —5H **39**
Trent Rd. *Nott* —5B **46**
Trentside. *Bees* —2G **65**
Trentside N. *W Bri* —3A **58**
Trentside S. *W Bri* —2A **58**
Trent S. Ind. Pk. *Nott* —6C **46**
Trent St. *Long E* —5G **63**
Trent St. *Nott* —6H **45** (6F **5**)
Trent Va. Rd. *Bees* —1G **65**
Trent Valley Vw. *Nott* —6C **34**
Trentview Ct. *Nott* —1B **58**
Trent Vw. Gdns. *Rad T* —4G **49**
Tressall Clo. *Ilk* —1C **40**
Trevelyan Rd. *W Bri* —2B **58**
Trevino Gdns. *Nott* —5E **21**
Trevone Av. *S'fd* —5G **53**
Trevor Rd. *Bees* —6F **55**
Trevor Rd. *W Bri* —5C **58**
Trevose Gdns. *Nott* —4H **33**
Treyford Clo. *Nott* —1E **67**
Triangle, The. *Ilk* —3C **40**
  (in two parts)
Tricornia Dri. *Nott* —3H **31**
Trigg Ct. *Los* —1A **14**
Tring Va. *Nott* —3E **33**
Trinity Av. *Nott* —6C **44**
Trinity Clo. *Ilk* —4A **28**
Trinity Cres. *Lamb* —6C **24**
Trinity Row. *Nott* —4G **45** (3D **4**)
Trinity Sq. *Nott* —4G **45** (3E **5**)
Trinity Wlk. *Nott* —4G **45** (3E **5**)
Trinstead Way. *Nott* —6G **21**
Triumph Rd. *Nott* —4B **44**
Trivett Sq. *Nott* —5H **45** (5G **5**)
Troon Clo. *Kimb* —6G **17**
Trough La. *Watn* —5H **17**
Trough Rd. *Watn* —5H **17**
Troutbeck. *Cotg* —2G **71**
Troutbeck Cres. *Bees* —3C **54**
Trowell Av. *Ilk* —4C **40**
Trowell Av. *Nott* —4B **42**
Trowell Gdns. *Nott* —4C **42**
Trowell Gro. *Long E* —3D **62**
Trowell Gro. *Trow* —6F **41**
Trowell Pk. Dri. *Trow* —1F **53**
Trowell Rd. *Nott* —5B **42**
Trowell Rd. *S'fd* —1G **53**
Trueman Gdns. *Arn* —1D **34**
Trueman St. *Ilk* —3B **28**
Truman Clo. *Nott* —3H **45** (1F **5**)
Truman Dri. *Huck* —5G **7**
Trumans Rd. *Nott* —2H **57**

Truman St. *Kimb* —6F **17**
Truro Cres. *Nott* —2C **44**
Tudor Clo. *Colw* —4G **47**
Tudor Clo. *Long E* —4F **63**
Tudor Ct. *Huck* —6C **6**
Tudor Ct. *S'fd* —6F **53**
Tudor Falls. *Hean* —2C **14**
Tudor Gro. *Nott* —2F **45**
Tudor Pl. *Ilk* —4G **39**
Tudor Rd. *W Bri* —4B **58**
Tudor Sq. *W Bri* —4B **58**
Tudwal Clo. *Nott* —6E **21**
Tudwal Wlk. *Nott* —6E **21**
Tulip Av. *Nott* —2H **45**
Tulip Rd. *Aws* —2D **28**
Tunnel Rd. *Nott* —5E **45** (5A **4**)
Tunstall Cres. *Nott* —6G **31**
Tunstall Dri. *Nott* —3D **32**
Tunstall Rd. *Wd'p* —3B **34**
Turnberry Clo. *Bees* —5C **54**
Turnberry Clo. *Ilk* —5G **27**
Turnberry Ct. *Edw* —2E **69**
Turnberry Rd. *Nott* —1B **32**
Turner Av. *Lan M* —2E **15**
Turner Clo. *S'fd* —5G **53**
Turner Dri. *Gilt* —6D **16**
Turner Rd. *Long E* —3E **73**
Turner St. *Huck* —4G **7**
Turneys Ct. *Nott* —1A **58**
Turney St. *Nott* —2H **57**
Turnpike La. *Bees* —3G **55**
Turnstone Wharf. *Nott* —1D **56**
Turpin Av. *Ged* —4F **35**
Turrell Ct. *Bramc* —2D **54**
Turton Clo. *Lan M* —2E **15**
Tuxford Wlk. *Nott* —3B **46**
Twells Clo. *Nott* —2B **46**
Twitchell, The. *Bees* —1E **65**
Twycross Rd. *Nott* —6F **21**
Twyford Clo. *Hean* —5A **14**
Twyford Clo. *W Hal* —1B **38**
Twyford Gdns. *Nott* —1C **66**
Twyford Rd. *Long E* —3B **72**
Tyburn Clo. *Arn* —4E **21**
Tynedale Clo. *Long E* —1C **72**
Tynedale Clo. *Nott* —6B **32**
Tyne Gdns. *Huck* —2D **18**

Ulldale Ct. *Bees* —1B **64**
Ullscarf Clo. *W Bri* —6E **59**
Ullswater Clo. *Gam* —5F **59**
Ullswater Clo. *Ged* —5H **35**
Ullswater Cres. *Bees* —2C **54**
Ullswater Dri. *Huck* —4F **7**
Union Clo. *L'by* —1G **7**
Union Rd. *Ilk* —2A **40**
Union Rd. *Nott* —4G **45** (2E **5**)
(in two parts)
Union St. *Bees* —5F **55**
Union St. *Bing* —5E **51**
Union St. *Long E* —5G **63**
Unity Cres. *Nott* —5E **35**
University Boulevd. *Bees & Nott*
—3H **55**
University Pk. —3A **56**
Uplands Ct. *Nott* —3F **43**
Upminster Dri. *Arn* —4B **22**
Upminster Dri. *Nut* —3D **30**
Up. Barn Clo. *Hean* —3D **14**
Up. Canaan. *Rud* —5H **67**
Up. College St. *Nott* —4F **45** (3B **4**)
Up. Dunstead Rd. *Lan M* —2F **15**
Up. Eldon St. *Nott* —5A **46** (4H **5**)
Up. Nelson St. *Hean* —3B **14**
Up. Orchard St. *S'fd* —4G **53**
Up. Parliament St. *Nott*
—4F **45** (3C **4**)
Up. Wellington St. *Long E* —4E **63**
Uppingham Cres. *W Bri* —6H **57**
Uppingham Gdns. *Nott* —1H **57**
Upton Clo. *Hean* —4E **15**
Upton Dri. *Nott* —2H **33**
Upton M. *Nott* —1D **46**
Utile Gdns. *Nott* —6G **19**

Vale Clo. *Eastw* —3D **16**
Vale Cres. N. *Nott* —3B **44**

Vale Cres. S. *Nott* —3B **44**
Vale Gdns. *Colw* —4F **47**
Valerian Way. *Bing* —5C **50**
Vale Rd. *Colw* —4G **47**
Valeside Gdns. *Colw* —4G **47**
Vale, The. *Ilk* —4A **28**
Valetta Rd. *Arn* —6D **22**
Valley Ct. *Nott* —2H **33**
Valley Dri. *Newt* —4D **16**
Valley Farm Ct. *Nott* —5E **21**
Valley Gdns. *W Bri* —6E **59**
Valley Rd. *Bees* —6A **54**
Valley Rd. *Cltn* —6D **34**
(in two parts)
Valley Rd. *Ilk* —4A **40**
Valley Rd. *Kimb* —6F **17**
Valley Rd. *Nott* —5D **32**
Valley Rd. *Rad T* —4G **49**
Valley Rd. *W Bri* —6C **58**
Valley Vw. *Ilk* —4A **40**
Valmont Rd. *Bees* —3A **54**
Valmont Rd. *Nott* —4E **33**
Vancouver Av. *Rad T* —1E **61**
Vanguard Rd. *Long E* —2G **73**
Varden Av. *Bees* —2G **55**
Varney Rd. *Nott* —2D **66**
Vaughan Av. *Huck* —2A **8**
Vaughan Rd. *Bees* —1A **64**
Vedonis Pk. *Huck* —6G **7**
Venn Ct. *Bees* —5F **55**
Ventnor Ri. *Nott* —3D **32**
Venus Clo. *Nott* —2C **32**
Verbena Clo. *Nott* —2H **45**
Verder Gro. *Nott* —5C **20**
Vere St. *Nott* —6H **19**
Verne Clo. *Cltn* —2E **47**
Vernon Av. *Bees* —5F **55**
Vernon Av. *Cltn* —1H **47**
Vernon Av. *Nott* —3F **57**
Vernon Av. *Old B* —4C **32**
Vernon Ct. *Nut* —4F **31**
Vernon Dri. *Nut* —4F **31**
Vernon Pk. Dri. *Nott* —4C **32**
Vernon Pl. *Nott* —3B **32**
Vernon Rd. *Nott* —3B **32**
Vernon St. *Ilk* —3B **28**
Vernon St. *Nott* —4F **45** (3B **4**)
Verona Av. *Colw* —3H **47**
Veronica Dri. *Cltn* —6F **35**
Veronica Dri. *Gilt* —5E **17**
Veronica Wlk. *Nott* —4A **66**
Vicarage Av. *Ilk* —3H **27**
Vicarage Clo. *Nott* —4D **32**
(Perry Rd.)
Vicarage Clo. *Nott* —3G **45**
(St Anne's Way)
Vicarage Dri. *Bur J* —3E **37**
Vicarage Gdns. *Hean* —4D **14**
Vicarage Grn. *Edw* —2D **68**
Vicarage La. *Rad T* —6E **49**
Vicarage La. *Rud* —6G **67**
Vicarage St. *Bees* —5E **55**
Vicarage St. *Ilk* —3H **27**
Vickers St. *Nott* —1H **45**
Victor Cres. *Sand* —1E **63**
Victoria Av. *Hean* —4B **14**
Victoria Av. *Nott* —5B **46**
Victoria Bus. Pk. *N'fld* —3B **48**
Victoria Cen. E. *Nott* —4G **45**
(off Clinton St. E.)
Victoria Cen. S. *Nott*
(off Lincoln St.) —4G **45** (3E **5**)
Victoria Clo. *Arn* —3B **22**
Victoria Clo. *Ilk* —6A **28**
Victoria Ct. *Long E* —5G **63**
Victoria Cres. *Nott* —5H **33**
Victoria Embkmt. *Nott* —2G **57**
Victoria Gdns. *Watn* —4A **18**
Victoria Gro. *L'by* —1H **7**
Victoria Leisure Cen. —3G **5**
Victoria Pk. Leisure Cen.
—6A **28**
Victoria Pk. Way. *N'fld* —3B **48**
Victoria Rd. *Bing* —4G **51**
Victoria Rd. *Bun* —6A **78**
Victoria Rd. *N'fld* —2H **47**
Victoria Rd. *Nott* —4F **33**
Victoria Rd. *Sand* —6D **52**
Victoria Rd. *W Bri* —4A **58**

Victoria Shop. Cen. *Nott*
—4G **45** (3E **5**)
Victoria St. *Eastw* —2B **16**
Victoria St. *Ged* —6H **35**
Victoria St. *Huck* —3F **7**
Victoria St. *Ilk* —3B **28**
Victoria St. *Kimb* —1A **30**
Victoria St. *Lan M* —2G **15**
Victoria St. *Long E* —2D **72**
Victoria St. *Nott* —5G **45** (4E **5**)
Victoria St. *Rad T* —6F **49**
Victoria St. *S'fd* —4F **53**
Victoria Ter. *Nott* —5A **46**
Victor Ter. *Nott* —5G **33**
Victory Clo. *Long E* —1G **73**
Victory Rd. *Bees* —1G **65**
Vigar Ct. *Bees* —5G **55**
Village Clo. *Edw* —2D **68**
Village Rd. *Clif* —3A **66**
Village St. *Edw* —2C **68**
Village, The. *Dal A* —6D **38**
Village, The. *W Hal* —2B **38**
Villa Rd. *Keyw* —3H **79**
Villa Rd. *Nott* —2G **45**
Villa St. *Bees* —4F **55**
Villiers Rd. *W Bri* —5C **58**
Villiers Rd. *Wd'p* —3H **33**
Vincent Av. *Bees* —6F **55**
Vincent Av. *Ilk* —1B **40**
Vincent Gdns. *Nott* —2C **44**
Vine Cres. *Sand* —5D **52**
Vine Farm Clo. *Cotg* —2E **71**
Vine Farm Clo. *Ilk* —3H **39**
Vines Cross. *Nott* —1E **55**
Vine Ter. *Huck* —4H **7**
Violet Av. *Newt* —5D **16**
Violet Clo. *Nott* —4B **32**
Violet Rd. *Cltn* —5F **35**
Violet Rd. *W Bri* —3C **58**
Vista, The. *S'fd* —6G **53**
Vivian Av. *Nott* —1F **45**
Vulcan Clo. *Nott* —3C **32**
Vyse Dri. *Long E* —1D **72**

Waddington Dri. *W Bri* —1H **67**
Wade Av. *Ilk* —2C **40**
Wades Way. *Bing* —6G **51**
Wadham Rd. *Wd'p* —2A **34**
Wadhurst Gdns. *Nott*
—3A **46** (1G **5**)
Wadhurst Gro. *Nott* —1D **54**
Wadsworth Rd. *S'fd* —3H **53**
Wainfleet Clo. *Ilk* —4G **27**
Waingrove. *Nott* —2E **67**
Wakefield Av. *Rad T* —5G **49**
Wakefield Cft. *Ilk* —4G **27**
Walbrook Clo. *Nott* —4G **31**
Walcote Dri. *W Bri* —1G **67**
Walcott Grn. *Nott* —4B **66**
Waldeck Rd. *Nott* —6F **33**
Waldemar Gro. *Bees* —5G **55**
Waldron Clo. *Nott* —1H **57**
Walesby Cres. *Nott* —3A **44**
Walgrave Wlk. *Nott* —6F **21**
Walker Clo. *Ilk* —5C **40**
Walker Gro. *S'fd* —5G **53**
Walkers Clo. *Bing* —5E **51**
Walker St. *Eastw* —3C **16**
Walker St. *Nott* —4A **46** (3H **5**)
Walker's Yd. *Rad T* —6F **49**
Wlk. Mill Dri. *Huck* —2H **7**
Wallace Av. *Cltn* —2H **47**
Wallace Gdns. *Bees* —3H **63**
Wallace St. *Got* —5H **75**
Wallan St. *Nott* —3C **44**
Wallet St. *N'fld* —2A **48**
Wallet St. *Nott* —1H **57**
Wallett Av. *Bees* —3F **55**
Wallis St. *Nott* —3C **32**
Walnut Clo. *Ilk* —2C **40**
Walnut Dri. *Bees* —3B **54**
Walnut Gro. *C'tn* —3H **11**
Walnut Gro. *Rad T* —6F **49**
Walnut Tree Gdns. *Nott* —6F **19**
Walsham Clo. *Bees* —3C **64**
Walsingham Rd. *Wd'p* —2C **34**
Walter St. *Nott* —3E **45** (1A **4**)
Waltham Clo. *W Bri* —5D **58**

Walton Av. *Nott* —4B **46**
Walton Ct. *Cltn* —2G **47**
(in two parts)
Walton Ct. *W Hal* —1B **38**
Walton Cres. *Cltn* —2G **47**
Walton Dri. *Keyw* —4H **79**
Walton M. *Nott* —2B **46**
Walton Rd. *Arn* —4C **22**
Walton St. *Long E* —5F **63**
Wansbeck Clo. *Nott* —4E **45**
Wansford Av. *Arn* —4B **22**
Wanstead Way. *Nott* —4C **20**
Ward Av. *Huck* —2F **7**
Ward Av. *Nott* —4D **34**
Wardle Gro. *Arn* —5C **22**
Wardlow Rd. *Ilk* —4A **28**
Ward's La. *Breas* —5A **62**
Ward St. *Nott* —1C **44**
Wareham Clo. *Nott* —4G **31**
Wareham Clo. *W Bri* —6G **57**
Warkton Clo. *Bees* —6C **54**
Warner St. *Nott* —4C **44**
Warren Av. *Nott* —5E **33**
Warren Av. *S'fd* —4F **53**
Warren Ct. *S'fd* —4F **53**
Warrender Clo. *Bees* —2C **54**
Warrener Gro. *Nott* —5C **20**
Warrenhill Clo. *Arn* —6G **21**
Warren La. *Locki* —5C **72**
(in two parts)
Warren Rd. *Huck* —6D **6**
Warren, The. *Cotg* —3F **71**
Warrington Rd. *Nott* —6A **20**
Warser Ga. *Nott* —5H **45** (4F **5**)
Warsop Clo. *Strel* —5D **30**
Warton Av. *Nott* —1B **46**
Warwick Av. *Bees* —3F **55**
Warwick Av. *Wd'p* —2A **34**
Warwick Dri. *Ilk* —4G **27**
Warwick Gdns. *Cotg* —4F **71**
Warwick Rd. *Long E* —6H **63**
Warwick Rd. *Nott* —5H **33**
Warwick St. *Nott* —1C **56**
Wasdale Clo. *W Bri* —6E **59**
Washdyke La. *Huck* —2D **6**
Washington Ct. *Arn* —6B **22**
Washington Dri. *S'fd* —2H **53**
Wasnidge Clo. *Nott* —4H **45** (2G **5**)
Wasnidge Wlk. *Nott* —4H **45** (1G **5**)
Watchwood Gro. *C'tn* —3H **11**
Watcombe Cir. *Nott* —5F **33**
Watcombe Rd. *Nott* —6G **33**
Watendlath Clo. *W Bri* —6E **59**
Waterdown Rd. *Nott* —4B **66**
Waterford St. *Nott* —4C **32**
Waterhouse La. *Ged* —5A **36**
Water La. *Oxt* —1B **12**
Water La. *Rad T* —6E **49**
Waterloo Cres. *Nott* —3E **45**
Waterloo La. *Trow* —3H **41**
Waterloo Promenade. *Nott* —3E **45**
(in two parts)
Waterloo Rd. *Bees* —6G **55**
Waterloo Rd. *L'by* —1G **7**
Waterloo Rd. *Nott* —3E **45** (1A **4**)
Watermeadows, The. *Long E*
—5D **62**
Water Orton Clo. *Bees* —2G **63**
Waterside Clo. *Gam* —5E **59**
Waterside Clo. *Sand* —2D **62**
Waterside Gdns. *Nott* —2C **56**
Waterway St. *Nott* —1H **57**
(in two parts)
Waterway St. W. *Nott* —1G **57**
Waterway, The. *Sand* —1E **63**
Watford Rd. *Nott* —5H **31**
Watkinson St. *Hean* —3B **14**
Watkin St. *Nott* —3G **45** (1E **5**)
Watnall Rd. *Huck* —3D **18**
Watnall Rd. *Nut* —1C **30**
Watney Factory Units. *Huck* —6F **7**
Watson Av. *Hean* —3D **14**
Watson Av. *Nott* —3D **46**
Waveney Clo. *Arn* —1C **34**
Waverley Av. *Bees* —5G **55**
Waverley Av. *Ged* —6A **36**
Waverley Mt. *Nott* —3E **45**
Waverley St. *Long E* —5G **63**
Waverley St. *Nott* —3E **45** (1A **4**)